Myths of the Norsemen

From the Eddas and Sagas

H. A. Guerber

Alpha Editions

This edition published in 2020

ISBN : 9789354151286 (Paperback)
ISBN : 9789354150791 (Hardback)

Design and Setting By
Alpha Editions
www.alphaedis.com
email - alphaedis@gmail.com

CONTENTS

CONTENTS

LIST OF ILLUSTRATIONS

vii

LIST OF ILLUSTRATIONS

LIST OF ILLUSTRATIONS

INTRODUCTION

*T*HE *prime importance of the rude fragments of poetry preserved in early Icelandic literature will now be disputed by none, but there has been until recent times an extraordinary indifference to the wealth of religious tradition and mythical lore which they contain.*

The long neglect of these precious records of our heathen ancestors is not the fault of the material in which all that survives of their religious beliefs is enshrined, for it may safely be asserted that the Edda is as rich in the essentials of national romance and race-imagination, rugged though it be, as the more graceful and idyllic mythology of the South. Neither is it due to anything weak in the conception of the deities themselves, for although they may not rise to great spiritual heights, foremost students of Icelandic literature agree that they stand out rude and massive as the Scandinavian mountains. They exhibit "a spirit of victory, superior to brute force, superior to mere matter, a spirit that fights and overcomes."[1] "Even were some part of the matter of their myths taken from others, yet the Norsemen have given their gods a noble, upright, great spirit, and placed them upon a high level that is all their own."[2] "In fact these old Norse songs have a truth in them, an inward perennial truth and greatness.

[1] " Northern Mythology," Kauffmann.
[2] Halliday Sparling.

INTRODUCTION

It is a greatness not of mere body and gigantic bulk, but a rude greatness of soul." [1]

The introduction of Christianity into the North brought with it the influence of the Classical races, and this eventually supplanted the native genius, so that the alien mythology and literature of Greece and Rome have formed an increasing part of the mental equipment of the northern peoples in proportion as the native literature and tradition have been neglected.

Undoubtedly Northern mythology has exercised a deep influence upon our customs, laws, and language, and there has been, therefore, a great unconscious inspiration flowing from these into English literature. The most distinctive traits of this mythology are a peculiar grim humour, to be found in the religion of no other race, and a dark thread of tragedy which runs throughout the whole woof, and these characteristics, touching both extremes, are writ large over English literature.

But of conscious influence, compared with the rich draught of Hellenic inspiration, there is little to be found, and if we turn to modern art the difference is even more apparent.

This indifference may be attributed to many causes, but it was due first to the fact that the religious beliefs of our pagan ancestors were not held with any real tenacity. Hence the success of the more or less considered policy of the early Christian missionaries to confuse the heathen beliefs, and merge them in the

[1] Carlyle, " Heroes and Hero Worship."

new faith, an interesting example of which is to be seen in the transference to the Christian festival of Easter of the attributes of the pagan goddess Eástre, from whom it took even the name. Northern mythology was in this way arrested ere it had attained its full development, and the progress of Christianity eventually relegated it to the limbo of forgotten things. Its comprehensive and intelligent scheme, however, in strong contrast with the disconnected mythology of Greece and Rome, formed the basis of a more or less rational faith which prepared the Norseman to receive the teaching of Christianity, and so helped to bring about its own undoing.

The religious beliefs of the North are not mirrored with any exactitude in the Elder Edda. Indeed only a travesty of the faith of our ancestors has been preserved in Norse literature. The early poet loved allegory, and his imagination rioted among the conceptions of his fertile muse. " His eye was fixed on the mountains till the snowy peaks assumed human features and the giant of the rock or the ice descended with heavy tread; or he would gaze at the splendour of the spring, or of the summer fields, till Freya with the gleaming necklace stepped forth, or Sif with the flowing locks of gold."[1]

We are told nothing as to sacrificial and religious rites, and all else is omitted which does not provide material for artistic treatment. The so-called Northern Mythology, therefore, may be regarded as

[1] " Northern Mythology," Kauffmann.

*a precious relic of the beginning of Northern poetry,
rather than as a representation of the religious beliefs
of the Scandinavians, and these literary fragments
bear many signs of the transitional stage wherein the
confusion of the old and new faiths is easily apparent.*

*But notwithstanding the limitations imposed by
long neglect it is possible to reconstruct in part a plan
of the ancient Norse beliefs, and the general reader
will derive much profit from Carlyle's illuminating
study in " Heroes and Hero-worship." " A be-
wildering, inextricable jungle of delusions, confusions,
falsehoods and absurdities, covering the whole field of
Life !" he calls them, with all good reason. But
he goes on to show, with equal truth, that at the soul
of this crude worship of distorted nature was a
spiritual force seeking expression. What we probe
without reverence they viewed with awe, and not
understanding it, straightway deified it, as all
children have been apt to do in all stages of the
world's history. Truly they were hero-worshippers
after Carlyle's own heart, and scepticism had no
place in their simple philosophy.*

*It was the infancy of thought gazing upon a
universe filled with divinity, and believing heartily
with all sincerity. A large-hearted people reaching
out in the dark towards ideals which were better
than they knew. Ragnarok was to undo their gods
because they had stumbled from their higher
standards.*

We have to thank a curious phenomenon for the

preservation of so much of the old lore as we still possess. While foreign influences were corrupting the Norse language, it remained practically unaltered in Iceland, which had been colonised from the mainland by the Norsemen who had fled thither to escape the oppression of Harold Fairhair after his crushing victory of Hafrsfirth. These people brought with them the poetic genius which had already manifested itself, and it took fresh root in that barren soil. Many of the old Norse poets were natives of Iceland, and in the early part of the Christian era, a supreme service was rendered to Norse literature by the Christian priest, Sæmund, who industriously brought together a large amount of pagan poetry in a collection known as the Elder Edda, which is the chief foundation of our present knowledge of the religion of our Norse ancestors. Icelandic literature remained a sealed book, however, until the end of the eighteenth century, and very slowly since that time it has been winning its way in the teeth of indifference, until there are now signs that it will eventually come into its own. "To know the old Faith," says Carlyle, "brings us into closer and clearer relation with the Past—with our own possessions in the Past. For the whole Past is the possession of the Present ; the Past had always something true, and is a precious possession."

The weighty words of William Morris regarding the Volsunga Saga may also be fitly quoted as an introduction to the whole of this collection of " Myths of

the Norsemen": "This is the great story of the
North, which should be to all our race what the
Tale of Troy was to the Greeks—to all our race
first, and afterwards, when the change of the world
has made our race nothing more than a name of what
has been—a story too—then should it be to those that
come after us no less than the Tale of Troy has been
to us."

CHAPTER I: THE BEGINNING

Myths of Creation

ALTHOUGH the Aryan inhabitants of Northern Europe are supposed by some authorities to have come originally from the plateau of Iran, in the heart of Asia, the climate and scenery of the countries where they finally settled had great influence in shaping their early religious beliefs, as well as in ordering their mode of living.

The grand and rugged landscapes of Northern Europe, the midnight sun, the flashing rays of the aurora borealis, the ocean continually lashing itself into fury against the great cliffs and icebergs of the Arctic Circle, could not but impress the people as vividly as the almost miraculous vegetation, the perpetual light, and the blue seas and skies of their brief summer season. It is no great wonder, therefore, that the Icelanders, for instance, to whom we owe the most perfect records of this belief, fancied in looking about them that the world was originally created from a strange mixture of fire and ice.

Northern mythology is grand and tragical. Its principal theme is the perpetual struggle of the beneficent forces of Nature against the injurious, and hence it is not graceful and idyllic in character, like the religion of the sunny South, where the people could bask in perpetual sunshine, and the fruits of the earth grew ready to their hand.

It was very natural that the dangers incurred in hunting and fishing under these inclement skies, and the suffering entailed by the long cold winters when the sun never shines, made our ancestors contemplate cold and ice as malevolent spirits; and it was with equal reason that they invoked with special fervour the beneficent influences of heat and light.

MYTHS OF THE NORSEMEN

When questioned concerning the creation of the world, the Northern scalds, or poets, whose songs are preserved in the Eddas and Sagas, declared that in the beginning, when there was as yet no earth, nor sea, nor air, when darkness rested over all, there existed a powerful being called Allfather, whom they dimly conceived as uncreated as well as unseen, and that whatever he willed came to pass.

In the centre of space there was, in the morning of time, a great abyss called Ginnunga-gap, the cleft of clefts, the yawning gulf, whose depths no eye could fathom, as it was enveloped in perpetual twilight. North of this abode was a space or world known as Nifl-heim, the home of mist and darkness, in the centre of which bubbled the exhaustless spring Hvergelmir, the seething cauldron, whose waters supplied twelve great streams known as the Elivagar. As the water of these streams flowed swiftly away from its source and encountered the cold blasts from the yawning gulf, it soon hardened into huge blocks of ice, which rolled downward into the immeasurable depths of the great abyss with a continual roar like thunder.

South of this dark chasm, and directly opposite Nifl-heim, the realm of mist, was another world called Muspells-heim, the home of elemental fire, where all was warmth and brightness, and whose frontiers were continually guarded by Surtr, the flame giant. This giant fiercely brandished his flashing sword, and continually sent forth great showers of sparks, which fell with a hissing sound upon the ice-blocks in the bottom of the abyss, and partly melted them by their heat.

> "Great Surtur, with his burning sword,
> Southward at Muspel's gate kept ward,
> And flashes of celestial flame,
> Life-giving, from the fire-world came."
>
> *Valhalla (J. C. Jones).*

The Giant with the Flaming Sword
J. C. Dollman

Ymir and Audhumla

As the steam rose in clouds it again encountered the prevailing cold, and was changed into rime or hoar-frost, which, layer by layer, filled up the great central space. Thus by the continual action of cold and heat, and also probably by the will of the uncreated and unseen, a gigantic creature called Ymir or Orgelmir (seething clay), the personification of the frozen ocean, came to life amid the ice-blocks in the abyss, and as he was born of rime he was called a Hrim-thurs, or ice-giant.

> " In early times,
> When Ymir lived,
> Was sand, nor sea,
> Nor cooling wave ;
> No earth was found,
> Nor heaven above ;
> One chaos all,
> And nowhere grass."
>
> *Sæmund's Edda* (*Henderson's tr.*).

Groping about in the gloom in search of something to eat, Ymir perceived a gigantic cow called Audhumla (the nourisher), which had been created by the same agency as himself, and out of the same materials. Hastening towards her, Ymir noticed with pleasure that from her udder flowed four great streams of milk, which would supply ample nourishment.

All his wants were thus satisfied ; but the cow, looking about her for food in her turn, began to lick the salt off a neighbouring ice-block with her rough tongue. This she continued to do until first the hair of a god appeared and then the whole head emerged from its icy envelope, until by-and-by Buri (the producer) stepped forth entirely free.

While the cow had been thus engaged, Ymir, the

3

giant, had fallen asleep, and as he slept a son and daughter were born from the perspiration under his armpit, and his feet produced the six-headed giant Thrudgelmir, who, shortly after his birth, brought forth in his turn the giant Bergelmir, from whom all the evil frost giants are descended.

> " Under the armpit grew,
> 'Tis said of Hrim-thurs,
> A girl and boy together;
> Foot with foot begat,
> Of that wise Jötun,
> A six-headed son."
>
> *Sæmund's Edda* (*Thorpe's tr.*).

Odin, Vili, and Ve

When these giants became aware of the existence of the god Buri, and of his son Börr (born), whom he had immediately produced, they began waging war against them, for as the gods and giants represented the opposite forces of good and evil, there was no hope of their living together in peace. The struggle continued evidently for ages, neither party gaining a decided advantage, until Börr married the giantess Bestla, daughter of Bolthorn (the thorn of evil), who bore him three powerful sons, Odin (spirit), Vili (will), and Ve (holy). These three sons immediately joined their father in his struggle against the hostile frost-giants, and finally succeeded in slaying their deadliest foe, the great Ymir. As he sank down lifeless the blood gushed from his wounds in such floods that it produced a great deluge, in which all his race perished, with the exception of Bergelmir, who escaped in a boat and went with his wife to the confines of the world.

> " And all the race of Ymir thou didst drown,
> Save one, Bergelmer: he on shipboard fled
> Thy deluge, and from him the giants sprang."
>
> *Balder Dead* (*Matthew Arnold*).

THE CREATION OF THE EARTH

Here he took up his abode, calling the place Jötun-heim (the home of the giants), and here he begat a new race of frost-giants, who inherited his dislikes, continued the feud, and were always ready to sally forth from their desolate country and raid the territory of the gods.

The gods, in Northern mythology called Æsir (pillars and supporters of the world), having thus triumphed over their foes, and being no longer engaged in perpetual warfare, now began to look about them, with intent to improve the desolate aspect of things and fashion a habitable world. After due consideration Börr's sons rolled Ymir's great corpse into the yawning abyss, and began to create the world out of its various component parts.

The Creation of the Earth

Out of the flesh they fashioned Midgard (middle garden), as the earth was called. This was placed in the exact centre of the vast space, and hedged all round with Ymir's eyebrows for bulwarks or ramparts. The solid portion of Midgard was surrounded by the giant's blood or sweat, which formed the ocean, while his bones made the hills, his flat teeth the cliffs, and his curly hair the trees and all vegetation.

Well pleased with the result of their first efforts at creation, the gods now took the giant's unwieldy skull and poised it skilfully as the vaulted heavens above earth and sea ; then scattering his brains throughout the expanse beneath they fashioned from them the fleecy clouds.

> " Of Ymir's flesh
> Was earth created,
> Of his blood the sea,
> Of his bones the hills,

5

Of his hair trees and plants,
Of his skull the heavens,
And of his brows
The gentle powers
Formed Midgard for the sons of men ;
But of his brain
The heavy clouds are
All created."

Norse Mythology (*R. B. Anderson*).

To support the heavenly vault, the gods stationed the strong dwarfs, Nordri, Sudri, Austri, Westri, at its four corners, bidding them sustain it upon their shoulders, and from them the four points of the compass received their present names of North, South, East, and West. To give light to the world thus created, the gods studded the heavenly vault with sparks secured from Muspells-heim, points of light which shone steadily through the gloom like brilliant stars. The most vivid of these sparks, however, were reserved for the manufacture of the sun and moon, which were placed in beautiful golden chariots.

" And from the flaming world, where Muspel reigns,
Thou sent'st and fetched'st fire, and madest lights :
Sun, moon, and stars, which thou hast hung in heaven,
Dividing clear the paths of night and day."

Balder Dead (*Matthew Arnold*).

When all these preparations had been finished, and the steeds Arvakr (the early waker) and Alsvin (the rapid goer) were harnessed to the sun-chariot, the gods, fearing lest the animals should suffer from their proximity to the ardent sphere, placed under their withers great skins filled with air or with some refrigerant substance. They also fashioned the shield Svalin (the cooler), and placed it in front of the car to shelter them from the sun's direct rays, which would else have

6

burned them and the earth to a cinder. The moon-car was, similarly, provided with a fleet steed called Alsvider (the all-swift) ; but no shield was required to protect him from the mild rays of the moon.

Mani and Sol

The chariots were ready, the steeds harnessed and impatient to begin what was to be their daily round, but who should guide them along the right road ? The gods looked about them, and their attention was attracted to the two beautiful offspring of the giant Mundilfari. He was very proud of his children, and had named them after the newly created orbs, Mani (the moon) and Sol (the sun). Sol, the Sun-maid, was the spouse of Glaur (glow), who was probably one of Surtr's sons.

The names proved to be happily bestowed, as the brother and sister were given the direction of the steeds of their bright namesakes. After receiving due counsel from the gods, they were transferred to the sky, and day by day they fulfilled their appointed duties and guided their steeds along the heavenly paths.

> " Know that Mundilfær is hight
> Father to the moon and sun ;
> Age on age shall roll away,
> While they mark the months and days."
> *Hávamál* (*W. Taylor's tr.*).

The gods next summoned Nott (night), a daughter of Norvi, one of the giants, and entrusted to her care a dark chariot, drawn by a sable steed, Hrim-faxi (frost mane), from whose waving mane the dew and hoar-frost dropped down upon the earth.

> " Hrim-faxi is the sable steed,
> From the east who brings the night,
> Fraught with the showering joys of love :

As he champs the foamy bit,
Drops of dew are scattered round
To adorn the vales of earth."
Vafthrudni's-mal (*W. Taylor's tr.*).

The goddess of night had thrice been married, and by her first husband, Naglfari, she had had a son named Aud; by her second, Annar, a daughter Jörd (earth); and by her third, the god Dellinger (dawn), another son, of radiant beauty, was now born to her, and he was given the name of Dag (day).

As soon as the gods became aware of this beautiful being's existence they provided a chariot for him also, drawn by the resplendent white steed Skin-faxi (shining mane), from whose mane bright beams of light shone forth in every direction, illuminating all the world, and bringing light and gladness to all.

" Forth from the east, up the ascent of heaven,
Day drove his courser with the shining mane."
Balder Dead (*Matthew Arnold*).

The Wolves Sköll and Hati

But as evil always treads close upon the footsteps of good, hoping to destroy it, the ancient inhabitants of the Northern regions imagined that both Sun and Moon were incessantly pursued by the fierce wolves Sköll (repulsion) and Hati (hatred), whose sole aim was to overtake and swallow the brilliant objects before them, so that the world might again be enveloped in its primeval darkness.

" Sköll the wolf is named
That the fair-faced goddess
To the ocean chases;
Another Hati hight
He is Hrodvitnir's son;
He the bright maid of heaven shall precede."
Sæmuna's Edda (*Thorpe's tr.*).

The Wolves pursuing Sol and Mani

J. C. Dollman

THE WOLVES SKOLL AND HATI

At times, they said, the wolves overtook and tried to swallow their prey, thus producing an eclipse of the radiant orbs. Then the terrified people raised such a deafening clamour that the wolves, frightened by the noise, hastily dropped them. Thus rescued, Sun and Moon resumed their course, fleeing more rapidly than before, the hungry monsters rushing along in their wake, lusting for the time when their efforts would prevail and the end of the world would come. For the Northern nations believed that as their gods had sprung from an alliance between the divine element (Börr) and the mortal (Bestla), they were finite, and doomed to perish with the world they had made.

> "But even in this early morn
> Faintly foreshadowed was the dawn
> Of that fierce struggle, deadly shock,
> Which yet should end in Ragnarok;
> When Good and Evil, Death and Life,
> Beginning now, end then their strife."
> *Valhalla* (*J. C. Jones*).

Mani was accompanied also by Hiuki, the waxing, and Bil, the waning, moon, two children whom he had snatched from earth, where a cruel father forced them to carry water all night. Our ancestors fancied they saw these children, the original " Jack and Jill," with their pail, darkly outlined upon the moon.

The gods not only appointed Sun, Moon, Day, and Night to mark the procession of the year, but also called Evening, Midnight, Morning, Forenoon, Noon, and Afternoon to share their duties, making Summer and Winter the rulers of the seasons. Summer, a direct descendant of Svasud (the mild and lovely), inherited his sire's gentle disposition, and was loved by all except Winter, his deadly enemy, the son of Vindsual, himself

9

a son of the disagreeable god Vasud, the personification of the icy wind.

> " Vindsual is the name of him
> Who begat the winter's god ;
> Summer from Suasuthur sprang :
> Both shall walk the way of years,
> Till the twilight of the gods."
>
> *Vafthrudni's-mal (W. Taylor's tr.).*

The cold winds continually swept down from the north, chilling all the earth, and the Northmen imagined that these were set in motion by the great giant Hræ-svelgr (the corpse-swallower), who, clad in eagle plumes, sat at the extreme northern verge of the heavens, and that when he raised his arms or wings the cold blasts darted forth and swept ruthlessly over the face of the earth, blighting all things with their icy breath.

> " Hræ-svelger is the name of him
> Who sits beyond the end of heaven,
> And winnows wide his eagle-wings,
> Whence the sweeping blasts have birth."
>
> *Vafthrudni's-mal (W. Taylor's tr.).*

Dwarfs and Elves

While the gods were occupied in creating the earth and providing for its illumination, a whole host of maggot-like creatures had been breeding in Ymir's flesh. These uncouth beings now attracted divine attention. Summoning them into their presence, the gods first gave them forms and endowed them with superhuman intelligence, and then divided them into two large classes. Those which were dark, treacherous, and cunning by nature were banished to Svart-alfa-heim, the home of the black dwarfs, situated underground, whence they were never allowed to come forth during the day, under penalty of being turned into stone. They were called Dwarfs, Trolls, Gnomes, or Kobolds, and spent all their time and energy in exploring the secret recesses of the earth. They collected gold, silver, and precious stones, which they stowed away in secret crevices, whence they could withdraw them at will. The remainder of these small creatures, including all that were fair, good, and useful, the gods called Fairies and Elves, and they sent them to dwell in the airy realm of Alf-heim (home of the light-elves), situated between heaven and earth, whence they could flit downward whenever they pleased, to attend to the plants and flowers, sport with the birds and butterflies, or dance in the silvery moonlight on the green.

Odin, who had been the leading spirit in all these undertakings, now bade the gods, his descendants, follow him to the broad plain called Idawold, far above the earth, on the other side of the great stream Ifing, whose waters never froze.

> " Ifing's deep and murky wave
> Parts the ancient sons of earth
> From the dwelling of the Goths:
> Open flows the mighty flood,
> Nor shall ice arrest its course
> While the wheel of Ages rolls."
> *Vafthrudni's-mal (W. Taylor's tr.).*

In the centre of the sacred space, which from the beginning of the world had been reserved for their own abode and called Asgard (home of the gods), the twelve Æsir (gods) and twenty-four Asynjur (goddesses) all assembled at the bidding of Odin. Then was held a great council, at which it was decreed that no blood should be shed within the limits of their realm, or peace-stead, but that harmony should reign there for ever. As a further result of the conference the gods set up a forge where they fashioned all their weapons

11

and the tools required to build the magnificent palaces of precious metals, in which they lived for many long years in a state of such perfect happiness that this period has been called the Golden Age.

The Creation of Man

Although the gods had from the beginning designed Midgard, or Mana-heim, as the abode of man, there were at first no human beings to inhabit it. One day Odin, Vili, and Ve, according to some authorities, or Odin, Hoenir (the bright one), and Lodur, or Loki (fire), started out together and walked along the sea-shore, where they found either two trees, the ash, Ask, and the elm, Embla, or two blocks of wood, hewn into rude semblances of the human form. The gods gazed at first upon the inanimate wood in silent wonder ; then, perceiving the use it could be put to, Odin gave these logs souls, Hoenir bestowed motion and senses, and Lodur contributed blood and blooming complexions.

Thus endowed with speech and thought, and with power to love and to hope and to work, and with life and death, the newly created man and woman were left to rule Midgard at will. They gradually peopled it with their descendants, while the gods, remembering they had called them into life, took a special interest in all they did, watched over them, and often vouchsafed their aid and protection.

The Tree Yggdrasil

Allfather next created a huge ash called Yggdrasil, the tree of the universe, of time, or of life, which filled all the world, taking root not only in the remotest depths of Nifl-heim, where bubbled the spring Hvergelmir, but also in Midgard, near Mimir's well (the ocean), and in Asgard, near the Urdar fountain.

From its three great roots the tree attained such a marvellous height that its topmost bough, called Lerad (the peace-giver), overshadowed Odin's hall, while the other wide-spreading branches towered over the other worlds. An eagle was perched on the bough Lerad, and between his eyes sat the falcon Vedfolnir, sending his piercing glances down into heaven, earth, and Niflheim, and reporting all that he saw.

As the tree Yggdrasil was ever green, its leaves never withering, it served as pasture-ground not only for Odin's goat Heidrun, which supplied the heavenly mead, the drink of the gods, but also for the stags Dain, Dvalin, Duneyr, and Durathor, from whose horns honey-dew dropped down upon the earth and furnished the water for all the rivers in the world.

In the seething cauldron Hvergelmir, close by the great tree, a horrible dragon, called Nidhug, continually gnawed the roots, and was helped in his work of destruction by countless worms, whose aim it was to kill the tree, knowing that its death would be the signal for the downfall of the gods.

> "Through all our life a tempter prowls malignant,
>   The cruel Nidhug from the world below.
>   He hates that asa-light whose rays benignant
>   On th' hero's brow and glitt'ring sword bright glow."
>   *Viking Tales of the North* (*R. B. Anderson*).

Scampering continually up and down the branches and trunk of the tree, the squirrel Ratatosk (branchborer), the typical busybody and tale-bearer, passed its time repeating to the dragon below the remarks of the eagle above, and *vice versa*, in the hope of stirring up strife between them.

The Bridge Bifröst

It was, of course, essential that the tree Yggdrasil should be maintained in a perfectly healthy condition, and this duty was performed by the Norns, or Fates, who daily sprinkled it with the holy waters from the Urdar fountain. This water, as it trickled down to earth through branches and leaves, supplied the bees with honey.

From either edge of Nifl-heim, arching high above Midgard, rose the sacred bridge, Bifröst (Asabru, the rainbow), built of fire, water, and air, whose quivering and changing hues it retained, and over which the gods travelled to and fro to the earth or to the Urdar well, at the foot of the ash Yggdrasil, where they daily assembled in council.

> " The gods arose
> And took their horses, and set forth to ride
> O'er the bridge Bifrost, where is Heimdall's watch,
> To the ash Igdrasil, and Ida's plain.
> Thor came on foot, the rest on horseback rode."
>
> *Balder Dead (Matthew Arnold).*

Of all the gods Thor only, the god of thunder, never passed over the bridge, for fear lest his heavy tread or the heat of his lightnings would destroy it. The god Heimdall kept watch and ward there night and day. He was armed with a trenchant sword, and carried a trumpet called Giallar-horn, upon which he generally blew a soft note to announce the coming or going of the gods, but upon which a terrible blast would be sounded when Ragnarok should come, and the frost-giants and Surtr combined to destroy the world.

> " Surt from the south comes
> With flickering flame ;
> Shines from his sword
> The Val-god's sun.

THE VANAS

The stony hills are dashed together,
The giantesses totter ;
Men tread the path of Hel,
And heaven is cloven."

Sæmund's Edda (Thorpe's tr.).

The Vanas

Now although the original inhabitants of heaven were the Æsir, they were not the sole divinities of the Northern races, who also recognised the power of the sea- and wind-gods, the Vanas, dwelling in Vana-heim and ruling their realms as they pleased. In early times, before the golden palaces in Asgard were built, a dispute arose between the Æsir and Vanas, and they resorted to arms, using rocks, mountains, and icebergs as missiles in the fray. But discovering ere long that in unity alone lay strength, they composed their differences and made peace, and to ratify the treaty they exchanged hostages.

It was thus that the Van, Niörd, came to dwell in Asgard with his two children, Frey and Freya, while the Asa, Hoenir, Odin's own brother, took up his abode in Vana-heim.

CHAPTER II : ODIN

The Father of Gods and Men

ODIN, Wuotan, or Woden was the highest and holiest god of the Northern races. He was the all-pervading spirit of the universe, the personification of the air, the god of universal wisdom and victory, and the leader and protector of princes and heroes. As all the gods were supposed to be descended from him, he was surnamed Allfather, and as eldest and chief among them he occupied the highest seat in Asgard. Known by the name of Hlidskialf, this chair was not only an exalted throne, but also a mighty watch-tower, from whence he could overlook the whole world and see at a glance all that was happening among gods, giants, elves, dwarfs, and men.

> " From the hall of Heaven he rode away
> To Lidskialf, and sate upon his throne,
> The mount, from whence his eye surveys the world.
> And far from Heaven he turned his shining orbs
> To look on Midgard, and the earth, and men."
> *Balder Dead (Matthew Arnold).*

Odin's Personal Appearance

None but Odin and his wife and queen Frigga were privileged to use this seat, and when they occupied it they generally gazed towards the south and west, the goal of all the hopes and excursions of the Northern nations. Odin was generally represented as a tall, vigorous man, about fifty years of age, either with dark curling hair or with a long grey beard and bald head. He was clad in a suit of grey, with a blue hood, and his muscular body was enveloped in a wide blue mantle flecked with grey—an emblem of the sky with its fleecy clouds. In his hand Odin generally carried the infal-
16

Odin   16

Sir E. Burne-Jones

By Permission of Frederick Hollyer

lible spear Gungnir, which was so sacred that an oath sworn upon its point could never be broken, and on his finger or arm he wore the marvellous ring, Draupnir, the emblem of fruitfulness, precious beyond compare. When seated upon his throne or armed for the fray, to mingle in which he would often descend to earth, Odin wore his eagle helmet; but when he wandered peacefully about the earth in human guise, to see what men were doing, he generally donned a broad-brimmed hat, drawn low over his forehead to conceal the fact that he possessed but one eye.

Two ravens, Hugin (thought) and Munin (memory), perched upon his shoulders as he sat upon his throne, and these he sent out into the wide world every morning, anxiously watching for their return at nightfall, when they whispered into his ears news of all they had seen and heard. Thus he was kept well informed about everything that was happening on earth.

> " Hugin and Munin
> Fly each day
> Over the spacious earth.
> I fear for Hugin
> That he come not back,
> Yet more anxious am I for Munin."
> *Norse Mythology* (*R. B. Anderson*).

At his feet crouched two wolves or hunting hounds, Geri and Freki, animals which were therefore considered sacred to him, and of good omen if met by the way. Odin always fed these wolves with his own hands from meat set before him. He required no food at all for himself, and seldom tasted anything except the sacred mead.

> " Geri and Freki
> The war-wont sates,
> The triumphant sire of hosts;

B

But on wine only
The famed in arms
Odin, ever lives."
Lay of Grimnir (*Thorpe's tr.*).

When seated in state upon his throne, Odin rested his feet upon a footstool of gold, the work of the gods, all of whose furniture and utensils were fashioned either of that precious metal or of silver.

Besides the magnificent hall Glads-heim, where stood the twelve seats occupied by the gods when they met in council, and Valaskialf, where his throne, Hlidskialf, was placed, Odin had a third palace in Asgard, situated in the midst of the marvellous grove Glasir, whose shimmering leaves were of red gold.

Valhalla

This palace, called Valhalla (the hall of the chosen slain), had five hundred and forty doors, wide enough to allow the passage of eight hundred warriors abreast, and above the principal gate were a boar's head and an eagle whose piercing glance penetrated to the far corners of the world. The walls of this marvellous building were fashioned of glittering spears, so highly polished that they illuminated the hall. The roof was of golden shields, and the benches were decorated with fine armour, the god's gifts to his guests. Here long tables afforded ample accommodation for the Einheriar, warriors fallen in battle, who were specially favoured by Odin.

" Easily to be known is,
By those who to Odin come,
The mansion by its aspect.
Its roof with spears is laid,
Its hall with shields is decked,
With corselets are its benches strewed."
Lay of Grimnir (*Thorpe's tr.*).

The Chosen Slain

K. Dielitz

THE FEAST OF THE HEROES

The ancient Northern nations, who deemed warfare the most honourable of occupations, and considered courage the greatest virtue, worshipped Odin principally as god of battle and victory. They believed that whenever a fight was impending he sent out his special attendants, the shield-, battle-, or wish-maidens, called Valkyrs (choosers of the slain), who selected from the dead warriors one-half of their number, whom they bore on their fleet steeds over the quivering rainbow bridge, Bifröst, into Valhalla. Welcomed by Odin's sons, Hermod and Bragi, the heroes were conducted to the foot of Odin's throne, where they received the praise due to their valour. When some special favourite of the god was thus brought into Asgard, Valfather (father of the slain), as Odin was called when he presided over the warriors, would sometimes rise from his throne and in person bid him welcome at the great entrance gate.

The Feast of the Heroes

Besides the glory of such distinction, and the enjoyment of Odin's beloved presence day after day, other more material pleasures awaited the warriors in Valhalla. Generous entertainment was provided for them at the long tables, where the beautiful white-armed virgins, the Valkyrs, having laid aside their armour and clad themselves in pure white robes, waited upon them with assiduous attention. These maidens, nine in number ccording to some authorities, brought the heroes great horns full of delicious mead, and set before them huge portions of boar's flesh, upon which they feasted heartily. The usual Northern drink was beer or ale, but our ancestors fancied this beverage too coarse for the heavenly sphere. They therefore imagined that Valfather kept his table liberally supplied with mead or hydromel, which was daily furnished in great abundance

19

by his she-goat Heidrun, who continually browsed on the tender leaves and twigs on Lerad, Yggdrasil's topmost branch.

> " Rash war and perilous battle, their delight ;
> And immature, and red with glorious wounds,
> Unpeaceful death their choice: deriving thence
> A right to feast and drain immortal bowls,
> In Odin's hall ; whose blazing roof resounds
> The genial uproar of those shades who fall
> In desperate fight, or by some brave attempt."
>
> *Liberty (James Thomson).*

The meat upon which the Einheriar feasted was the flesh of the divine boar Sæhrimnir, a marvellous beast, daily slain by the cook Andhrimnir, and boiled in the great cauldron Eldhrimnir ; but although Odin's guests had true Northern appetites and gorged themselves to the full, there was always plenty of meat for all.

> " Andhrimnir cooks
> In Eldhrimnir
> Sæhrimnir ;
> 'Tis the best of flesh ;
> But few know
> What the einherjes eat."
>
> *Lay of Grimnir (Anderson's version).*

Moreover, the supply was exhaustless, for the boar always came to life again before the time of the next meal. This miraculous renewal of supplies in the larder was not the only wonderful occurrence in Valhalla, for it is related that the warriors, after having eaten and drunk to satiety, always called for their weapons, armed themselves, and rode out into the great courtyard, where they fought against one another, repeating the feats of arms for which they were famed on earth, and recklessly dealing terrible wounds, which, however,

20

A Viking Foray

J. C. Dollman

By Arrangement with the Artist

were miraculously and completely healed as soon as the dinner horn sounded.

> " All the chosen guests of Odin
> Daily ply the trade of war;
> From the fields of festal fight
> Swift they ride in gleaming arms,
> And gaily, at the board of gods,
> Quaff the cup of sparkling ale
> And eat Sæhrimni's vaunted flesh."
> *Vafthrudni's-mal (W. Taylor's tr.).*

Whole and happy at the sound of the horn, and bearing one another no grudge for cruel thrusts given and received, the Einheriar would ride gaily back to Valhalla to renew their feasts in Odin's beloved presence, while the white-armed Valkyrs, with flying hair, glided gracefully about, constantly filling their horns or their favourite drinking vessels, the skulls of their enemies, while the scalds sang of war and of stirring Viking forays.

> "And all day long they there are hack'd and hewn
> 'Mid dust, and groans, and limbs lopped off, and blood ;
> But all at night return to Odin's hall
> Woundless and fresh : such lot is theirs in heaven."
> *Balder Dead (Matthew Arnold).*

Fighting and feasting thus, the heroes were said to spend their days in perfect bliss, while Odin delighted in their strength and number, which, however, he foresaw would not avail to prevent his downfall when the day of the last battle should dawn.

As such pleasures were the highest a Northern warrior's fancy could paint, it was very natural that all fighting men should love Odin, and early in life should dedicate themselves to his service. They vowed to die arms in hand, if possible, and even wounded themselves

21

with their own spears when death drew near, if they had been unfortunate enough to escape death on the battlefield and were threatened with "straw death," as they called decease from old age or sickness.

> " To Odin then true-fast
> Carves he fair runics,—
> Death-runes cut deep on his arm and his breast."
> *Viking Tales of the North* (*R. B. Anderson*).

In reward for this devotion Odin watched with special care over his favourites, giving them gifts, a magic sword, a spear, or a horse, and making them invincible until their last hour had come, when he himself appeared to claim or destroy the gift he had bestowed, and the Valkyrs bore the heroes to Valhalla.

> " He gave to Hermod
> A helm and corselet,
> And from him Sigmund
> A sword received."
> *Lay of Hyndla* (*Thorpe's tr.*).

Sleipnir

When Odin took an active part in war, he generally rode his eight-footed grey steed, Sleipnir, and bore a white shield. His glittering spear flung over the heads of the combatants was the signal for the fray to commence, and he would dash into the midst of the ranks shouting his warcry : " Odin has you all ! "

> "And Odin donned
> His dazzling corslet and his helm of gold,
> And led the way on Sleipnir."
> *Balder Dead* (*Matthew Arnold*).

At times he used his magic bow, from which he would shoot ten arrows at once, every one invariably bringing down a foe. Odin was also supposed to

22

inspire his favourite warriors with the renowned "Berserker rage" (bare sark or shirt), which enabled them, although naked, weaponless, and sore beset, to perform unheard-of feats of valour and strength, and move about as with charmed lives.

As Odin's characteristics, like the all-pervading elements, were multitudinous, so also were his names, of which he had no less than two hundred, almost all descriptive of some phase of his activities. He was considered the ancient god of seamen and of the wind.

> "Mighty Odin,
> Norsemen hearts we bend to thee!
> Steer our barks, all-potent Woden,
> O'er the surging Baltic Sea."
>
> *Vail.*

The Wild Hunt

Odin, as wind-god, was pictured as rushing through mid-air on his eight-footed steed, from which originated the oldest Northern riddle, which runs as follows: "*Who are the two who ride to the Thing? Three eyes have they together, ten feet, and one tail: and thus they travel through the lands.*" And as the souls of the dead were supposed to be wafted away on the wings of the storm, Odin was worshipped as the leader of all disembodied spirits. In this character he was most generally known as the Wild Huntsman, and when people heard the rush and roar of the wind they cried aloud in superstitious fear, fancying they heard and saw him ride past with his train, all mounted on snorting steeds, and accompanied by baying hounds. And the passing of the Wild Hunt, known as Woden's Hunt, the Raging Host, Gabriel's Hounds, or Asgardreia, was also considered a presage of such misfortune as pestilence or war.

23

MYTHS OF THE NORSEMEN

"The Rhine flows bright; but its waves ere long
   Must hear a voice of war,
And a clash of spears our hills among,
   And a trumpet from afar ;
And the brave on a bloody turf must lie,
For the Huntsman hath gone by !"

               The Wild Huntsman (Mrs. Hemans).

It was further thought that if any were so sacrilegious as to join in the wild halloo in mockery, they would be immediately snatched up and whirled away with the vanishing host, while those who joined in the halloo with implicit good faith would be rewarded by the sudden gift of a horse's leg, hurled at them from above, which, if carefully kept until the morrow, would be changed into a lump of gold.

Even after the introduction of Christianity the ignorant Northern folk still dreaded the on-coming storm, declaring that it was the Wild Hunt sweeping across the sky.

"And ofttimes will start,
For overhead are sweeping Gabriel's hounds,
   Doomed with their impious lord the flying hart
To chase forever on aëreal grounds."

               Sonnet (Wordsworth).

Sometimes it left behind a small black dog, which, cowering and whining upon a neighbouring hearth, had to be kept for a whole year and carefully tended unless it could be exorcised or frightened away. The usual recipe, the same as for the riddance of change-lings, was to brew beer in egg-shells, and this performance was supposed so to startle the spectral dog that he would fly with his tail between his legs, exclaiming that, although as old as the Behmer, or Bohemian forest, he had never before beheld such an uncanny sight.

24

THE WILD HUNT

"I am as old
As the Behmer wold,
And have in my life
Such a brewing not seen."
Old Saying (*Thorpe's tr.*)

The object of this phantom hunt varied greatly, and was either a visonary boar or wild horse, white-breasted maidens who were caught and borne away bound only once in seven years, or the wood nymphs, called Moss Maidens, who were thought to represent the autumn leaves torn from the trees and whirled away by the wintry gale.

In the middle ages, when the belief in the old heathen deities was partly forgotten, the leader of the Wild Hunt was no longer Odin, but Charlemagne, Frederick Barbarossa, King Arthur, or some Sabbath-breaker, like the Squire of Rodenstein or Hans von Hackelberg, who, in punishment for his sins, was condemned to hunt for ever through the realms of air.

As the winds blew fiercest in autumn and winter, Odin was supposed to prefer hunting during that season, especially during the time between Christmas and Twelfth-night, and the peasants were always careful to leave the last sheaf or measure of grain out in the fields to serve as food for his horse.

This hunt was of course known by various names in the different countries of Northern Europe ; but as the tales told about it are all alike, they evidently originated in the same old heathen belief, and to this day ignorant people of the North fancy that the baying of a hound on a stormy night is an infallible presage of death.

"Still, still shall last the dreadful chase,
Till time itself shall have an end ;
By day, they scour earth's cavern'd space,
At midnight's witching hour, ascend.

MYTHS OF THE NORSEMEN

"This is the horn, and hound, and horse
  That oft the lated peasant hears ;
Appall'd, he signs the frequent cross,
  When the wild din invades his ears.

"The wakeful priest oft drops a tear
  For human pride, for human woe,
When, at his midnight mass, he hears
  The infernal cry of ' Holla, ho ! ' "
                                    Sir Walter Scott.

The Wild Hunt, or Raging Host of Germany, was
called Herlathing in England, from the mythical king
Herla, its supposed leader ; in Northern France it bore
the name of *Mesnée d'Hellequin,* from Hel, goddess of
death ; and in the middle ages it was known as Cain's
Hunt or Herod's Hunt, these latter names being given
because the leaders were supposed to be unable to find
rest on account of the iniquitous murders of Abel, of
John the Baptist, and of the Holy Innocents.

In Central France the Wild Huntsman, whom we
have already seen in other countries as Odin, Charlemagne, Barbarossa, Rodenstein, von Hackelberg, King
Arthur, Hel, one of the Swedish kings, Gabriel, Cain,
or Herod, is also called the Great Huntsman of Fontainebleau (*le Grand Veneur de Fontainebleau*), and people
declare that on the eve of Henry IV.'s murder, and
also just before the outbreak of the great French
Revolution, his shouts were distinctly heard as he swept
across the sky.

It was generally believed among the Northern nations
that the soul escaped from the body in the shape of a
mouse, which crept out of a corpse's mouth and ran
away, and it was also said to creep in and out of the
mouths of people in a trance. While the soul was
absent, no effort or remedy could recall the patient to
life ; but as soon as it had come back animation
returned.

26

THE PIED PIPER

The Pied Piper

As Odin was the leader of all disembodied spirits, he was identified in the middle ages with the Pied Piper of Hamelin. According to mediæval legends, Hamelin was so infested by rats that life became unbearable, and a large reward was offered to any who would rid the town of these rodents. A piper, in parti-coloured garments, offered to undertake the commission, and the terms being accepted, he commenced to play through the streets in such wise that, one and all, the rats were beguiled out of their holes until they formed a vast procession. There was that in the strains which compelled them to follow, until at last the river Weser was reached, and all were drowned in its tide.

> " And ere three shrill notes the pipe uttered,
>   You heard as if an army muttered ;
>   And the muttering grew to a grumbling ;
>   And the grumbling grew to a mighty rumbling ;
>   And out of the houses the rats came tumbling.
>   Great rats, small rats, lean rats, brawny rats,
>   Brown rats, black rats, grey rats, tawny rats,
>   Grave old plodders, gay young friskers,
>   Fathers, mothers, uncles, cousins,
>   Cocking tails and pricking whiskers,
>   Families by tens and dozens,
>   Brothers, sisters, husbands, wives—
>   Followed the Piper for their lives.
>   From street to street he piped advancing,
>   And step for step they followed dancing,
>   Until they came to the river Weser,
>   Wherein all plunged and perished ! "
>   *Robert Browning.*

As the rats were all dead, and there was no chance of their returning to plague them, the people of Hamelin refused to pay the reward, and they bade the piper do his worst. He took them at their word, and a few moments later the weird strains of the magic flute again arose, and this time it was the children who swarmed out of the houses and merrily followed the piper.

> " There was a rustling that seemed like a bustling
> Of merry crowds justling at pitching and hustling;
> Small feet were pattering, wooden shoes clattering,
> Little hands clapping and little tongues chattering,
> And, like fowls in a farmyard when barley is scattering,
> Out came all the children running.
> All the little boys and girls,
> With rosy cheeks and flaxen curls,
> And sparkling eyes and teeth like pearls,
> Tripping and skipping, ran merrily after
> The wonderful music with shouting and laughter."
>
> *Robert Browning.*

The burghers were powerless to prevent the tragedy, and as they stood spellbound the piper led the children out of the town to the Koppelberg, a hill on the confines of the town, which miraculously opened to receive the procession, and only closed again when the last child had passed out of sight. This legend probably originated the adage " to pay the piper." The children were never seen in Hamelin again, and in commemoration of this public calamity all official decrees have since been dated so many years after the Pied Piper's visit.

> "They made a decree that lawyers never
> Should think their records dated duly
> If, after the day of the month and year,
> These words did not as well appear,
> 'And so long after what happened here
> On the Twenty-second of July,
> Thirteen hundred and seventy-six:'
> And the better in memory to fix
> The place of the children's last retreat,
> They called it the Pied Piper Street—
> Where any one playing on pipe or tabor
> Was sure for the future to lose his labour."
>
> *Robert Browning.*

The Pied Piper of Hamelin
H. Kaulbach

BISHOP HATTO

In this myth Odin is the piper, the shrill tones of the flute are emblematic of the whistling wind, the rats represent the souls of the dead, which cheerfully follow him, and the hollow mountain into which he leads the children is typical of the grave.

Bishop Hatto

Another German legend which owes its existence to this belief is the story of Bishop Hatto, the miserly prelate, who, annoyed by the clamours of the poor during a time of famine, had them burned alive in a deserted barn, like the rats whom he declared they resembled, rather than give them some of the precious grain which he had laid up for himself.

> " ' I' faith, 'tis an excellent bonfire ! ' quoth he,
> ' And the country is greatly obliged to me
> For ridding it in these times forlorn
> Of rats that only consume the corn.' "
>
> *Robert Southey.*

Soon after this terrible crime had been accomplished the bishop's retainers reported the approach of a vast swarm of rats. These, it appears, were the souls of the murdered peasants, which had assumed the forms of the rats to which the bishop had likened them. His efforts to escape were vain, and the rats pursued him even into the middle of the Rhine, to a stone tower in which he took refuge from their fangs. They swam to the tower, gnawed their way through the stone walls, and, pouring in on all sides at once, they found the bishop and devoured him alive.

> " And in at the windows, and in at the door,
> And through the walls, helter-skelter they pour,
> And down from the ceiling, and up through the floor,
> From the right and the left, from behind and before,

29

From within and without, from above and below,
And all at once to the Bishop they go.
They have whetted their teeth against the stones ;
And now they pick the Bishop's bones ;
They gnaw'd the flesh from every limb,
For they were sent to do judgment on him!"

Robert Southey.

The red glow of the sunset above the Rat Tower near Bingen on the Rhine is supposed to be the reflection of the hell fire in which the wicked bishop is slowly roasting in punishment for his heinous crime.

Irmin

In some parts of Germany Odin was considered to be identical with the Saxon god Irmin, whose statue, the Irminsul, near Paderborn, was destroyed by Charlemagne in 772. Irmin was said to possess a ponderous brazen chariot, in which he rode across the sky along the path which we know as the Milky Way, but which the ancient Germans designated as Irmin's Way. This chariot, whose rumbling sound occasionally became perceptible to mortal ears as thunder, never left the sky, where it can still be seen in the constellation of the Great Bear, which is also known in the North as Odin's, or Charles's, Wain.

" The Wain, who wheels on high
His circling course, and on Orion waits ;
Sole star that never bathes in the Ocean wave."

Homer's Iliad (Derby's tr.).

Mimir's Well

To obtain the great wisdom for which he is so famous, Odin, in the morn of time, visited Mimir's (Memor, memory) spring, " the fountain of all wit and wisdom," in whose liquid depths even the future was clearly mirrored, and besought the old man who guarded it to

30

let him have a draught. But Mimir, who well knew
the value of such a favour (for his spring was considered
the source or headwater of memory), refused the boon
unless Odin would consent to give one of his eyes in
exchange.

The god did not hesitate, so highly did he prize the
draught, but immediately plucked out one of his eyes,
which Mimir kept in pledge, sinking it deep down into
his fountain, where it shone with mild lustre, leaving
Odin with but one eye, which is considered emblematic
of the sun.

> " Through our whole lives we strive towards the sun;
> That burning forehead is the eye of Odin.
> His second eye, the moon, shines not so bright;
> It has he placed in pledge in Mimer's fountain,
> That he may fetch the healing waters thence,
> Each morning, for the strengthening of this eye."
> *Oehlenschläger (Howitt's tr.).*

Drinking deeply of Mimir's fount, Odin gained the
knowledge he coveted, and he never regretted the
sacrifice he had made, but as further memorial of that
day broke off a branch of the sacred tree Yggdrasil,
which overshadowed the spring, and fashioned from it
his beloved spear Gungnir.

> " A dauntless god
> Drew for drink to its gleam,
> Where he left in endless
> Payment the light of an eye.
> From the world-ash
> Ere Wotan went he broke a bough ;
> For a spear the staff
> He split with strength from the stem."
> *Dusk of the Gods, Wagner (Forman's tr.).*

But although Odin was now all-wise, he was sad and
oppressed, for he had gained an insight into futurity,

31

and had become aware of the transitory nature of all things, and even of the fate of the gods, who were doomed to pass away. This knowledge so affected his spirits that he ever after wore a melancholy and contemplative expression.

To test the value of the wisdom he had thus obtained, Odin went to visit the most learned of all the giants, Vafthrudnir, and entered with him into a contest of wit, in which the stake was nothing less than the loser's head.

> " Odin rose with speed, and went
> To contend in runic lore
> With the wise and crafty Jute.
> To Vafthrudni's royal hall
> Came the mighty king of spells."
> *Vafthrudni's-mal* (*W. Taylor's tr.*).

Odin and Vafthrudnir

On this occasion Odin had disguised himself as a Wanderer, by Frigga's advice, and when asked his name declared it was Gangrad. The contest of wit immediately began, Vafthrudnir questioning his guest concerning the horses which carried Day and Night across the sky, the river Ifing separating Jötun-heim from Asgard, and also about Vigrid, the field where the last battle was to be fought.

All these questions were minutely answered by Odin, who, when Vafthrudnir had ended, began the interrogatory in his turn, and received equally explicit answers about the origin of heaven and earth, the creation of the gods, their quarrel with the Vanas, the occupations of the heroes in Valhalla, the offices of the Norns, and the rulers who were to replace the Æsir when they had all perished with the world they had created. But when, in conclusion, Odin bent near the giant and softly inquired what words Allfather whispered to his dead son Balder as he lay upon his funeral pyre, Vafthrudnir

32

suddenly recognised his divine visitor. Starting back in dismay, he declared that no one but Odin himself could answer that question, and that it was now quite plain to him that he had madly striven in a contest of wisdom and wit with the king of the gods, and fully deserved the penalty of failure, the loss of his head.

> " Not the man of mortal race
> Knows the words which thou hast spoken
> To thy son in days of yore.
> I hear the coming tread of death ;
> He soon shall raze the runic lore,
> And knowledge of the rise of gods,
> From his ill-fated soul who strove
> With Odin's self the strife of wit,
> Wisest of the wise that breathe :
> Our stake was life, and thou hast won."
> *Vafthrudni's-mal* (*W. Taylor's tr.*).

As is the case with so many of the Northern myths, which are often fragmentary and obscure, this one ends here, and none of the scalds informs us whether Odin really slew his rival, nor what was the answer to his last question ; but mythologists have hazarded the suggestion that the word whispered by Odin in Balder's ear, to console him for his untimely death, must have been " resurrection."

Invention of Runes

Besides being god of wisdom, Odin was god and inventor of runes, the earliest alphabet used by Northern nations, which characters, signifying mystery, were at first used for divination, although in later times they served for inscriptions and records. Just as wisdom could only be obtained at the cost of sacrifice, Odin himself relates that he hung nine days and nights from the sacred tree Yggdrasil, gazing down into the immeasurable depths of

Nifl-heim, plunged in deep thought, and self-wounded
with his spear, ere he won the knowledge he sought.

> " I know that I hung
> On a wind-rocked tree
> Nine whole nights,
> With a spear wounded,
> And to Odin offered
> Myself to myself;
> On that tree
> Of which no one knows
> From what root it springs."
>
> *Odin's Rune-Song (Thorpe's tr.)*.

When he had fully mastered this knowledge, Odin cut
magic runes upon his spear Gungnir, upon the teeth of
his horse Sleipnir, upon the claws of the bear, and upon
countless other animate and inanimate things. And because he had thus hung over the abyss for such a long
space of time, he was ever after considered the patron
divinity of all who were condemned to be hanged or
who perished by the noose.

After obtaining the gift of wisdom and runes, which
gave him power over all things, Odin also coveted the
gift of eloquence and poetry, which he acquired in a
manner which we shall relate in a subsequent chapter.

Geirrod and Agnar

Odin, as has already been stated, took great interest
in the affairs of mortals, and, we are told, was specially
fond of watching King Hrauding's handsome little sons,
Geirrod and Agnar, when they were about eight and
ten years of age respectively. One day these little lads
went fishing, and a storm suddenly arose which blew
their boat far out to sea, where it finally stranded upon
an island, upon which dwelt a seeming old couple, who
in reality were Odin and Frigga in disguise. They

34

had assumed these forms in order to indulge a sudden passion for the close society of their *protégés*. The lads were warmly welcomed and kindly treated, Odin choosing Geirrod as his favourite, and teaching him the use of arms, while Frigga petted and made much of little Agnar. The boys tarried on the island with their kind protectors during the long, cold winter season; but when spring came, and the skies were blue, and the sea calm, they embarked in a boat which Odin provided, and set out for their native shore. Favoured by gentle breezes, they were soon wafted thither; but as the boat neared the strand Geirrod quickly sprang out and pushed it far back into the water, bidding his brother sail away into the evil spirit's power. At that self-same moment the wind veered, and Agnar was indeed carried away, while his brother hastened to his father's palace with a lying tale as to what had happened to his brother. He was joyfully received as one from the dead, and in due time he succeeded his father upon the throne.

Years passed by, during which the attention of Odin had been claimed by other high considerations, when one day, while the divine couple were seated on the throne Hlidskialf, Odin suddenly remembered the winter's sojourn on the desert island, and he bade his wife notice how powerful his pupil had become, and taunted her because her favourite Agnar had married a giantess and had remained poor and of no consequence. Frigga quietly replied that it was better to be poor than hardhearted, and accused Geirrod of lack of hospitality—one of the most heinous crimes in the eyes of a Northman. She even went so far as to declare that in spite of all his wealth he often ill-treated his guests.

When Odin heard this accusation he declared that he

would prove the falsity of the charge by assuming the guise of a Wanderer and testing Geirrod's generosity. Wrapped in his cloud-hued raiment, with slouch hat and pilgrim staff,—

> " Wanderer calls me the world,
> Far have I carried my feet,
> On the back of the earth
> I have boundlessly been,"—
>
> *Wagner* (*Forman's tr.*).

Odin immediately set out by a roundabout way, while Frigga, to outwit him, immediately despatched a swift messenger to warn Geirrod to beware of a man in wide mantle and broad-brimmed hat, as he was a wicked enchanter who would work him ill.

When, therefore, Odin presented himself before the king's palace he was dragged into Geirrod's presence and questioned roughly. He gave his name as Grimnir, but refused to tell whence he came or what he wanted, so as this reticence confirmed the suspicion suggested to the mind of Geirrod, he allowed his love of cruelty full play, and commanded that the stranger should be bound between two fires, in such wise that the flames played around him without quite touching him, and he remained thus eight days and nights, in obstinate silence, without food. Now Agnar had returned secretly to his brother's palace, where he occupied a menial position, and one night when all was still, in pity for the suffering of the unfortunate captive, he conveyed to his lips a horn of ale. But for this Odin would have had nothing to drink—the most serious of all trials to the god.

At the end of the eighth day, while Geirrod, seated upon his throne, was gloating over his prisoner's sufferings, Odin began to sing—softly at first, then louder and louder, until the hall re-echoed with his triumphant

36

Odin
B. E. Fogelberg

notes—a prophecy that the king, who had so long enjoyed the god's favour, would soon perish by his own sword.

> " The fallen by the sword
> Ygg shall now have ;
> Thy life is now run out :
> Wroth with thee are the Dísir:
> Odin thou now shalt see :
> Draw near to me if thou canst."
>
> *Sæmund's Edda* (*Thorpe's tr.*).

As the last notes died away the chains dropped from his hands, the flames flickered and went out, and Odin stood in the midst of the hall, no longer in human form, but in all the power and beauty of a god.

On hearing the ominous prophecy Geirrod hastily drew his sword, intending to slay the insolent singer ; but when he beheld the sudden transformation he started in dismay, tripped, fell upon the sharp blade, and perished as Odin had just foretold. Turning to Agnar, who, according to some accounts, was the king's son, and not his brother, for these old stories are often strangely confused, Odin bade him ascend the throne in reward for his humanity, and, further to repay him for the timely draught of ale, he promised to bless him with all manner of prosperity.

On another occasion Odin wandered to earth, and was absent so long that the gods began to think that they would not see him in Asgard again. This encouraged his brothers Vili and Ve, who by some mythologists are considered as other personifications of himself, to usurp his power and his throne, and even, we are told, to espouse his wife Frigga.

> " Be thou silent, Frigg !
> Thou art Fiörgyn's daughter
> And ever hast been fond of men,

Since Ve and Vili, it is said,
Thou, Vidrir's wife, didst
Both to thy bosom take."
Sæmund's Edda (Thorpe's tr.).

May-Day Festivals

But upon Odin's return the usurpers vanished for ever ; and in commemoration of the disappearance of the false Odin, who had ruled seven months and had brought nothing but unhappiness to the world, and of the return of the benevolent deity, the heathen Northmen formerly celebrated yearly festivals, which were long continued as May Day rejoicings. Until very lately there was always, on that day, a grand procession in Sweden, known as the May Ride, in which a flower-decked May king (Odin) pelted with blossoms the fur-enveloped Winter (his supplanter), until he put him to ignominious flight. In England also the first of May was celebrated as a festive occasion, in which Maypole dances, May queens, Maid Marian, and Jack in the Green played prominent parts.

As personification of heaven, Odin, of course, was the lover and spouse of the earth, and as to them the earth bore a threefold aspect, the Northmen depicted him as a polygamist, and allotted to him several wives. The first among these was Jörd (Erda), the primitive earth, daughter of Night or of the giantess Fiorgyn. She bore him his famous son Thor, the god of thunder. The second and principal wife was Frigga, a personification of the civilised world. She gave him Balder, the gentle god of spring, Hermod, and, according to some authorities, Tyr. The third wife was Rinda, a personification of the hard and frozen earth, who reluctantly yields to his warm embrace, but finally gives birth to Vali, the emblem of vegetation.

Odin is also said to have married Saga or Laga, the

38

goddess of history (hence our verb " to say "), and to have daily visited her in the crystal hall of Sokvabek, beneath a cool, ever-flowing river, to drink its waters and listen to her songs about olden times and vanished races.

> " Sokvabek hight the fourth dwelling;
> Over it flow the cool billows;
> Glad drink there Odin and Saga
> Every day from golden cups."
>
> *Norse Mythology* (*R. B. Anderson*).

His other wives were Grid, the mother of Vidar; Gunlod, the mother of Bragi ; Skadi ; and the nine giantesses who simultaneously bore Heimdall—all of whom play more or less important parts in the various myths of the North.

The Historical Odin

Besides this ancient Odin, there was a more modern, semi-historical personage of the same name, to whom all the virtues, powers, and adventures of his predecessor have been attributed. He was the chief of the Æsir, inhabitants of Asia Minor, who, sore pressed by the Romans, and threatened with destruction or slavery, left their native land about 70 B.C., and migrated into Europe. This Odin is said to have conquered Russia, Germany, Denmark, Norway, and Sweden, leaving a son on the throne of each conquered country. He also built the town of Odensö. He was welcomed in Sweden by Gylfi, the king, who gave him a share of the realm, and allowed him to found the city of Sigtuna, where he built a temple and introduced a new system of worship. Tradition further relates that as his end drew near, this mythical Odin assembled his followers, publicly cut himself nine times in the breast with his spear,—a ceremony called " carving Geir odds,"—and

39

told them he was about to return to his native land Asgard, his old home, where he would await their coming,
to share with him a life of feasting, drinking, and fighting.

According to another account, Gylfi, having heard of
the power of the Æsir, the inhabitants of Asgard, and
wishing to ascertain whether these reports were true,
journeyed to the south. In due time he came to Odin's
palace, where he was expected, and where he was deluded
by the vision of Har, Iafn-har, and Thridi, three
divinities, enthroned one above the other. The gate-
keeper, Gangler, answered all his questions, and gave
him a long explanation of Northern mythology, which
is recorded in the Younger Edda, and then, having
finished his instructions, suddenly vanished with the
palace amid a deafening noise.

According to other very ancient poems, Odin's sons,
Weldegg, Beldegg, Sigi, Skiold, Sæming, and Yngvi,
became kings of East Saxony, West Saxony, Franconia,
Denmark, Norway, and Sweden, and from them are
descended the Saxons, Hengist and Horsa, and the
royal families of the Northern lands. Still another
version relates that Odin and Frigga had seven sons,
who founded the Anglo-Saxon heptarchy. In the
course of time this mysterious king was confounded
with the Odin whose worship he introduced, and all his
deeds were attributed to the god.

Odin was worshipped in numerous temples, but
especially in the great fane at Upsala, where the most
solemn festivals were held, and where sacrifices were
offered. The victim was generally a horse, but in
times of pressing need human offerings were made,
even the king being once offered up to avert a famine.

> " Upsal's temple, where the North
> Saw Valhal's halls fair imag'd here on earth."
> *Viking Tales of the North* (R. B. *Anderson*).

THE HISTORICAL ODIN

The first toast at every festival here was drunk in his honour, and, besides the first of May, one day in every week was held sacred to him, and, from his Saxon name, Woden, was called Woden's day, whence the English word "Wednesday" has been derived. It was customary for the people to assemble at his shrine on festive occasions, to hear the songs of the scalds, who were rewarded for their minstrelsy by the gift of golden bracelets or armlets, which curled up at the ends and were called " Odin's serpents."

There are but few remains of ancient Northern art now extant, and although rude statues of Odin were once quite common they have all disappeared, as they were made of wood—a perishable substance, which in the hands of the missionaries, and especially of Olaf the Saint, the Northern iconoclast, was soon reduced to ashes.

> "There in the Temple, carved in wood,
> The image of great Odin stood."
> *Saga of King Olaf* (*Longfellow*).

Odin himself is supposed to have given his people a code of laws whereby to govern their conduct, in a poem called Hávamál, or the High Song, which forms part of the Edda. In this lay he taught the fallibility of man, the necessity for courage, temperance, independence, and truthfulness, respect for old age, hospitality, charity, and contentment, and gave instructions for the burial of the dead.

> "At home let a man be cheerful,
> And toward a guest liberal;
> Of wise conduct he should be,
> Of good memory and ready speech;
> If much knowledge he desires,
> He must often talk on what is good."
> *Hávamál* (*Thorpe's tr.*).

CHAPTER III : FRIGGA

The Queen of the Gods

FRIGGA, or Frigg, daughter of Fiorgyn and sister of Jörd, according to some mythologists, is considered by others as a daughter of Jörd and Odin, whom she eventually married. This wedding caused such general rejoicing in Asgard, where the goddess was greatly beloved, that ever after it was customary to celebrate its anniversary with feast and song, and the goddess being declared patroness of marriage, her health was always proposed with that of Odin and Thor at wedding feasts.

Frigga was goddess of the atmosphere, or rather of the clouds, and as such was represented as wearing either snow-white or dark garments, according to her somewhat variable moods. She was queen of the gods, and she alone had the privilege of sitting on the throne Hlidskialf, beside her august husband. From thence she too could look over all the world and see what was happening, and, according to the belief of our ancestors, she possessed the knowledge of the future, which, however, no one could ever prevail upon her to reveal, thus proving that Northern women could keep a secret inviolate.

> " Of me the gods are sprung;
> And all that is to come I know, but lock
> In my own breast, and have to none reveal'd."
> *Balder Dead* (*Matthew Arnold*).

She was generally represented as a tall, beautiful, and stately woman, crowned with heron plumes, the symbol of silence or forgetfulness, and clothed in pure white robes, secured at the waist by a golden girdle, from which hung a bunch of keys, the distinctive sign

42

Frigga spinning the Clouds
J. C. Dollman

of the Northern housewife, whose special patroness she was said to be. Although she often appeared beside her husband, Frigga preferred to remain in her own palace, called Fensalir, the hall of mists or of the sea, where she diligently plied her wheel or distaff, spinning golden thread or weaving long webs of bright-coloured clouds.

In order to perform this work she made use of a marvellous jewelled spinning wheel or distaff, which at night shone brightly in the sky as a constellation, known in the North as Frigga's Spinning Wheel, while the inhabitants of the South called the same stars Orion's Girdle.

To her hall Fensalir the gracious goddess invited husbands and wives who had led virtuous lives on earth, so that they might enjoy each other's companionship even after death, and never be called upon to part again.

> " There in the glen, Fensalir stands, the house
> Of Frea, honour'd mother of the gods,
> And shows its lighted windows and the open doors."
> *Balder Dead* (*Matthew Arnold*).

Frigga was therefore considered the goddess of conjugal and motherly love, and was specially worshipped by married lovers and tender parents. This exalted office did not entirely absorb her thoughts however, for we are told that she was very fond of dress, and whenever she appeared before the assembled gods her attire was rich and becoming, and her jewels chosen with much taste.

The Stolen Gold

Frigga's love of adornment once led her sadly astray, for, in her longing to possess some new ornament, she secretly purloined a piece of gold from a statue representing her husband, which had just been placed

43

in his temple. The stolen metal was entrusted to the dwarfs, with instructions to fashion a marvellous necklace for her use. This, when finished, was so resplendent that it greatly enhanced her charms, and even increased Odin's love for her. But when he discovered the theft of the gold he angrily summoned the dwarfs and bade them reveal who had dared to touch his statue. Unwilling to betray the queen of the gods, the dwarfs remained obstinately silent, and, seeing that no information could be elicited from them, Odin commanded that the statue should be placed above the temple gate, and set to work to devise runes which should endow it with the power of speech and enable it to denounce the thief. When Frigga heard these tidings she trembled with fear, and implored her favourite attendant, Fulla, to invent some means of protecting her from Allfather's wrath. Fulla, who was always ready to serve her mistress, immediately departed, and soon returned, accompanied by a hideous dwarf, who promised to prevent the statue from speaking if Frigga would only deign to smile graciously upon him. This boon having been granted, the dwarf hastened off to the temple, caused a deep sleep to fall upon the guards, and while they were thus unconscious, pulled the statue down from its pedestal and broke it to pieces, so that it could never betray Frigga's theft, in spite of all Odin's efforts to give it the power of speech.

Odin, discovering this sacrilege on the morrow, was very angry indeed ; so angry that he left Asgard and utterly disappeared, carrying away with him all the blessings which he had been wont to shower upon gods and men. According to some authorities, his brothers, as we have already seen, took advantage of his absence to assume his form and secure possession of his throne and wife ; but although they looked exactly like him they could not restore the lost blessings, and allowed the ice-giants, or Jotuns, to invade the earth and bind it fast in their cold fetters. These wicked giants pinched the leaves and buds till they all shrivelled up, stripped the trees bare, shrouded the earth in a great white coverlet, and veiled it in impenetrable mists.

But at the end of seven weary months the true Odin relented and returned, and when he saw all the evil that had been done he drove the usurpers away, forced the frost-giants to relax their grip of the earth and to release her from her icy bonds, and again showered all his blessings down upon her, cheering her with the light of his smile.

Odin Outwitted

As has already been seen, Odin, although god of wit and wisdom, was sometimes no match for his wife Frigga, who, womanlike, was sure to obtain her way by some means. On one occasion the august pair were seated upon Hlidskialf, gazing with interest upon the Winilers and Vandals, who were preparing for a battle which was to decide which people should henceforth have supremacy. Odin gazed with satisfaction upon the Vandals, who were loudly praying to him for victory; but Frigga watched the movements of the Winilers with more attention, because they had entreated her aid. She therefore turned to Odin and coaxingly inquired whom he meant to favour on the morrow; he, wishing to evade her question, declared he would not decide, as it was time for bed, but would give the victory to those upon whom his eyes first rested in the morning.

This answer was shrewdly calculated, for Odin knew that his couch was so turned that upon waking he would face the Vandals, and he intended looking out from thence, instead of waiting until he had mounted his throne. But, although so cunningly contrived, this plan was frustrated by Frigga, who, divining his purpose, waited until he was sound asleep, and then noiselessly turned his couch so that he should face her favourites. Then she sent word to the Winilers to dress their women in armour and send them out in battle array at dawn, with their long hair carefully combed down over their cheeks and breasts.

> " Take thou thy women-folk,
> Maidens and wives:
> Over your ankles
> Lace on the white war-hose ;
> Over your bosoms
> Link up the hard mail-nets ;
> Over your lips
> Plait long tresses with cunning ;—
> So war beasts full-bearded
> King Odin shall deem you,
> When off the grey sea-beach
> At sunrise ye greet him."
> *The Longbeards' Saga* (*Charles Kingsley*).

These instructions were carried out with scrupulous exactness, and when Odin awoke the next morning his first conscious glance fell upon their armed host, and he exclaimed in surprise, " What Longbeards are those ? " (In German the ancient word for long beards was *Langobarden*, which was the name used to designate the Lombards.) Frigga, upon hearing this exclamation, which she had foreseen, immediately cried out in triumph that Allfather had given them a new name, and was in honour bound to follow the usual Northern custom and give also a baptismal gift.

> " 'A name thou hast given them,
> Shames neither thee nor them,
> Well can they wear it.

FULLA

Give them the victory,
First have they greeted thee;
Give them the victory,
Yoke-fellow mine ! ' "
The Longbeards' Saga (Charles Kingsley).

Odin, seeing he had been so cleverly outwitted, made
no demur, and in memory of the victory which his
favour vouchsafed to them the Winilers retained the
name given by the king of the gods, who ever after
watched over them with special care, giving them many
blessings, among others a home in the sunny South, on
the fruitful plains of Lombardy.

Fulla

Frigga had, as her own special attendants, a number
of beautiful maidens, among whom were Fulla (Volla),
her sister, according to some authorities, to whom she
entrusted her jewel casket. Fulla always presided over
her mistress's toilet, was privileged to put on her golden
shoes, attended her everywhere, was her confidante, and
often advised her how best to help the mortals who
implored her aid. Fulla was very beautiful indeed, and
had long golden hair, which she wore flowing loose over
her shoulders, restrained only by a golden circlet or
snood. As her hair was emblematic of the golden grain,
this circlet represented the binding of the sheaf. Fulla
was also known as Abundia, or Abundantia, in some
parts of Germany, where she was considered the symbol
of the fulness of the earth.

Hlin, Frigga's second attendant, was the goddess of
consolation, sent out to kiss away the tears of mourners
and pour balm into hearts wrung by grief. She also
listened with ever-open ears to the prayers of mortals,
carrying them to her mistress, and advising her at times
how best to answer them and give the desired relief.

47

Gna

Gna was Frigga's swift messenger. Mounted upon her fleet steed Hofvarpnir (hoof-thrower), she would travel with marvellous rapidity through fire and air, over land and sea, and was therefore considered the personification of the refreshing breeze. Darting thus to and fro, Gna saw all that was happening upon earth, and told her mistress all she knew. On one occasion, as she was passing over Hunaland, she saw King Rerir, a lineal descendant of Odin, sitting mournfully by the shore, bewailing his childlessness. The queen of heaven, who was also goddess of childbirth, upon hearing this took an apple (the emblem of fruitfulness) from her private store, gave it to Gna, and bade her carry it to the king. With the rapidity of the element she personified, Gna darted away, and as she passed over Rerir's head, she dropped her apple into his lap with a radiant smile.

> " 'What flies up there, so quickly driving past ?'
> Her answer from the clouds, as rushing by :
> 'I fly not, nor do drive, but hurry fast,
> Hoof-flinger swift through cloud and mist and sky.' "
> *Asgard and the Gods* (*Wagner-Macdowall*).

The king pondered for a moment upon the meaning of this sudden apparition and gift, and then hurried home, his heart beating high with hope, and gave the apple to his wife to eat. In due season, to his intense joy, she bore him a son, Volsung, the great Northern hero, who became so famous that he gave his name to all his race.

Lofn, Vjofn, and Syn

Besides the three above mentioned, Frigga had other attendants in her train. There was the mild and gracious maiden Lofn (praise or love), whose duty it was to remove all obstacles from the path of lovers.

GEFJON

" My lily tall, from her saddle bearing,
  I led then forth through the temple, faring
  To th' altar-circle where, priests among,
  Lofn's vows she took with unfalt'ring tongue."
                    Viking Tales of the North (R B. Anderson).

Vjofn's duty was to incline obdurate hearts to love, to maintain peace and concord among mankind, and to reconcile quarrelling husbands and wives.   Syn (truth) guarded the door of Frigga's palace, refusing to open it to those who were not allowed to come in.   When she had once shut the door upon a would-be intruder no appeal would avail to change her decision.   She therefore presided over all tribunals and trials, and whenever a thing was to be vetoed the usual formula was to declare that Syn was against it.

Gefjon

Gefjon was also one of the maidens in Frigga's palace, and to her were entrusted all those who died unwedded, whom she received and made happy for ever.

According to some authorities, Gefjon did not remain a virgin herself, but married one of the giants, by whom she had four sons.   This same tradition goes on to declare that Odin sent her before him to visit Gylfi, King of Sweden, and to beg for some land which she might call her own.   The king, amused at her request, promised her as much land as she could plough around in one day and night. Gefjon, nothing daunted, changed her four sons into oxen, harnessed them to a plough, and began to cut a furrow so wide and deep that the king and his courtiers were amazed.   But Gefjon continued her work without showing any signs of fatigue, and when she had ploughed all around a large piece of land forcibly wrenched it away, and made her

D   49 oxen drag it down into the sea, where she made it fast and called it Seeland.

> " Gefjon drew from Gylfi,
> Rich in stored up treasure,
> The land she joined to Denmark.
> Four heads and eight eyes bearing,
> While hot sweat trickled down them,
> The oxen dragged the reft mass
> That formed this winsome island."
>
> *Norse Mythology* (*R. B. Anderson*).

As for the hollow she left behind her, it was quickly filled with water and formed a lake, at first called Logrum (the sea), but now known as Mälar, whose every indentation corresponds with the headlands of Seeland. Gefjon then married Skiold, one of Odin's sons, and became the ancestress of the royal Danish race of Skioldungs, dwelling in the city of Hleidra or Lethra, which she founded, and which became the principal place of sacrifice for the heathen Danes.

Eira, Vara, Vör and Snotra

Eira, also Frigga's attendant, was considered a most skilful physician. She gathered simples all over the earth to cure both wounds and diseases, and it was her province to teach the science to women, who were the only ones to practise medicine among the ancient nations of the North.

> " Gaping wounds are bound by Eyra."
>
> *Valhalla* (*J. C. Jones*).

Vara heard all oaths and punished perjurers, while she rewarded those who faithfully kept their word. Then there were also Vör (faith), who knew all that was to occur throughout the world, and Snotra, goddess of virtue, who had mastered all knowledge.

With such a galaxy of attendants it is little wonder

50

that Frigga was considered a powerful deity ; but in spite of the prominent place she occupied in Northern religion, she had no special temple nor shrine, and was but little worshipped except in company with Odin.

Holda

While Frigga was not known by this name in Southern Germany, there were other goddesses worshipped there, whose attributes were so exactly like hers, that they were evidently the same, although they bore very different names in the various provinces. Among them was the fair goddess Holda (Hulda or Frau Holle), who graciously dispensed many rich gifts. As she presided over the weather, the people were wont to declare when the snowflakes fell that Frau Holle was shaking her bed, and when it rained, that she was washing her clothes, often pointing to the white clouds as her linen which she had put out to bleach. When long grey strips of clouds drifted across the sky they said she was weaving, for she was supposed to be also a very diligent weaver, spinner, and housekeeper. It is said she gave flax to mankind and taught them how to use it, and in the Tyrol the following story is told about the way in which she bestowed this invaluable gift :

The Discovery of Flax

There was once a peasant who daily left his wife and children in the valley to take his sheep up the mountain to pasture ; and as he watched his flock grazing on the mountain-side, he often had opportunity to use his cross-bow and bring down a chamois, whose flesh would furnish his larder with food for many a day.

While pursuing a fine animal one day he saw it disappear behind a boulder, and when he came to the spot, he was amazed to see a doorway in the neighbouring

51

glacier, for in the excitement of the pursuit he had climbed higher and higher, until he was now on top of the mountain, where glittered the everlasting snow.

The shepherd boldly passed through the open door, and soon found himself in a wonderful jewelled cave hung with stalactites, in the centre of which stood a beautiful woman, clad in silvery robes, and attended by a host of lovely maidens crowned with Alpine roses. In his surprise, the shepherd sank to his knees, and as in a dream heard the queenly central figure bid him choose anything he saw to carry away with him. Although dazzled by the glow of the precious stones around him, the shepherd's eyes constantly reverted to a little nosegay of blue flowers which the gracious apparition held in her hand, and he now timidly proffered a request that it might become his. Smiling with pleasure, Holda, for it was she, gave it to him, telling him he had chosen wisely and would live as long as the flowers did not droop and fade. Then, giving the shepherd a measure of seed which she told him to sow in his field, the goddess bade him begone; and as the thunder pealed and the earth shook, the poor man found himself out upon the mountain-side once more, and slowly wended his way home to his wife, to whom he told his adventure and showed the lovely blue flowers and the measure of seed.

The woman reproached her husband bitterly for not having brought some of the precious stones which he so glowingly described, instead of the blossoms and seed; nevertheless the man proceeded to sow the latter, and he found to his surprise that the measure supplied seed enough for several acres.

Soon the little green shoots began to appear, and one moonlight night, while the peasant was gazing upon them, as was his wont, for he felt a curious attraction

Tannhauser and Frau Venus

J. Wagrez

to the field which he had sown, and often lingered there wondering what kind of grain would be produced, he saw a misty form hover above the field, with hands outstretched as if in blessing. At last the field blossomed, and countless little blue flowers opened their calyxes to the golden sun. When the flowers had withered and the seed was ripe, Holda came once more to teach the peasant and his wife how to harvest the flax —for such it was—and from it to spin, weave, and bleach linen. As the people of the neighbourhood willingly purchased both linen and flax-seed, the peasant and his wife soon grew very rich indeed, and while he ploughed, sowed, and harvested, she spun, wove, and bleached the linen. The man lived to a good old age, and saw his grandchildren and great-grandchildren grow up around him. All this time his carefully treasured bouquet had remained fresh as when he first brought it home, but one day he saw that during the night the flowers had drooped and were dying.

Knowing what this portended, and that he too must die, the peasant climbed the mountain once more to the glacier, and found again the doorway for which he had often vainly searched. He entered the icy portal, and was never seen or heard of again, for, according to the legend, the goddess took him under her care, and bade him live in her cave, where his every wish was gratified.

Tannhäuser

According to a mediæval tradition, Holda dwelt in a cave in the Hörselberg, in Thuringia, where she was known as Frau Venus, and was considered as an enchantress who lured mortals into her realm, where she detained them for ever, steeping their senses in all manner of sensual pleasures. The most famous of her victims was Tannhäuser, who, after he had lived under her spell for a season, experienced a revulsion of feeling which loosened her bonds over his spirit and induced anxious thoughts concerning his soul. He escaped from her power and hastened to Rome to confess his sins and seek absolution. But when the Pope heard of his association with one of the pagan goddesses whom the priests taught were nothing but demons, he declared that the knight could no more hope for pardon than to see his staff bear buds and bloom.

> " Hast thou within the nets of Satan lain ?
> Hast thou thy soul to her perdition pledged ?
> Hast thou thy lip to Hell's Enchantress lent,
> To drain damnation from her reeking cup ?
> Then know that sooner from the withered staff
> That in my hand I hold green leaves shall spring,
> Than from the brand in hell-fire scorched rebloom
> The blossoms of salvation."
>
> *Tannhäuser* (*Owen Meredith*).

Crushed with grief at this pronouncement, Tannhäuser fled, and, despite the entreaties of his faithful friend, Eckhardt, no great time elapsed ere he returned to the Hörselberg, where he vanished within the cave. He had no sooner disappeared, however, than the Pope's messengers arrived, proclaiming that he was pardoned, for the withered staff had miraculously bloomed, thus proving to all that there was no sin too heinous to be pardoned, providing repentance were sincere.

> " Dashed to the hip with travel, dewed with haste,
> A flying post, and in his hand he bore
> A withered staff o'erflourished with green leaves ;
> Who,—followed by a crowd of youth and eld,
> That sang to stun with sound the lark in heaven,
> ' A miracle ! a miracle from Rome !
> Glory to God that makes the bare bough green ! '—
> Sprang in the midst, and, hot for answer, asked
> News of the Knight Tannhäuser."
>
> *Tannhäuser* (*Owen Meredith*).

Eástre
Jacques Reich

54

EÁSTRE, THE GODDESS OF SPRING

Holda was also the owner of a magic fountain called Quickborn, which rivalled the famed fountain of youth, and of a chariot in which she rode from place to place when she inspected her domain. This vehicle having once suffered damage, the goddess bade a wheelwright repair it, and when he had finished told him to keep some chips as his pay. The man was indignant at such a meagre reward, and kept only a very few of the number ; but to his surprise he found these on the morrow changed to gold.

> "Fricka, thy wife—
> This way she reins her harness of rams.
> Hey ! how she whirls
> The golden whip ;
> The luckless beasts
> Unboundedly bleat ;
> Her wheels wildly she rattles;
> Wrath is lit in her look."
>
> *Wagner* (*Forman's tr.*).

Eástre, the Goddess of Spring

The Saxon goddess Eástre, or Ostara, goddess of spring, whose name has survived in the English word Easter, is also identical with Frigga, for she too is considered goddess of the earth, or rather of Nature's resurrection after the long death of winter. This gracious goddess was so dearly loved by the old Teutons, that even after Christianity had been introduced they retained so pleasant a recollection of her, that they refused to have her degraded to the rank of a demon, like many of their other divinities, and transferred her name to their great Christian feast. It had long been customary to celebrate this day by the exchange of presents of coloured eggs, for the egg is the type of the beginning of life ; so the early Christians continued to observe this rule, declaring, however, that the egg is also symbolical of the Resurrection. In various parts of Germany,

55

stone altars can still be seen, which are known as Easter-stones, because they were dedicated to the fair goddess Ostara. They were crowned with flowers by the young people, who danced gaily around them by the light of great bonfires,—a species of popular games practised until the middle of the present century, in spite of the priests' denunciations and of the repeatedly published edicts against them.

Bertha, the White Lady

In other parts of Germany, Frigga, Holda, or Ostara is known by the name of Brechta, Bertha, or the White Lady. She is best known under this title in Thuringia, where she was supposed to dwell in a hollow mountain, keeping watch over the Heimchen, souls of unborn children, and of those who died unbaptized. Here Bertha watched over agriculture, caring for the plants, which her infant troop watered carefully, for each babe was supposed to carry a little jar for that express purpose. While the goddess was duly respected and her retreat unmolested, she remained where she was; but tradition relates that she once left the country with her infant train dragging her plough, and settled else-where to continue her kind ministrations. Bertha is the legendary ancestress of several noble families, and she is supposed to be the same as the industrious queen of the same name, the mythical mother of Charlemagne, whose era has become proverbial, for in speaking of the Golden Age in France and Germany it is customary to say, " in the days when Bertha spun."

As this Bertha is supposed to have developed a very large and flat foot, from continually pressing the treadle of her wheel, she is often represented in mediæval art as a woman with a splay foot, and hence known as *la reine pédauque.*

56

BERTHA, THE WHITE LADY

As ancestress of the imperial house of Germany, the White Lady is supposed to appear in the palace before a death or misfortune in the family, and this superstition is still so rife in Germany, that the newspapers in 1884 contained the official report of a sentinel, who declared that he had seen her flit past him in one of the palace corridors.

As Bertha was renowned for her spinning, she naturally was regarded as the special patroness of that branch of female industry, and was said to flit through the streets of every village, at nightfall, during the twelve nights between Christmas and January 6, peering into every window to inspect the spinning of the household.

The maidens whose work had been carefully performed were rewarded by a present of one of her own golden threads or a distaff full of extra fine flax ; but wherever a careless spinner was found, her wheel was broken, her flax soiled, and if she had failed to honour the goddess by eating plenty of the cakes baked at that period of the year, she was cruelly punished.

In Mecklenburg, this same goddess is known as Frau Gode, or Wode, the female form of Wuotan or Odin, and her appearance is always considered the harbinger of great prosperity. She is also supposed to be a great huntress, and to lead the Wild Hunt, mounted upon a white horse, her attendants being changed into hounds and all manner of wild beasts.

In Holland she was called Vrou-elde, and from her the Milky Way is known by the Dutch as *Vrou-elden-straat;* while in parts of Northern Germany she was called Nerthus (Mother Earth). Her sacred car was kept on an island, presumably Rügen, where the priests guarded it carefully until she appeared to take a yearly journey throughout her realm to bless the land. The goddess, her face completely hidden by a thick veil, then sat in this car, which was drawn by two cows, and she was respectfully escorted by her priests. When she passed, the people did homage by ceasing all warfare, and laying aside their weapons. They donned festive attire, and began no quarrel until the goddess had again retired to her sanctuary. Then both car and goddess were bathed in a secret lake (the Schwartze See, in Rügen), which swallowed up the slaves who had assisted at the bathing, and once more the priests resumed their watch over the sanctuary and grove of Nerthus or Hlodyn, to await her next appearance.

In Scandinavia, this goddess was also known as Huldra, and boasted of a train of attendant wood-nymphs, who sometimes sought the society of mortals, to enjoy a dance upon the village green. They could always be detected, however, by the tip of a cow's tail which trailed from beneath their long snow-white garments. These Huldra folk were the special protectors of the cattle on the mountain-sides, and were said to surprise the lonely traveller, at times, by the marvellous beauty of the melodies they sang to beguile the hours at their tasks.

Huldra's Nymphs
B. E. Ward

CHAPTER IV : THOR

The Thunderer

ACCORDING to some mythologists, Thor, or Donar, is the son of Jörd (Erda) and of Odin, but others state that his mother was Frigga, queen of the gods. This child was very remarkable for his great size and strength, and very soon after his birth amazed the assembled gods by playfully lifting and throwing about ten great bales of bear skins. Although generally good-tempered, Thor would occasionally fly into a terrible rage, and as he was very dangerous at these times, his mother, unable to control him, sent him away from home and entrusted him to the care of Vingnir (the winged), and of Hlora (heat). These foster-parents, who are also considered as the personification of sheet-lightning, soon managed to control their troublesome charge, and brought him up so wisely, that the gods entertained a very grateful recollection of their kind offices. Thor himself, recognising all he owed them, assumed the names of Vingthor and Hlorridi, by which he is also known.

> " Cry on, Vingi-Thor,
> With the dancing of the ring-mail and the smitten shields of war."
> *Sigurd the Volsung* (*William Morris*)

Having attained his full growth and the age of reason, Thor was admitted to Asgard among the other gods, where he occupied one of the twelve seats in the great judgment hall. He was also given the realm of Thrud-vang or Thrud-heim, where he built a wonderful palace called Bilskirnir (lightning), the most spacious in all Asgard. It contained five hundred and forty halls for the accommodation of the thralls, who after death were welcomed to his home, where they received equal

59

treatment with their masters in Valhalla, for Thor was
the patron god of the peasants and lower classes.

> " Five hundred halls
> And forty more,
> Methinketh, hath
> Bowed Bilskirnir.
> Of houses roofed
> There's none I know
> My son's surpassing."
> *Sæmund's Edda* (*Percy's tr.*).

As he was god of thunder, Thor alone was never
allowed to pass over the wonderful bridge Bifröst,
lest he should set it aflame by the heat of his presence ;
and when he wished to join his fellow gods by the
Urdar fountain, under the shade of the sacred tree
Yggdrasil, he was forced to make his way thither on
foot, wading through the rivers Kormt and Ormt, and
the two streams Kerlaug, to the trysting place.

Thor, who was honoured as the highest god in
Norway, came second in the trilogy of all the other
countries, and was called " old Thor," because he is
supposed by some mythologists to have belonged to an
older dynasty of gods, and not on account of his actual
age, for he was represented and described as a man in
his prime, tall and well formed, with muscular limbs
and bristling red hair and beard, from which, in moments
of anger, the sparks flew in showers.

> " First, Thor with the bent brow,
>   In red beard muttering low,
>   Darting fierce lightnings from eyeballs that glow,
> Comes, while each chariot wheel
> Echoes in thunder peal,
>   As his dread hammer shock
>   Makes Earth and Heaven rock,
> Clouds rifting above, while Earth quakes below."
> *Valhalla* (*J. C. Jones*).

Thor

B. E. Fogelberg

The Northern races further adorned him with a crown, on each point of which was either a glittering star, or a steadily burning flame, so that his head was ever surrounded by a kind of halo of fire, his own element.

Thor's Hammer

Thor was the proud possessor of a magic hammer called Miölnir (the crusher) which he hurled at his enemies, the frost-giants, with destructive power, and which possessed the wonderful property of always returning to his hand, however far away he might hurl it.

> "I am the Thunderer!
> Here in my Northland,
> My fastness and fortress,
> Reign I forever!
>
> "Here amid icebergs
> Rule I the nations;
> This is my hammer,
> Miölnir the mighty;
> Giants and sorcerers
> Cannot withstand it!"
> *Saga of King Olaf* (*Longfellow*).

As this huge hammer, the emblem of the thunder-bolts, was generally red-hot, the god had an iron gauntlet called Iarn-greiper, which enabled him to grasp it firmly. He could hurl Miölnir a great distance, and his strength, which was always remarkable, was doubled when he wore his magic belt called Megin-giörd.

> "This is my girdle:
> Whenever I brace it,
> Strength is redoubled!"
> *Saga of King Olaf* (*Longfellow*)

Thor's hammer was considered so very sacred by the

ancient Northern people, that they were wont to make the sign of the hammer, as the Christians later taught them to make the sign of the cross, to ward off all evil influences, and to secure blessings. The same sign was also made over the newly born infant when water was poured over its head and a name given. The hammer was used to drive in boundary stakes, which it was considered sacrilegious to remove, to hallow the threshold of a new house, to solemnise a marriage, and, lastly, it played a part in the consecration of the funeral pyre upon which the bodies of heroes, together with their weapons and steeds, and, in some cases, with their wives and dependents, were burned.

In Sweden, Thor, like Odin, was supposed to wear a broad-brimmed hat, and hence the storm-clouds in that country are known as Thor's hat, a name also given to one of the principal mountains in Norway. The rumble and roar of the thunder were said to be the roll of his chariot, for he alone among the gods never rode on horseback, but walked, or drove in a brazen chariot drawn by two goats, Tanngniostr (tooth-cracker), and Tanngrisnr (tooth-gnasher), from whose teeth and hoofs the sparks constantly flew.

> "Thou camest near the next, O warrior Thor !
> Shouldering thy hammer, in thy chariot drawn,
> Swaying the long-hair'd goats with silver'd rein."
> *Balder Dead* (*Matthew Arnold*).

When the god thus drove from place to place, he was called Aku-thor, or Thor the charioteer, and in Southern Germany the people, fancying a brazen chariot alone inadequate to furnish all the noise they heard, declared it was loaded with copper kettles, which rattled and clashed, and therefore often called him, with disrespectful familiarity, the kettle-vendor.

Thor's Family

Thor was twice married; first to the giantess Iarnsaxa (iron stone), who bore him two sons, Magni (strength) and Modi (courage), both destined to survive their father and the twilight of the gods, and rule over the new world which was to rise like a phœnix from the ashes of the first. His second wife was Sif, the golden-haired, who also bore him two children, Lorride, and a daughter named Thrud, a young giantess renowned for her size and strength. True to the well-known affinity of contrast, Thrud was wooed by the dwarf Alvis, whom she rather favoured; and one evening, when this suitor, who, being a dwarf, could not face the light of day, presented himself in Asgard to sue for her hand, the assembled gods did not refuse their consent. They had scarcely signified their approbation, however, when Thor, who had been absent, suddenly appeared, and casting a glance of contempt upon the puny lover, declared he would have to prove that his knowledge atoned for his small stature, before he could win his bride.

To test Alvis's mental powers, Thor then questioned him in the language of the gods, Vanas, elves, and dwarfs, artfully prolonging his examination until sunrise, when the first beam of light, falling upon the unhappy dwarf, petrified him. There he stood, an enduring example of the gods' power, to serve as a warning to all other dwarfs who might dare to test it.

> " Ne'er in human bosom
> Have I found so many
> Words of the old time.
> Thee with subtlest cunning
> Have I yet befooled.
> Above ground standeth thou, dwarf
> By day art overtaken,
> Bright sunshine fills the hall."
> *Sæmund's Edda (Howitt's version).*

Sif, the Golden-haired

Sif, Thor's wife, was very vain of a magnificent head of long golden hair which covered her from head to foot like a brilliant veil; and as she too was a symbol of the earth, her hair was said to represent the long grass, or the golden grain covering the Northern harvest fields. Thor was very proud of his wife's beautiful hair; imagine his dismay, therefore, upon waking one morning, to find her shorn, and as bald and denuded of ornament as the earth when the grain has been garnered, and nothing but the stubble remains! In his anger, Thor sprang to his feet, vowing he would punish the perpetrator of this outrage, whom he immediately and rightly conjectured to be Loki, the archplotter, ever on the look-out for some evil deed to perform. Seizing his hammer, Thor went in search of Loki, who attempted to evade the irate god by changing his form. But it was all to no purpose; Thor soon overtook him, and without more ado caught him by the throat, and almost strangled him ere he yielded to his imploring signs and relaxed his powerful grip. When he could draw his breath, Loki begged forgiveness, but all his entreaties were vain, until he promised to procure for Sif a new head of hair, as beautiful as the first, and as luxuriant in growth.

> " And thence for Sif new tresses I'll bring
>   Of gold, ere the daylight's gone,
> So that she shall liken a field in spring,
>   With its yellow-flowered garment on."
>   *The Dwarfs*, Oehlenschläger (*Pigott's tr.*).

Then Thor consented to let the traitor go; so Loki rapidly crept down into the bowels of the earth, where Svart-alfa-heim was situated, to beg the dwarf Dvalin to

Sif and Thor

J. C. Dollman

64

fashion not only the precious hair, but a present for Odin and Frey, whose anger he wished to disarm.

His request was favourably received and the dwarf fashioned the spear Gungnir, which never failed in its aim, and the ship Skidbladnir, which, always wafted by favourable winds, could sail through the air as well as on the water, and which had this further magic property, that although it could contain the gods and all their steeds, it could be folded up into the very smallest compass and thrust in one's pocket. Lastly, he spun the finest golden thread, from which he fashioned the hair required for Sif, declaring that as soon as it touched her head it would grow fast there and become as her own.

> " Though they now seem dead, let them touch but her head,
>   Each hair shall the life-moisture fill ;
>   Nor shall malice nor spell henceforward prevail
>   Sif's tresses to work aught of ill."
>   *The Dwarfs*, Oehlenschläger (*Pigott's tr.*).

Loki was so pleased with these proofs of the dwarfs' skill that he declared the son of Ivald to be the most clever of smiths—words which were overheard by Brock, another dwarf, who exclaimed that he was sure his brother Sindri could produce three objects which would surpass those which Loki held, not only in intrinsic value, but also in magical properties. Loki immediately challenged the dwarf to show his skill, wagering his head against Brock's on the result of the undertaking.

Sindri, apprised of the wager, accepted Brock's offer to blow the bellows, warning him, however, that he must work persistently and not for a moment relax his efforts if he wished him to succeed; then he threw some gold in the fire, and went out to bespeak the favour of

E

the hidden powers. During his absence Brock diligently plied the bellows, while Loki, hoping to make
him pause, changed himself into a gadfly and cruelly
stung his hand. In spite of the pain, the dwarf kept
on blowing, and when Sindri returned, he drew out of
the fire an enormous wild boar, called Gullin-bursti,
because of its golden bristles, which had the power of
radiating light as it flitted across the sky, for it could
travel through the air with marvellous velocity.

> " And now, strange to tell, from the roaring fire
> Came the golden-haired Gullinbörst,
> To serve as a charger the sun-god Frey,
> Sure, of all wild boars this the first."
> *The Dwarfs, Oehlenschläger (Pigott's tr.).*

This first piece of work successfully completed, Sindri
flung some more gold on the fire and bade his brother
resume blowing, while he again went out to secure
magic assistance. This time Loki, still disguised as a
gadfly, stung the dwarf on his cheek ; but in spite of
the pain Brock worked on, and when Sindri returned,
he triumphantly drew out of the flames the magic ring
Draupnir, the emblem of fertility, from which eight
similar rings dropped every ninth night.

> " They worked it and turned it with wondrous skill,
> Till they gave it the virtue rare,
> That each thrice third night from its rim there fell
> Eight rings, as their parent fair."
> *The Dwarfs, Oehlenschläger (Pigott's tr.).*

Now a lump of iron was cast in the flames, and with
renewed caution not to forfeit their success by inatten-
tion, Sindri passed out, leaving Brock to ply the
bellows as before. Loki was now in desperation and
he prepared for a final effort. This time, still in the
guise of the gadfly, he stung the dwarf above the eye

until the blood began to flow in such a stream, that it prevented his seeing what he was doing. Hastily raising his hand for a second, Brock dashed aside the stream of blood ; but short as was the interruption it had worked irreparable harm, and when Sindri drew his work out of the fire he uttered an exclamation of disappointment for the hammer he had fashioned was short in the handle.

> " Then the dwarf raised his hand to his brow for the smart,
>   Ere the iron well out was beat,
> And they found that the haft by an inch was too short,
>   But to alter it then 'twas too late."
>   *The Dwarfs, Oehlenschläger (Pigott's tr.).*

Notwithstanding this mishap, Brock was sure of winning the wager and he did not hesitate to present himself before the gods in Asgard, where he gave Odin the ring Draupnir, Frey the boar Gullin-bursti, and Thor the hammer Miölnir, whose power none could resist.

Loki in turn gave the spear Gungnir to Odin, the ship Skidbladnir to Frey, and the golden hair to Thor ; but although the latter immediately grew upon Sif's head and was unanimously declared more beautiful than her own locks had ever been, the gods decreed that Brock had won the wager, on the ground that the hammer Miölnir, in Thor's hands, would prove invaluable against the frost giants on the last day.

> " And at their head came Thor,
> Shouldering his hammer, which the giants know."
>   *Balder Dead (Matthew Arnold).*

In order to save his head, Loki fled precipitately, but was overtaken by Thor, who brought him back and handed him over to Brock, telling him, however, that although Loki's head was rightfully his, he must not touch his neck. Hindered from obtaining full vengeance, the dwarf determined to punish Loki by sewing his lips together, and as his sword would not pierce them, he borrowed his brother's awl for the purpose. However, Loki, after enduring the gods' gibes in silence for a little while, managed to cut the string and soon after was as loquacious as ever.

In spite of his redoubtable hammer, Thor was not held in dread as the injurious god of the storm, who destroyed peaceful homesteads and ruined the harvest by sudden hail-storms and cloud-bursts. The Northmen fancied he hurled it only against ice giants and rocky walls, reducing the latter to powder to fertilise the earth and make it yield plentiful fruit to the tillers of the soil.

In Germany, where the eastern storms are always cold and blighting, while the western bring warm rains and mild weather, Thor was supposed to journey always from west to east, to wage war against the evil spirits which would fain have enveloped the country in impenetrable veils of mist and have bound it in icy fetters.

Thor's Journey to Jötun-heim

As the giants from Jötun-heim were continually sending out cold blasts of wind to nip the tender buds and hinder the growth of the flowers, Thor once made up his mind to go and force them to behave better. Accompanied by Loki he set out in his chariot, and after riding for a whole day the gods came at nightfall to the confines of the giant-world, where, seeing a peasant's hut, they resolved to stay for rest and refreshment.

Their host was hospitable but very poor, and Thor, seeing that he would scarcely be able to supply the

necessary food to satisfy his by no means small appetite, slew both his goats, which he cooked and made
ready to eat, inviting his host and family to partake
freely of the food thus provided, but cautioning them
to throw all the bones, without breaking them, into the
skins of the goats which he had spread out on the floor.

The peasant and his family ate heartily, but his son
Thialfi, encouraged by mischievous Loki, ventured to
break one of the bones and suck out the marrow,
thinking his disobedience would not be detected. On
the morrow, however, Thor, ready to depart, struck the
goat skins with his hammer Miölnir, and immediately
the goats sprang up as lively as before, except that one
seemed somewhat lame. Perceiving that his commands
had been disregarded, Thor would have slain the whole
family in his wrath. The culprit acknowledged his
fault, however, and the peasant offered to compensate
for the loss by giving the irate god not only his son
Thialfi, but also his daughter Roskva, to serve him for
ever.

Charging the man to take good care of the goats,
which he left there until he should return, and bidding
the young peasants accompany him, Thor now set out
on foot with Loki, and after walking all day found
himself at nightfall in a bleak and barren country,
which was enveloped in an almost impenetrable grey
mist. After seeking for some time, Thor saw through
the fog the uncertain outline of what looked like a
strangely-shaped house. Its open portal was so wide
and high that it seemed to take up all one side of the
house. Entering and finding neither fire nor light,
Thor and his companions flung themselves wearily
down on the floor to sleep, but were soon disturbed by
a peculiar noise, and a prolonged trembling of the
ground beneath them. Fearing lest the main roof

should fall during this earthquake, Thor and his companions took refuge in a wing of the building, where they soon fell sound asleep. At dawn, the god and his companions passed out, but they had not gone very far ere they saw the recumbent form of a sleeping giant, and perceived that the peculiar sounds which had disturbed their rest were produced by his snores. At that moment the giant awoke, arose, stretched himself, looked about him for his missing property, and a second later picked up the object which Thor and his companions had mistaken in the darkness for a house. They then perceived with amazement that this was nothing more than a huge mitten, and that the wing in which they had all slept was the separate place for the giant's great thumb! Learning that Thor and his companions were on their way to Utgard, as the giants' realm was also called, Skrymir, the giant, proposed to be their guide ; and after walking with them all day, he brought them at nightfall to a spot where he proposed to rest. Ere he composed himself for sleep, however, he offered them the provisions in his wallet. But, in spite of strenuous efforts, neither Thor nor his companions could unfasten the knots which Skrymir had tied.

> " Skrymir's thongs
> Seemed to thee hard,
> When at the food thou couldst not get,
> When, in full health, of hunger dying."
> Sæmund's Edda (Thorpe's tr.).

Utgard-loki

Angry because of his snoring, which kept them awake, Thor thrice dealt him fearful blows with his hammer. These strokes, instead of annihilating the monster, merely evoked sleepy comments to the effect that a leaf, a bit of bark, or a twig from a bird's nest overhead had fallen upon his face. Early on the morrow, Skrymir left Thor and his companions, pointing out the shortest road to Utgard-loki's castle, which was built of great ice blocks, with huge glittering icicles as pillars. The gods, slipping between the bars of the great gate, presented themselves boldly before the king of the giants, Utgard-loki, who, recognising them, immediately pretended to be greatly surprised at their small size, and expressed a wish to see for himself what they could do, as he had often heard their prowess vaunted.

Loki, who had fasted longer than he wished, immediately declared he was ready to eat for a wager with any one. So the king ordered a great wooden trough full of meat to be brought into the hall, and placing Loki at one end and his cook Logi at the other, he bade them see which would win. Although Loki did wonders, and soon reached the middle of the trough, he found that, whereas he had picked the bones clean, his opponent had devoured both them and the trough.

Smiling contemptuously, Utgard-loki said that it was evident they could not do much in the eating line, and this so nettled Thor that he declared if Loki could not eat like the voracious cook, he felt confident he could drain the biggest vessel in the house, such was his unquenchable thirst. Immediately a horn was brought in, and, Utgard-loki declaring that good drinkers emptied it at one draught, moderately thirsty persons at two, and small drinkers at three, Thor applied his lips to the rim. But, although he drank so deep that he thought he would burst, the liquid still came almost up to the rim when he raised his head. A second and third attempt to empty this horn proved equally unsuccessful. Thialfi then offered to run a race, but a young fellow named Hugi, who was matched against him, soon outstripped him, although Thialfi ran remarkably fast.

Thor proposed next to show his strength by lifting weights, and was challenged to pick up the giant's cat. Seizing an opportunity to tighten his belt Megin-giörd, which greatly enhanced his strength, he tugged and strained but was able only to raise one of its paws from the floor.

> " Strong is great Thor, no doubt, when Megingarder
> He braces tightly o'er his rock-firm loins."
> *Viking Tales of the North* (R. B. *Anderson*).

A last attempt on his part to wrestle with Utgard-loki's old nurse Elli, the only opponent deemed worthy of such a puny fellow, ended just as disastrously, and the gods, acknowledging they were beaten, were hospitably entertained. On the morrow they were escorted to the confines of Utgard, where the giant politely informed them that he hoped they would never call upon him again, as he had been forced to employ magic against them. He then went on to explain that he was the giant Skrymir, and that had he not taken the precaution to interpose a mountain between his head and Thor's blows, while he seemingly lay asleep, he would have been slain, as deep clefts in the mountain side, to which he pointed, testified to the god's strength. Next he informed them that Loki's opponent was Logi (wild fire) ; that Thialfi had run a race with Hugi (thought), than which no swifter runner exists ; that Thor's drinking horn was connected with the ocean, where his deep draughts had produced a perceptible ebb ; that the cat was in reality the terrible Midgard snake encircling the world, which Thor had nearly pulled out of the sea ; and that Elli, his nurse, was old age, whom none can resist. Having finished these

72

Thor and the Mountain   72
J. C. Dollman

explanations and cautioned them never to return or he
would defend himself by similar delusions, Utgard-loki
vanished, and although Thor angrily brandished his
hammer, and would have destroyed his castle, such a
mist enveloped it that it could not be seen, and the
thunder god was obliged to return to Thrud-vang
without having administered his purposed salutary
lesson to the race of giants.

> " The strong-armed Thor
> Full oft against Jotunheim did wend,
> But spite his belt celestial, spite his gauntlets,
> Utgard-Loki still his throne retains ;
> Evil, itself a force, to force yields never."
> *Viking Tales of the North* (*R. B. Anderson*).

Thor and Hrungnir

Odin himself was once dashing through the air on
his eight-footed steed Sleipnir, when he attracted the
attention of the giant Hrungnir, who proposed a race,
declaring that Gullfaxi, his steed, could rival Sleipnir in
speed. In the heat of the race, Hrungnir did not
notice the direction in which they were going, until, in
the vain hope of overtaking Odin, he urged his steed
to the very gates of Valhalla. Discovering then where
he was, the giant grew pale with fear, for he knew he
had jeopardised his life by venturing into the stronghold
of the gods, his hereditary foes.

The Æsir, however, were too honourable to take
even an enemy at a disadvantage, and, instead of doing
him harm, they asked him into their banqueting-halls,
where he proceeded to indulge in liberal potations of
the heavenly mead set before him. He soon grew so
excited that he began to boast of his power, declaring
he would come some day and take possession of Asgard,
which he would destroy, together with the gods, save

only Freya and Sif, upon whom he gazed with an admiring leer.

The gods, knowing he was not responsible, let him talk unmolested; but Thor, coming home just then from one of his journeys, and hearing his threat to carry away the beloved Sif, flew into a terrible rage. He furiously brandished his hammer, with intent to annihilate the boaster. This the gods would not permit, however, and they quickly threw themselves between the irate Thunderer and their guest, imploring Thor to respect the sacred rights of hospitality, and not to desecrate their peace-stead by shedding blood.

Thor was at last induced to bridle his wrath, but he demanded that Hrungnir should appoint a time and place for a holmgang, as a Northern duel was generally called. Thus challenged, Hrungnir promised to meet Thor at Griottunagard, the confines of his realm, three days later, and departed somewhat sobered by the fright he had experienced. When his fellow giants heard how rash he had been, they chided him sorely; but they took counsel together in order to make the best of a bad situation. Hrungnir told them that he was to have the privilege of being accompanied by a squire, whom Thialfi would engage in fight, wherefore they proceeded to construct a creature of clay, nine miles long, and proportionately wide, whom they called Mokerkialfi (mist wader). As they could find no human heart big enough to put in this monster's breast, they secured that of a mare, which, however, kept fluttering and quivering with apprehension. The day of the duel arrived. Hrungnir and his squire were on the ground awaiting the arrival of their respective opponents. The giant had not only a flint heart and skull, but also a shield and club of the same substance, and therefore deemed himself well-nigh invincible. Thialfi came before his

74

master and soon after there was a terrible rumbling and shaking which made the giant apprehensive that his enemy would come up through the ground and attack him from underneath. He therefore followed a hint from Thialfi and stood upon his shield.

A moment later, however, he saw his mistake, for, while Thialfi attacked Mokerkialfi with a spade, Thor came with a rush upon the scene and flung his hammer full at his opponent's head. Hrungnir, to ward off the blow, interposed his stone club, which was shivered into pieces that flew all over the earth, supplying all the flint stones thereafter to be found, and one fragment sank deep intoThor's forehead. As the god dropped fainting to the ground, his hammer crashed against the head of Hrungnir, who fell dead beside him, in such a position that one of his ponderous legs was thrown over the recumbent god.

> " Thou now remindest me
> How I with Hrungnir fought,
> That stout-hearted Jotun,
> Whose head was all of stone;
> Yet I made him fall
> And sink before me."
>
> *Sæmund's Edda (Thorpe's tr.)*.

Thialfi, who, in the meanwhile, had disposed of the great clay giant with its cowardly mare's heart, now rushed to his master's assistance, but his efforts were unavailing, nor could the other gods, whom he quickly summoned, raise the pinioning leg. While they were standing there, helplessly wondering what they should do next, Thor's little son Magni came up. According to varying accounts, he was then only three days or three years old, but he quickly seized the giant's foot, and, unaided, set his father free, declaring that had he only been summoned sooner he would easily have disposed of both giant and squire. This exhibition of strength made the gods marvel greatly, and helped them to recognise the truth of the various predictions, which one and all declared that their descendants would be mightier than they, would survive them, and would rule in their turn over the new heaven and earth.

To reward his son for his timely aid, Thor gave him the steed Gullfaxi (golden-maned), to which he had fallen heir by right of conquest, and Magni ever after rode this marvellous horse, which almost equalled the renowned Sleipnir in speed and endurance.

Groa, the Sorceress

After vainly trying to remove the stone splinter from his forehead, Thor sadly returned home to Thrud-vang, where Sif's loving efforts were equally unsuccessful. She therefore resolved to send for Groa (green-making), a sorceress, noted for her skill in medicine and for the efficacy of her spells and incantations. Groa immediately signified her readiness to render every service in her power to the god who had so often benefited her, and solemnly began to recite powerful runes, under whose influence Thor felt the stone grow looser and looser. His delight at the prospect of a speedy deliverance made Thor wish to reward the enchantress forthwith, and knowing that nothing could give greater pleasure to a mother than the prospect of seeing a long-lost child, he proceeded to tell her that he had recently crossed the Elivagar, or ice streams, to rescue her little son Orvandil (germ) from the frost giants' cruel power, and had succeeded in carrying him off in a basket. But, as the little rogue would persist in sticking one of his bare toes through a hole in the basket, it had been frost-bitten, and Thor, accidentally breaking it off, had flung it up into the sky, to shine as a star, known in the North as " Orvandil's Toe."

Delighted with these tidings, the prophetess paused in her incantations to express her joy, but, having forgotten just where she left off, she was unable to continue her spell, and the flint stone remained embedded in Thor's forehead, whence it could never be dislodged.

Of course, as Thor's hammer always did him such good service, it was the most prized of all his possessions, and his dismay was very great when he awoke one morning and found it gone. His cry of anger and disappointment soon brought Loki to his side, and to him Thor confided the secret of his loss, declaring that were the giants to hear of it, they would soon attempt to storm Asgard and destroy the gods.

> " Wroth waxed Thor, when his sleep was flown,
> And he found his trusty hammer gone;
> He smote his brow, his beard he shook,
> The son of earth 'gan round him look;
> And this the first word that he spoke:
> ' Now listen what I tell thee, Loke;
> Which neither on earth below is known,
> Nor in heaven above: my hammer's gone."
> *Thrym's Quida (Herbert's tr.).*

Thor and Thrym

Loki declared he would try to discover the thief and recover the hammer, if Freya would lend him her falcon plumes, and he immediately hastened off to Folkvang to borrow them. His errand was successful and in the form of a bird he then winged his flight across the river Ifing, and over the barren stretches of Jötun-heim, where he suspected that the thief would be found. There he saw Thrym, prince of the frost giants and god of the destructive thunder-storm, sitting alone on a hill-side. Artfully questioning him, he soon learned that Thrym had stolen the hammer and had buried it deep underground. Moreover, he found that there was little hope of its being restored unless Freya were brought to him arrayed as a bride.

> " I have the Thunderer's hammer bound
> Fathoms eight beneath the ground ;
> With it shall no one homeward tread
> Till he bring me Freya to share my bed."
>
> *Thrym's Quida (Herbert's tr.).*

Indignant at the giant's presumption, Loki returned to Thrud-vang, but Thor declared it would be well to visit Freya and try to prevail upon her to sacrifice herself for the general good. But when the Æsir told the goddess of beauty what they wished her to do, she flew into such a passion that even her necklace burst. She told them that she would never leave her beloved husband for any god, much less to marry a detested giant and dwell in Jötun-heim, where all was dreary in the extreme, and where she would soon die of longing for the green fields and flowery meadows, in which she loved to roam. Seeing that further persuasions would be useless, Loki and Thor returned home and there deliberated upon another plan for recovering the hammer. By Heimdall's advice, which, however, was only accepted with extreme reluctance, Thor borrowed and put on Freya's clothes together with her necklace, and enveloped himself in a thick veil. Loki, having attired himself as handmaiden, then mounted with him in the goat-drawn chariot, and the strangely attired pair set out for Jötun-heim, where they intended to play the respective parts of the goddess of beauty and her attendant.

78

THOR AND THRYM

" Home were driven
Then the goats,
And hitched to the car;
Hasten they must—
The mountains crashed,
The earth stood in flames:
Odin's son
Rode to Jotun-heim."

Norse Mythology (*R. B. Anderson*).

Thrym welcomed his guests at the palace door, over-joyed at the thought that he was about to secure undisputed possession of the goddess of beauty, for whom he had long sighed in vain. He quickly led them to the banqueting-hall, where Thor, the bride elect, distinguished himself by eating an ox, eight huge salmon, and all the cakes and sweets provided for the women, washing down these miscellaneous viands with the contents of two barrels of mead.

The giant bridegroom watched these gastronomic feats with amazement, whereupon Loki, in order to reassure him, confidentially whispered that the bride was so deeply in love with him that she had not been able to taste a morsel of food for more than eight days. Thrym then sought to kiss the bride, but drew back appalled at the fire of her glance, which Loki explained as a burning glance of love. The giant's sister, claiming the usual gifts, was not even noticed ; wherefore Loki again whispered to the wondering Thrym that love makes people absent-minded. Intoxicated with passion and mead, which he, too, had drunk in liberal quantities, the bridegroom now bade his servants produce the sacred hammer to consecrate the marriage, and as soon as it was brought he himself laid it in the pretended Freya's lap. The next moment a powerful hand closed over the short handle, and soon the giant, his sister,

79

and all the invited guests, were slain by the terrible Thor.

> " ' Bear in the hammer to plight the maid ;
> Upon her lap the bruiser lay,
> And firmly plight our hands and fay.'
> The Thunderer's soul smiled in his breast ;
> When the hammer hard on his lap was placed,
> Thrym first, the king of the Thursi, he slew,
> And slaughtered all the giant crew."
>
> *Thrym's Quida (Herbert's tr.).*

Leaving a smoking heap of ruins behind them, the gods then drove rapidly back to Asgard, where the borrowed garments were given back to Freya, much to the relief of Thor, and the Æsir rejoiced at the recovery of the precious hammer. When next Odin gazed upon that part of Jötun-heim from his throne Hlidskialf, he saw the ruins covered with tender green shoots, for Thor, having conquered his enemy, had taken possession of his land, which henceforth would no longer remain barren and desolate, but would bring forth fruit in abundance.

Thor and Geirrod

Loki once borrowed Freya's falcon-garb and flew off in search of adventures to another part of Jötun-heim, where he perched on top of the gables of Geirrod's house. He soon attracted the attention of this giant, who bade one of his servants catch the bird. Amused at the fellow's clumsy attempts to secure him, Loki flitted about from place to place, only moving just as the giant was about to lay hands upon him, when, miscalculating his distance, he suddenly found himself a captive.

Attracted by the bird's bright eyes, Geirrod looked closely at it and concluded that it was a god in disguise.

and finding that he could not force him to speak, he locked him in a cage, where he kept him for three whole months without food or drink. Conquered at last by hunger and thirst, Loki revealed his identity, and obtained his release by promising that he would induce Thor to visit Geirrod without his hammer, belt, or magic gauntlet. Loki then flew back to Asgard, and told Thor that he had been royally entertained, and that his host had expressed a strong desire to see the powerful thunder-god, of whom he had heard such wonderful tales. Flattered by this artful speech, Thor was induced to consent to a friendly journey to Jötunheim, and the two gods set out, leaving the three marvellous weapons at home. They had not gone far, however, ere they came to the house of the giantess Grid, one of Odin's many wives. Seeing Thor unarmed, she warned him to beware of treachery and lent him her own girdle, staff, and glove. Some time after leaving her, Thor and Loki came to the river Veimer, which the Thunderer, accustomed to wading, prepared to ford, bidding Loki and Thialfi cling fast to his belt.

In the middle of the stream, however, a sudden cloud-burst and freshet overtook them; the waters began to rise and roar, and although Thor leaned heavily upon his staff, he was almost swept away by the force of the raging current.

> " Wax not, Veimer,
> Since to wade I desire
> To the realm of the giants !
> Know, if thou waxest,
> Then waxes my asa-might
> As high as the heavens."
> *Norse Mythology* (*R. B. Anderson*).

Thor now became aware of the presence, up stream, of Geirrod's daughter Gialp, and rightly suspecting that

F   81 she was the cause of the storm, he picked up a huge boulder and flung it at her, muttering that the best place to dam a river was at its source. The missile had the desired effect, for the giantess fled, the waters abated, and Thor, exhausted but safe, pulled himself up on the opposite bank by a little shrub, the mountain-ash or sorb. This has since been known as "Thor's salvation," and occult powers have been attributed to it. After resting awhile Thor and his companions resumed their journey ; but upon arriving at Geirrod's house the god was so exhausted that he sank wearily upon the only chair in sight. To his surprise, however, he felt it rising beneath him, and fearful lest he should be crushed against the rafters, he pushed the borrowed staff against the ceiling and forced the chair downward with all his might. Then followed a terrible cracking, sudden cries, and moans of pain ; and when Thor came to investigate, it appeared that the giant's daughters, Gialp and Greip, had slipped under his chair with intent treacherously to slay him, and they had reaped a righteous retribution and both lay crushed to death.

> " Once I employed
> My asa-might
> In the realm of giants,
> When Gialp and Greip,
> Geirrod's daughters,
> Wanted to lift me to heaven."
> *Norse Mythology* (*R. B. Anderson*).

Geirrod now appeared and challenged Thor to a test of strength and skill, but without waiting for a pre-concerted signal, he flung a red-hot wedge at him. Thor, quick of eye and a practised catcher, caught the missile with the giantess's iron glove, and hurled it back at his opponent. Such was the force of the god, that the missile passed, not only through the pillar behind which the giant had taken refuge, but through him and the wall of the house, and buried itself deep in the earth without.

Thor then strode up to the giant's corpse, which at the blow from his weapon had been petrified into stone, and set it up in a conspicuous place, as a monument of his strength and of the victory he had won over his redoubtable foes, the mountain giants.

The Worship of Thor

Thor's name has been given to many of the places he was wont to frequent, such as the principal harbour of the Faroe Islands, and to families which claim to be descended from him. It is still extant in such names as Thunderhill in Surrey, and in the family names of Thorburn and Thorwaldsen, but is most conspicuous in the name of one of the days of the week, Thor's day or Thursday.

> " Over the whole earth
> Still is it Thor's day ! "
> *Saga of King Olaf* (*Longfellow*).

Thor was considered a pre-eminently benevolent deity, and it was for that reason that he was so widely worshipped and that temples to his worship arose at Moeri, Hlader, Godey, Gothland, Upsala, and other places, where the people never failed to invoke him for a favourable year at Yule-tide, his principal festival. It was customary on this occasion to burn a great log of oak, his sacred tree, as an emblem of the warmth and light of summer, which would drive away the darkness and cold of winter.

Brides invariably wore red, Thor's favourite colour, which was considered emblematical of love, and for the same reason betrothal rings in the North were almost always set with a red stone.

Thor's temples and statues, like Odin's, were fashioned of wood, and the greater number of them were destroyed during the reign of King Olaf the Saint. According to ancient chronicles, this monarch forcibly converted his subjects. He was specially incensed against the inhabitants of a certain province, because they worshipped a rude image of Thor, which they decked with golden ornaments, and before which they set food every evening, declaring the god ate it, as no trace of it was left in the morning.

The people, being called upon in 1030 to renounce this idol in favour of the true God, promised to consent if the morrow were cloudy ; but when after a whole night spent by Olaf in ardent prayer, there followed a cloudy day, the obstinate people declared they were not yet convinced of his God's power, and would only believe if the sun shone on the next day.

Once more Olaf spent the night in prayer, but at dawn, to his great chagrin, the sky was overcast. Nevertheless, he assembled the people near Thor's statue, and after secretly bidding his principal attendant to smash the idol with his battle-axe if the people turned their eyes away but for a moment, he began to address them. Suddenly, while all were listening to him, Olaf pointed to the horizon, where the sun was slowly breaking its way through the clouds, and exclaimed, " Behold our God ! " The people one and all turned to see what he meant, and the attendant seized this opportunity for attacking the idol, which yielded easily to his blows, and a host of mice and other vermin scattered hastily from its hollow interior. Seeing now that the food placed before their god had been devoured by noxious animals only, the people ceased to revere Thor, and definitely accepted the faith which King Olaf had so long and vainly pressed upon them.

CHAPTER V: TYR

The God of War

TYR Tiu, or Ziu was the son of Odin, and, according to different mythologists, his mother was Frigga, queen of the gods, or a beautiful giantess whose name is unknown, but who was a personification of the raging sea. He is the god of martial honour, and one of the twelve principal deities of Asgard. Although he appears to have had no special dwelling there, he was always welcome to Vingolf or Valhalla, and occupied one of the twelve thrones in the great council hall of Glads-heim.

> "The hall Glads-heim, which is built of gold;
> Where are in circle, ranged twelve golden chairs,
> And in the midst one higher, Odin's Throne."
> *Balder Dead (Matthew Arnold).*

As the God of courage and of war, Tyr was frequently invoked by the various nations of the North, who cried to him, as well as to Odin, to obtain victory. That he ranked next to Odin and Thor is proved by his name, Tiu, having been given to one of the days of the week, Tiu's day, which in modern English has become Tuesday. Under the name of Ziu, Tyr was the principal divinity of the Suabians, who originally called their capital, the modern Augsburg, Ziusburg. This people, venerating the god as they did, were wont to worship him under the emblem of a sword, his distinctive attribute, and in his honour held great sword dances, where various figures were performed. Sometimes the participants forming two long lines, crossed their swords, point upward, and challenged the boldest among their number to take a flying leap over them. At other times the warriors joined their sword points closely

85

together in the shape of a rose or wheel, and when this figure was complete invited their chief to stand on the navel thus formed of flat, shining steel blades, and then they bore him upon it through the camp in triumph. The sword point was further considered so sacred that it became customary to register oaths upon it.

> " . . . Come hither, gentlemen,
> And lay your hands again upon my sword ;
> Never to speak of this that you have heard,
> Swear by my sword."
>
> *Hamlet* (*Shakespeare*).

A distinctive feature of the worship of this god among the Franks and some other Northern nations was that the priests called Druids or Godi offered up human sacrifices upon his altars, generally cutting the bloody- or spread-eagle upon their victims, that is to say, making a deep incision on either side of the back-bone, turning the ribs thus loosened inside out, and tearing out the viscera through the opening thus made. Of course only prisoners of war were treated thus, and it was considered a point of honour with north European races to endure this torture without a moan. These sacrifices were made upon rude stone altars called dolmens, which can still be seen in Northern Europe. As Tyr was considered the patron god of the sword, it was deemed indispensable to engrave the sign or rune representing him upon the blade of every sword—an observance which the Edda enjoined upon all those who were desirous of obtaining victory.

> " Sig-runes thou must know,
> If victory (*sigr*) thou wilt have,
> And on thy sword's hilt rist them ;
> Some on the chapes,
> Some on the guard,
> And twice name the name of Tyr."
>
> *Lay of Sigdrifa* (*Thorpe's tr.*).

TYR'S SWORD

Tyr was identical with the Saxon god Saxnot (from *sax*, a sword), and with Er, Heru, or Cheru, the chief divinity of the Cheruski, who also considered him god of the sun, and deemed his shining sword blade an emblem of its rays.

> " This very sword a ray of light
> Snatched from the Sun ! "
> *Valhalla (J. C. Jones)*.

Tyr's Sword

According to an ancient legend, Cheru's sword, which had been fashioned by the same dwarfs, sons of Ivald, who had also made Odin's spear, was held very sacred by his people, to whose care he had entrusted it, declaring that those who possessed it were sure to have the victory over their foes. But although carefully guarded in the temple, where it was hung so that it reflected the first beams of the morning sun, it suddenly and mysteriously disappeared one night. A Vala, druidess, or prophetess, consulted by the priests, revealed that the Norns had decreed that whoever wielded it would conquer the world and come to his death by it ; but in spite of all entreaties she refused to tell who had taken it or where it might be found. Some time after this occurrence a tall and dignified stranger came to Cologne, where Vitellius, the Roman prefect, was feasting, and called him away from his beloved dainties. In the presence of the Roman soldiery he gave him the sword, telling him it would bring him glory and renown, and finally hailed him as emperor. The cry was taken up by the assembled legions, and Vitellius, without making any personal effort to secure the honour, found himself elected Emperor of Rome.

The new ruler, however, was so absorbed in indulging

his taste for food and drink that he paid but little heed to the divine weapon. One day while leisurely making his way towards Rome he carelessly left it hanging in the antechamber to his pavilion. A German soldier seized this opportunity to substitute in its stead his own rusty blade, and the besotted emperor did not notice the exchange. When he arrived at Rome, he learned that the Eastern legions had named Vespasian emperor, and that he was even then on his way home to claim the throne.

Searching for the sacred weapon to defend his rights, Vitellius now discovered the theft, and, overcome by superstitious fears, did not even attempt to fight. He crawled away into a dark corner of his palace, whence he was ignominiously dragged by the enraged populace to the foot of the Capitoline Hill. There the prophecy was duly fulfilled, for the German soldier, who had joined the opposite faction, coming along at that moment, cut off Vitellius' head with the sacred sword.

The German soldier now changed from one legion to another, and travelled over many lands ; but wherever he and his sword were found, victory was assured. After winning great honour and distinction, this man, having grown old, retired from active service to the banks of the Danube, where he secretly buried his treasured weapon, building his hut over its resting-place to guard it as long as he might live. When he lay on his deathbed he was implored to reveal where he had hidden it, but he persistently refused to do so, saying that it would be found by the man who was destined to conquer the world, but that he would not be able to escape the curse. Years passed by. Wave after wave the tide of barbarian invasion swept over that part of the country, and last of all came the terrible Huns under the leadership of Attila, the "Scourge of God." As he passed

A Foray

A. Malmstrom

along the river, he saw a peasant mournfully examining his cow's foot, which had been wounded by some sharp instrument hidden in the long grass, and when search was made the point of a buried sword was found sticking out of the soil.

Attila, seeing the beautiful workmanship and the fine state of preservation of this weapon, immediately exclaimed that it was Cheru's sword, and brandishing it above his head he announced that he would conquer the world. Battle after battle was fought by the Huns, who, according to the Saga, were everywhere victorious, until Attila, weary of warfare, settled down in Hungary, taking to wife the beautiful Burgundian princess Ildico, whose father he had slain. This princess, resenting the murder of her kin and wishing to avenge it, took advantage of the king's state of intoxication upon his wedding night to secure possession of the divine sword, with which she slew him in his bed, once more fulfilling the prophecy uttered so many years before.

The magic sword again disappeared for a long time, to be unearthed once more, for the last time, by the Duke of Alva, Charles V.'s general, who shortly after won the victory of Mühlberg (1547). The Franks were wont to celebrate yearly martial games in honour of the sword ; but it is said that when the heathen gods were renounced in favour of Christianity, the priests transferred many of their attributes to the saints, and that this sword became the property of the Archangel St. Michael, who has wielded it ever since.

Tyr, whose name was synonymous with bravery and wisdom, was also considered by the ancient Northern people to have the white-armed Valkyrs, Odin's attendants, at his command, and they thought that he it was who designated the warriors whom they should transfer to Valhalla to aid the gods on the last day.

MYTHS OF THE NORSEMEN

" The god Tyr sent
Gondul and Skogul
To choose a king
Of the race of Ingve,
To dwell with Odin
In roomy Valhal."

Norse Mythology (*R. B. Anderson*).

The Story of Fenris

Tyr was generally spoken of and represented as one-armed, just as Odin was called one-eyed. Various explanations are offered by different authorities ; some claim that it was because he could give the victory only to one side ; others, because a sword has but one blade. However this may be, the ancients preferred to account for the fact in the following way :

Loki married secretly at Jötun-heim the hideous giantess Angur-boda (anguish boding), who bore him three monstrous children—the wolf Fenris, Hel, the parti-coloured goddess of death, and Iörmungandr, a terrible serpent. He kept the existence of these monsters secret as long as he could ; but they speedily grew so large that they could no longer remain confined in the cave where they had come to light. Odin, from his throne Hlidskialf, soon became aware of their existence, and also of the disquieting rapidity with which they increased in size. Fearful lest the monsters, when they had gained further strength, should invade Asgard and destroy the gods, Allfather determined to get rid of them, and striding off to Jötun-heim, he flung Hel into the depths of Nifl-heim, telling her she could reign over the nine dismal worlds of the dead. He then cast Iörmungandr into the sea, where he attained such immense proportions that at last he encircled the earth and could bite his own tail.

90

THE STORY OF FENRIS

"Into mid-ocean's dark depths hurled,
Grown with each day to giant size,
The serpent soon inclosed the world,
With tail in mouth, in circle-wise ;
Held harmless still
By Odin's will."

Valhalla (J. C. Jones).

None too well pleased that the serpent should attain such fearful dimensions in his new element, Odin resolved to lead Fenris to Asgard, where he hoped, by kindly treatment, to make him gentle and tractable. But the gods one and all shrank in dismay when they saw the wolf, and none dared approach to give him food except Tyr, whom nothing daunted. Seeing that Fenris daily increased in size, strength, voracity, and fierceness, the gods assembled in council to deliberate how they might best dispose of him. They unanimously decided that as it would desecrate their peacesteads to slay him, they would bind him fast so that he could work them no harm.

With that purpose in view, they obtained a strong chain named Læding, and then playfully proposed to Fenris to bind this about him as a test of his vaunted strength. Confident in his ability to release himself, Fenris patiently allowed them to bind him fast, and when all stood aside, with a mighty effort he stretched himself and easily burst the chain asunder.

Concealing their chagrin, the gods were loud in praise of his strength, but they next produced a much stronger fetter, Droma, which, after some persuasion, the wolf allowed them to fasten around him as before. Again a short, sharp struggle sufficed to burst this bond, and it is proverbial in the North to use the figurative expressions, "to get loose out of Læding," and "to dash out of Droma," whenever great difficulties have to be surmounted.

" Twice did the Æsir strive to bind,
Twice did they fetters powerless find ;
Iron or brass of no avail,
Naught, save through magic, could prevail."
Valhalla (J. C. Jones).

The gods, perceiving now that ordinary bonds, however strong, would never prevail against the Fenris
wolf's great strength, bade Skirnir, Frey's servant, go
down to Svart-alfa-heim and bid the dwarfs fashion a
bond which nothing could sever.

By magic arts the dark elves manufactured a slender
silken rope from such impalpable materials as the sound
of a cat's footsteps, a woman's beard, the roots of a
mountain, the longings of the bear, the voice of fishes,
and the spittle of birds, and when it was finished they
gave it to Skirnir, assuring him that no strength would
avail to break it, and that the more it was strained the
stronger it would become.

" Gleipnir, at last,
By Dark Elves cast,
In Svart-alf-heim, with strong spells wrought,
To Odin was by Skirnir brought :
As soft as silk, as light as air,
Yet still of magic power most rare."
Valhalla (J. C. Jones).

Armed with this bond, called Gleipnir, the gods went
with Fenris to the Island of Lyngvi, in the middle of
Lake Amsvartnir, and again proposed to test his
strength. But although Fenris had grown still
stronger, he mistrusted the bond which looked so
slight. He therefore refused to allow himself to be
bound, unless one of the Æsir would consent to put
his hand in his mouth, and leave it there, as a pledge
of good faith, and that no magic arts were to be used
against him.

92

The Binding of Fenris
Dorothy Hardy

THE STORY OF FENRIS

The gods heard the decision with dismay, and all drew back except Tyr, who, seeing that the others would not venture to comply with this condition, boldly stepped forward and thrust his hand between the monster's jaws. The gods now fastened Gleipnir securely around Fenris's neck and paws, and when they saw that his utmost efforts to free himself were fruitless, they shouted and laughed with glee. Tyr, however, could not share their joy, for the wolf, finding himself captive, bit off the god's hand at the wrist, which since then has been known as the wolf's joint.

LOKI.

" Be silent, Tyr !
Thou couldst never settle
A strife 'twixt two ;
Of thy right hand also
I must mention make,
Which Fenris from thee took.

TYR.

I of a hand am wanting,
But thou of honest fame ;
Sad is the lack of either.
Nor is the wolf at ease :
He in bonds must abide
Until the gods' destruction."

Sæmund's Edda (*Thorpe's tr.*)

Deprived of his right hand, Tyr was now forced to use the maimed arm for his shield, and to wield his sword with his left hand ; but such was his dexterity that he slew his enemies as before.

The gods, in spite of the wolf's struggles, drew the end of the fetter Gelgia through the rock Gioll, and fastened it to the boulder Thviti, which was sunk deep in the ground. Opening wide his fearful jaws, Fenris uttered such terrible howls that the gods, to silence

93

him, thrust a sword into his mouth, the hilt resting upon his lower jaw and the point against his palate. The blood then began to pour out in such streams that it formed a great river, called Von. The wolf was destined to remain thus chained fast until the last day, when he would burst his bonds and would be free to avenge his wrongs.

> " The wolf Fenrir,
> Freed from the chain,
> Shall range the earth."
> *Death-song of Hâkon (W. Taylor's tr.).*

While some mythologists see in this myth an emblem of crime restrained and made innocuous by the power of the law, others see the underground fire, which kept within bounds can injure no one, but which unfettered fills the world with destruction and woe. Just as Odin's second eye is said to rest in Mimir's well, so Tyr's second hand (sword) is found in Fenris's jaws. He has no more use for two weapons than the sky for two suns.

The worship of Tyr is commemorated in sundry places (such as Tübingen, in Germany), which bear more or less modified forms of his name. The name has also been given to the aconite, a plant known in Northern countries as "Tyr's helm."

CHAPTER VI: BRAGI

The Origin of Poetry

AT the time of the dispute between the Æsir and Vanas, when peace had been agreed upon, a vase was brought into the assembly into which both parties solemnly spat. From this saliva the gods created Kvasir, a being renowned for his wisdom and goodness, who went about the world answering all questions asked him, thus teaching and benefiting mankind. The dwarfs, hearing about Kvasir's great wisdom, coveted it, and finding him asleep one day, two of their number, Fialar and Galar, treacherously slew him, and drained every drop of his blood into three vessels—the kettle Od-hroerir (inspiration) and the bowls Son (expiation) and Boden (offering). After duly mixing this blood with honey, they manufactured from it a sort of beverage so inspiring that any one who tasted it immediately became a poet, and could sing with a charm which was certain to win all hearts.

Now, although the dwarfs had brewed this marvellous mead for their own consumption, they did not even taste it, but hid it away in a secret place, while they went in search of further adventures. They had not gone very far ere they found the giant Gilling also sound asleep, lying on a steep bank, and they maliciously rolled him into the water, where he perished. Then hastening to his dwelling, some climbed on the roof, carrying a huge millstone, while the others, entering, told the giantess that her husband was dead. This news caused the poor creature great grief, and she rushed out of the house to view Gilling's remains. As she passed through the door, the wicked dwarfs rolled the millstone down upon her head, and killed her. According to another account, the dwarfs invited the

95

giant to go fishing with them, and succeeded in slaying him by sending him out in a leaky vessel, which sank beneath his weight.

The double crime thus committed did not long remain unpunished, for Gilling's brother, Suttung, quickly went in search of the dwarfs, determined to avenge him. Seizing them in his mighty grasp, the giant conveyed them to a shoal far out at sea, where they would surely have perished at the next high tide had they not succeeded in redeeming their lives by promising to deliver to the giant their recently brewed mead. As soon as Suttung set them ashore, they therefore gave him the precious compound, which he entrusted to his daughter Gunlod, bidding her guard it night and day, and allow neither gods nor mortals to have so much as a taste. The better to fulfil this command, Gunlod carried the three vessels into the hollow mountain, where she kept watch over them with the most scrupulous care, nor did she suspect that Odin had discovered their place of concealment, thanks to the sharp eyes of his ever-vigilant ravens Hugin and Munin.

The Quest of the Draught

As Odin had mastered the runic lore and had tasted the waters of Mimir's fountain, he was already the wisest of gods ; but learning of the power of the draught of inspiration manufactured out of Kvasir's blood, he became very anxious to obtain possession of the magic fluid. With this purpose in view he therefore donned his broad-brimmed hat, wrapped himself in his cloud-hued cloak, and journeyed off to Jötun-heim. On his way to the giant's dwelling he passed by a field where nine ugly thralls were busy making hay. Odin paused for a moment, watching them at their work, and noticing that their scythes seemed very dull indeed, he proposed to whet them, an offer which the thralls eagerly accepted.

Drawing a whetstone from his bosom, Odin proceeded to sharpen the nine scythes, skilfully giving them such a keen edge that the thralls, delighted, begged that they might have the stone. With good-humoured acquiescence, Odin tossed the whetstone over the wall; but as the nine thralls simultaneously sprang forward to catch it, they wounded one another with their keen scythes. In anger at their respective carelessness, they now began to fight, and did not pause until they were all either mortally wounded or dead.

Quite undismayed by this tragedy, Odin continued on his way, and shortly after came to the house of the giant Baugi, a brother of Suttung, who received him very hospitably. In the course of conversation, Baugi informed him that he was greatly embarrassed, as it was harvest time and all his workmen had just been found dead in the hayfield.

Odin, who on this occasion had given his name as Bolwerk (evil doer), promptly offered his services to the giant, promising to accomplish as much work as the nine thralls, and to labour diligently all the summer in exchange for one single draught of Suttung's magic mead when the busy season was ended. This bargain was immediately concluded, and Baugi's new servant, Bolwerk, worked incessantly all the summer long, more than fulfilling his contract, and safely garnering all the grain before the autumn rains began to fall. When the first days of winter came, Bolwerk presented himself before his master, claiming his reward. But Baugi hesitated and demurred, saying he dared not openly ask his brother Suttung for the draught of inspiration, but would try to obtain it by guile. Together, Bolwerk and Baugi then proceeded to the mountain where

G

Gunlod dwelt, and as they could find no other mode of entering the secret cave, Odin produced his trusty auger, called Rati, and bade the giant bore with all his might to make a hole through which he might crawl into the interior.

Baugi silently obeyed, and after a few moments' work withdrew the tool, saying that he had pierced through the mountain, and that Odin would have no difficulty in slipping through. But the god, mistrusting this statement, merely blew into the hole, and when the dust and chips came flying into his face, he sternly bade Baugi resume his boring and not attempt to deceive him again. The giant did as he was told, and when he withdrew his tool again, Odin ascertained that the hole was really finished. Changing himself into a snake, he wriggled through with such remarkable rapidity that he managed to elude the sharp auger, which Baugi treacherously thrust into the hole after him, intending to kill him.

> " Rati's mouth I caused
> To make a space,
> And to gnaw the rock ;
> Over and under me
> Were the Jötun's ways :
> Thus I my head did peril."
>
> *Hávamál (Thorpe's tr.).*

The Rape of the Draught

Having reached the interior of the mountain, Odin reassumed his usual godlike form and starry mantle, and then presented himself in the stalactite-hung cave before the beautiful Gunlod. He intended to win her love as a means of inducing her to grant him a sip from each of the vessels confided to her care.

Won by his passionate wooing, Gunlod consented to become his wife, and after he had spent three whole days with her in this retreat, she brought out the vessels

98

from their secret hiding-place, and told him he might take a sip from each.

> " And a draught obtained
> Of the precious mead,
> Drawn from Od-hroerir."
> *Odin's Rune-Song* (*Thorpe's tr.*).

Odin made good use of this permission and drank so deeply that he completely drained all three vessels. Then, having obtained all that he wanted, he emerged from the cave and, donning his eagle plumes, rose high into the blue, and, after hovering for a moment over the mountain top, winged his flight towards Asgard.

He was still far from the gods' realm when he became aware of a pursuer, and, indeed, Suttung, having also assumed the form of an eagle, was coming rapidly after him with intent to compel him to surrender the stolen mead. Odin therefore flew faster and faster, straining every nerve to reach Asgard before the foe should overtake him, and as he drew near the gods anxiously watched the race.

Seeing that Odin would only with difficulty be able to escape, the Æsir hastily gathered all the combustible materials they could find, and as he flew over the ramparts of their dwelling, they set fire to the mass or fuel, so that the flames, rising high, singed the wings of Suttung, as he followed the god, and he fell into the very midst of the fire, where he was burned to death.

As for Odin, he flew to where the gods had prepared vessels for the stolen mead, and disgorged the draught of inspiration in such breathless haste that a few drops fell and were scattered over the earth. There they became the portion of rhymesters and poetasters, the gods reserving the main draught for their own consumption, and only occasionally vouchsafing a taste to some favoured mortal, who, immediately after, would win world-wide renown by his inspired songs.

> "Of a well-assumed form
> I made good use :
> Few things fail the wise ;
> For Od-hroerir
> Is now come up
> To men's earthly dwellings."
> *Hávamál* (*Thorpe's tr.*).

As men and gods owed the priceless gift to Odin, they were ever ready to express to him their gratitude, and they not only called it by his name, but they worshipped him as patron of eloquence, poetry, and song, and of all scalds.

The God of Music

Although Odin had thus won the gift of poetry, he seldom made use of it himself. It was reserved for his son Bragi, the child of Gunlod, to become the god of poetry and music, and to charm the world with his songs.

> "White-bearded bard, ag'd
> Bragi, his gold harp
> Sweeps—and yet softer
> Stealeth the day."
> *Viking Tales of the North* (*R. B. Anderson*).

As soon as Bragi was born in the stalactite-hung cave where Odin had won Gunlod's affections, the dwarfs presented him with a magical golden harp, and, setting him on one of their own vessels, they sent him out into the wide world. As the boat gently passed out of subterranean darkness, and floated over the threshold of Nain, the realm of the dwarf of death, Bragi, the fair and immaculate young god, who until then had shown no signs of life, suddenly sat up, and, seizing the golden harp beside him, he began to sing the

100

Idun

B. E. Ward

wondrous song of life, which rose at times to heaven, and then sank down to the dread realm of Hel, goddess of death.

> " Yggdrasil's ash is
> Of all trees most excellent,
> And of all ships, Skidbladnir ;
> Of the Æsir, Odin,
> And of horses, Sleipnir ;
> Bifröst of bridges,
> And of scalds, Bragi."
>
> *Lay of Grimnir* (*Thorpe's tr.*).

While he played the vessel was wafted gently over sunlit waters, and soon touched the shore. Bragi then proceeded on foot, threading his way through the bare and silent forest, playing as he walked. At the sound of his tender music the trees began to bud and bloom, and the grass underfoot was gemmed with countless flowers.

Here he met Idun, daughter of Ivald, the fair goddess of immortal youth, whom the dwarfs allowed to visit the earth from time to time, when, at her approach, nature invariably assumed its loveliest and gentlest aspect.

It was only to be expected that two such beings should feel attracted to each other, and Bragi soon won this fair goddess for his wife. Together they hastened to Asgard, where both were warmly welcomed and where Odin, after tracing runes on Bragi's tongue, decreed that he should be the heavenly minstrel and composer of songs in honour of the gods and of the heroes whom he received in Valhalla.

Worship of Bragi

As Bragi was god of poetry, eloquence, and song, the Northern races also called poetry by his name, and scalds of either sex were frequently designated as Bragamen or Braga-women. Bragi was greatly honoured by all the Northern races, and hence his health was always drunk on solemn or festive occasions, but especially at funeral feasts and at Yuletide celebrations.

When it was time to drink this toast, which was served in cups shaped like a ship, and was called the Bragaful, the sacred sign of the hammer was first made over it. Then the new ruler or head of the family solemnly pledged himself to some great deed of valour, which he was bound to execute within the year, unless he wished to be considered destitute of honour. Following his example, all the guests were then wont to make similar vows and declare what they would do ; and as some of them, owing to previous potations, talked rather too freely of their intentions on these occasions, this custom seems to connect the god's name with the vulgar but very expressive English verb " to brag."

In art, Bragi is generally represented as an elderly man, with long white hair and beard, and holding the golden harp from which his fingers could draw such magic strains.

CHAPTER VII: IDUN

The Apples of Youth

IDUN, the personification of spring or immortal youth, who, according to some mythologists, had no birth and was never to taste death, was warmly welcomed by the gods when she made her appearance in Asgard with Bragi. To further win their affections she promised them a daily taste of the marvellous apples which she bore in her casket, and which had the power of conferring immortal youth and loveliness upon all who partook of them.

> " The golden apples
> Out of her garden
> Have yielded you a dower of youth,
> Ate you them every day."
> *Wagner (Forman's tr.).*

Thanks to this magic fruit, the Scandinavian gods, who, because they sprang from a mixed race, were not all immortal, warded off the approach of old age and disease, and remained vigorous, beautiful, and young through countless ages. These apples were therefore considered very precious indeed, and Idun carefully treasured them in her magic casket. No matter how many she drew out, the same number always remained for distribution at the feast of the gods, to whom alone she vouchsafed a taste, although dwarfs and giants were eager to obtain possession of the fruit.

> " Bright Iduna, Maid immortal !
> Standing at Valhalla's portal,
> In her casket has rich store
> Of rare apples gilded o'er ;
> Those rare apples, not of Earth,
> Ageing Æsir give fresh birth."
> *Valhalla (J. C. Jones).*

The Story of Thiassi

One day, Odin, Hoenir, and Loki started out upon one of their usual excursions to earth, and, after wandering for a long while, they found themselves in a deserted region, where they could discover no hospitable dwelling. Weary and very hungry, the gods, perceiving a herd of oxen, slew one of the beasts, and, kindling a fire, they sat down beside it to rest while waiting for their meat to cook.

To their surprise, however, in spite of the roaring flames the carcass remained quite raw. Realising that some magic must be at work, they looked about them to discover what could hinder their cookery, when they perceived an eagle perched upon a tree above them. Seeing that he was an object of suspicion to the wayfarers, the bird addressed them and admitted that he it was who had prevented the fire from doing its accustomed work, but he offered to remove the spell if they would give him as much food as he could eat. The gods agreed to do this, whereupon the eagle, swooping downward, fanned the flames with his huge wings, and soon the meat was cooked. The eagle then made ready to carry off three quarters of the ox as his share, but this was too much for Loki, who seized a great stake lying near at hand, and began to belabour the voracious bird, forgetting that it was skilled in magic arts. To his great dismay one end of the stake stuck fast to the eagle's back, the other to his hands, and he found himself dragged over stones and through briers, sometimes through the air, his arms almost torn out of their sockets. In vain he cried for mercy and implored the eagle to let him go; the bird flew on, until he promised any ransom his captor might ask in exchange for his release.

Loki and Thiassi

Dorothy Hardy

THE STORY OF THIASSI

The seeming eagle, who was the storm giant Thiassi, at last agreed to release Loki upon one condition. He made him promise upon the most solemn of oaths that he would lure Idun out of Asgard, so that Thiassi might obtain possession of her and of her magic fruit.

Released at last, Loki returned to Odin and Hoenir, to whom, however, he was very careful not to confide the condition upon which he had obtained his freedom; and when they had returned to Asgard he began to plan how he might entice Idun outside of the gods' abode. A few days later, Bragi being absent on one of his minstrel journeys, Loki sought Idun in the groves of Brunnaker, where she had taken up her abode, and by artfully describing some apples which grew at a short distance, and which he mendaciously declared were exactly like hers, he lured her away from Asgard with a crystal dish full of fruit, which she intended to compare with that which he extolled. No sooner had Idun left Asgard, however, than the deceiver Loki forsook her, and ere she could return to the shelter of the heavenly abode the storm giant Thiassi swept down from the north on his eagle wings, and catching her up in his cruel talons, he bore her swiftly away to his barren and desolate home of Thrym-heim.

> "Thrymheim the sixth is named,
> Where Thiassi dwelt,
> That all-powerful Jötun."
> *Lay of Grimnir* (*Thorpe's tr.*).

Isolated from her beloved companions, Idun pined, grew pale and sad, but persistently refused to give Thiassi the smallest bite of her magic fruit, which, as he well knew, would make him beautiful and renew his strength and youth.

" All woes that fall
On Odin's hall
Can be traced to Loki base.
From out Valhalla's portal
'Twas he who pure Iduna lured,—
Whose casket fair
Held apples rare
That render gods immortal,—
And in Thiassi's tower immured."

Valhalla (*J. C. Jones*).

Time passed. The gods, thinking that Idun had accompanied her husband and would soon return, at first paid no heed to her departure, but little by little the beneficent effect of the last feast of apples passed away. They began to feel the approach of old age, and saw their youth and beauty disappear; so, becoming alarmed, they began to search for the missing goddess.

Close investigation revealed the fact that she had last been seen in Loki's company, and when Odin sternly called him to account, he was forced to admit that he had betrayed her into the storm-giant's power.

" By his mocking, scornful mien,
Soon in Valhal it was seen
'Twas the traitor Loki's art
Which had led Idun apart
To gloomy tower
And Jotun power."

Valhalla (*J. C. Jones*).

The Return of Idun

The attitude of the gods now became very menacing, and it was clear to Loki that if he did not devise means to restore the goddess, and that soon, his life would be in considerable danger.

He assured the indignant gods, therefore, that he would leave no stone unturned in his efforts to secure

106

the release of Idun, and, borrowing Freya's falcon plumage, he flew off to Thrym-heim, where he found Idun alone, sadly mourning her exile from Asgard and her beloved Bragi. Changing the fair goddess into a nut according to some accounts, or according to others, into a swallow, Loki grasped her tightly between his claws, and then rapidly retraced his way to Asgard, hoping that he would reach the shelter of its high walls ere Thiassi returned from a fishing excursion in the Northern seas to which he had gone.

Meantime the gods had assembled on the ramparts of the heavenly city, and they were watching for the return of Loki with far more anxiety than they had felt for Odin when he went in search of Od-hroerir. Remembering the success of their ruse on that occasion, they had gathered great piles of fuel, which they were ready to set on fire at any moment.

Suddenly they saw Loki coming, but descried in his wake a great eagle. This was the giant Thiassi who had suddenly returned to Thrym-heim and found that his captive had been carried off by a falcon, in whom he readily recognised one of the gods. Hastily donning his eagle plumes he had given immediate chase and was rapidly overtaking his prey. Loki redoubled his efforts as he neared the walls of Asgard, and ere Thiassi overtook him he reached the goal and sank exhausted in the midst of the gods. Not a moment was lost in setting fire to the accumulated fuel, and as the pursuing Thiassi passed over the walls in his turn, the flames and smoke brought him to the ground crippled and half stunned, an easy prey to the gods, who fell ruthlessly upon him and slew him.

The Æsir were overjoyed at the recovery of Idun, and they hastened to partake of the precious apples which she had brought safely back. Feeling the return of their wonted strength and good looks with every mouthful they ate, they good-naturedly declared that it was no wonder if even the giants longed to taste the apples of perpetual youth. They vowed therefore that they would place Thiassi's eyes as a constellation in the heavens, in order to soften any feeling of anger which his kinsmen might experience upon learning that he had been slain.

> " Up I cast the eyes
> Of Allvaldi's son
> Into the heaven's serene:
> They are signs the greatest
> Of my deeds."
>
> Lay of Harbard (*Thorpe's tr.*).

The Goddess of Spring

The physical explanation of this myth is obvious. Idun, the emblem of vegetation, is forcibly carried away in autumn, when Bragi is absent and the singing of the birds has ceased. The cold wintry wind, Thiassi, detains her in the frozen, barren north, where she cannot thrive, until Loki, the south wind, brings back the seed or the swallow, which are both precursors of the returning spring. The youth, beauty, and strength conferred by Idun are symbolical of Nature's resurrection in spring after winter's sleep, when colour and vigour return to the earth, which had grown wrinkled and grey.

Idun Falls to the Nether World

As the disappearance of Idun (vegetation) was a yearly occurrence, we might expect to find other myths dealing with the striking phenomenon, and there is another favourite of the old scalds which, unfortunately, has come down to us only in a fragmentary and very incomplete form. According to this account, Idun was once sitting upon the branches of the sacred ash Yggdrasil when, growing suddenly faint, she loosed her hold and dropped to the ground beneath, and down to the lowest depths of Nifl-heim. There she lay, pale and motionless, gazing with fixed and horror-struck eyes upon the gruesome sights of Hel's realm, trembling violently the while, like one overcome by penetrating cold.

> " In the dales dwells
> The prescient Dis,
> From Yggdrasil's
> Ash sunk down,
> Of alfen race,
> Idun by name,
> The youngest of Ivaldi's
> Elder children.
> She ill brooked
> Her descent
> Under the hoar tree's
> Trunk confined.
> She would not happy be
> With Norvi's daughter,
> Accustomed to a pleasanter
> Abode at home."
> *Odin's Ravens' Song* (*Thorpe's tr.*).

Seeing that she did not return, Odin bade Bragi, Heimdall, and another of the gods go in search of her, giving them a white wolfskin to envelop her in, so that she should not suffer from the cold, and bidding them make every effort to rouse her from the stupor which his prescience told him had taken possession of her.

> " A wolf's skin they gave her,
> In which herself she clad."
> *Odin's Ravens' Song* (*Thorpe's tr.*).

Idun passively allowed the gods to wrap her in the warm wolfskin, but she persistently refused to speak of move, and from her strange manner her husband sadly suspected that she had had a vision of great ills. The tears ran continuously down her pallid cheeks, and Bragi, overcome by her unhappiness, at length bade the other gods return to Asgard without him, vowing that he would remain beside his wife until she was ready to leave Hel's dismal realm. The sight of her woe oppressed him so sorely that he had no heart for his usual merry songs, and the strings of his harp were mute while he remained in the underworld.

> ' That voice-like zephyr o'er flow'r meads creeping,
> Like Bragi's music his harp strings sweeping."
> *Viking Tales of the North* (*R. B. Anderson*).

In this myth Idun's fall from Yggdrasil is symbolical of the autumnal falling of the leaves, which lie limp and helpless on the cold bare ground until they are hidden from sight under the snow, represented by the wolfskin, which Odin, the sky, sends down to keep them warm ; and the cessation of the birds' songs is further typified by Bragi's silent harp.

CHAPTER VIII: NIÖRD

A Hostage with the Gods

WE have already seen how the Æsir and Vanas exchanged hostages after the terrible war they had waged against each other, and that while Hoenir, Odin's brother, went to live in Vanaheim, Niörd, with his two children, Frey and Freya, definitely took up his abode in Asgard.

> " In Vana-heim
> Wise powers him created,
> And to the gods a hostage gave."
> *Lay of Vafthrudnir (Thorpe's tr.).*

As ruler of the winds, and of the sea near the shore, Niörd was given the palace of Nôatûn, near the seashore, where, we are told, he stilled the terrible tempests stirred up by Ægir, god of the deep sea.

> " Niörd, the god of storms, whom fishers know;
> Not born in Heaven—he was in Van-heim rear'd,
> With men, but lives a hostage with the gods;
> He knows each frith, and every rocky creek
> Fringed with dark pines, and sands where sea-fowl scream."
> *Balder Dead (Matthew Arnola).*

He also extended his special protection over commerce and fishing, which two occupations could be pursued with advantage only during the short summer months, of which he was in a measure considered the personification.

The God of Summer

Niörd is represented in art as a very handsome god, in the prime of life, clad in a short green tunic, with a crown of shells and seaweed upon his head, or a brown-brimmed hat adorned with eagle or heron plumes. As personification of the summer, he was invoked to still the raging storms which desolated the coasts during the winter months. He was also implored to hasten the vernal warmth and thereby extinguish the winter fires.

As agriculture was practised only during the summer months, and principally along the fiords or sea inlets, Niörd was also invoked for favourable harvests, for he was said to delight in prospering those who placed their trust in him.

Niörd's first wife, according to some authorities, was his sister Nerthus, Mother Earth, who in Germany was identified with Frigga, as we have seen, but in Scandinavia was considered a separate divinity. Niörd was, however, obliged to part with her when summoned to Asgard, where he occupied one of the twelve seats in the great council hall, and was present at all the assemblies of the gods, withdrawing to Nôatûn only when his services were not required by the Æsir.

> " Nôatûn is the eleventh;
> There Niörd has
> Himself a dwelling made,
> Prince of men;
> Guiltless of sin,
> He rules o'er the high-built fane."
> *Lay of Grimnir* (*Thorpe's tr.*).

In his home by the seashore, Niörd delighted in watching the gulls fly to and fro, and in observing the graceful movements of the swans, his favourite birds, which were held sacred to him. He spent many an hour, too, gazing at the gambols of the gentle seals, which came to bask in the sunshine at his feet.

Skadi, Goddess of Winter

Shortly after Idun's return from Thrym-heim, and Thiassi's death within the bounds of Asgard, the assembled gods were greatly surprised and dismayed to see Skadi, the giant's daughter, appear one day in their midst, to demand satisfaction for her father's death. Although the daughter of an ugly old Hrim-thurs, Skadi, the goddess of winter, was very beautiful indeed, in her silvery armour, with her glittering spear, sharp-pointed arrows, short white hunting dress, white fur leggings, and broad snowshoes ; and the gods could not but recognise the justice of her claim, wherefore they offered the usual fine in atonement. Skadi, however, was so angry that she at first refused this compromise, and sternly demanded a life for a life, until Loki, wishing to appease her wrath, and thinking that if he could only make her cold lips relax in a smile the rest would be easy, began to play all manner of pranks. Fastening a goat to himself by an invisible cord, he went through a series of antics, which were reproduced by the goat ; and the sight was so grotesque that all the gods fairly shouted with merriment, and even Skadi was forced to smile.

Taking advantage of this softened mood, the gods pointed to the firmament where her father's eyes glowed like radiant stars in the northern hemisphere. They told her they had placed them there to show him all honour, and finally added that she might select as husband any of the gods present at the assembly, providing she were content to judge of their attractions by their naked feet.

Blindfolded, so that she could see only the feet of the gods standing in a circle around her, Skadi looked about her and her gaze fell upon a pair of beautifully formed feet. She felt sure they must belong to Balder, the god of light, whose bright face had charmed her, and she designated their owner as her choice.

When the bandage was removed, however, she dis-

covered to her chagrin that she had chosen Niörd, to
whom her troth was plighted ; but notwithstanding her
disappointment, she spent a happy honeymoon in Asgard, where all seemed to delight in doing her honour.
After this, Niörd took his bride home to Nôatûn, where
the monotonous sound of the waves, the shrieking of
the gulls, and the cries of the seals so disturbed Skadi's
slumbers that she finally declared it was quite impossible
for her to remain there any longer, and she implored
her husband to take her back to her native Thrym-heim.

> " Sleep could I not
> On my sea-strand couch,
> For screams of the sea fowl.
> There wakes me,
> When from the wave he comes,
> Every morning the mew."
>
> *Norse Mythology* (*R. B. Anderson*).

Niörd, anxious to please his new wife, consented to take
her to Thrym-heim and to dwell there with her nine
nights out of every twelve, providing she would spend the
remaining three with him at Nôatûn ; but when he
reached the mountain region, the soughing of the wind
in the pines, the thunder of the avalanches, the cracking
of the ice, the roar of the waterfalls, and the howling
of the wolves appeared to him as unbearable as the
sound of the sea had seemed to his wife, and he could
not but rejoice each time when his period of exile was
ended, and he found himself again at Nôatûn.

> " Am weary of the mountains ;
> Not long was I there,
> Only nine nights ;
> The howl of the wolves
> Methought sounded ill
> To the song of the swans."
>
> *Norse Mythology* (*R. B. Anderson*).

THE PARTING OF NIÖRD AND SKADI

The Parting of Niörd and Skadi

For some time, Niörd and Skadi, who are the personifications of summer and winter, alternated thus, the wife spending the three short summer months by the sea, and he reluctantly remaining with her in Thrymheim during the nine long winter months. But, concluding at last that their tastes would never agree, they decided to part for ever, and returned to their respective homes, where each could follow the occupations which custom had endeared to them.

> " Thrym-heim it's called,
> Where Thjasse dwelled,
> That stream-mighty giant;
> But Skade now dwells,
> Pure bride of the gods,
> In her father's old mansion."
> *Norse Mythology* (*R. B. Anderson*).

Skadi now resumed her wonted pastime of hunting, leaving her realm again only to marry the semi-historical Odin, to whom she bore a son called Sæming, the first king of Norway, and the supposed founder of the royal race which long ruled that country.

According to other accounts, however, Skadi eventually married Uller, the winter-god. As Skadi was a skilful marksman, she is represented with bow and arrow, and, as goddess of the chase, she is generally accompanied by one of the wolf-like Eskimo dogs so common in the North. Skadi was invoked by hunters and by winter travellers, whose sleighs she would guide over the snow and ice, thus helping them to reach their destination in safety.

Skadi's anger against the gods, who had slain her father, the storm giant, is an emblem of the unbending rigidity of the ice-enveloped earth, which, softened at

115

last by the frolicsome play of Loki (the heat lightning), smiles, and permits the embrace of Niörd (summer). His love, however, cannot hold her for more than three months of the year (typified in the myth by nights), as she is always secretly longing for the wintry storms and for her wonted activities among the mountains.

The Worship of Niörd

Niörd was supposed to bless the vessels passing in and out of port, and his temples were situated by the sea-shore ; there oaths in his name were commonly sworn, and his health was drunk at every banquet, where he was invariably named with his son Frey.

As all aquatic plants were supposed to belong to him, the marine sponge was known in the North as " Niörd's glove," a name which was retained until lately, when the same plant has been popularly re-named the " Virgin's hand."

CHAPTER IX: FREY

The God of Fairyland

FREY, or Fro, as he was called in Germany, was the son of Niörd and Nerthus, or of Niörd and Skadi, and was born in Vana-heim. He therefore belonged to the race of the Vanas, the divinities of water and air, but was warmly welcomed in Asgard when he came thither as hostage with his father. As it was customary among the Northern nations to bestow some valuable gift upon a child when he cut his first tooth, the Æsir gave the infant Frey the beautiful realm of Alf-heim or Fairyland, the home of the Light Elves.

> " Alf-heim the gods to Frey
> Gave in days of yore
> For a tooth gift."
> *Sæmund's Edda (Thorpe's tr.).*

Here Frey, the god of the golden sunshine and the warm summer showers, took up his abode, charmed with the society of the elves and fairies, who implicitly obeyed his every order, and at a sign from him flitted to and fro, doing all the good in their power, for they were pre-eminently beneficent spirits.

Frey also received from the gods a marvellous sword (an emblem of the sunbeams), which had the power of fighting successfully, and of its own accord, as soon as it was drawn from its sheath. Frey wielded this princi-pally against the frost giants, whom he hated almost as much as did Thor, and because he carried this glittering weapon, he has sometimes been confounded with the sword-god Tyr or Saxnot.

> " With a short-shafted hammer fights conquering Thor ;
> Frey's own sword but an ell long is made."
> *Viking Tales of the North (R. B. Anderson).*

The dwarfs from Svart-alfa-heim gave Frey the golden-bristled boar Gullin-bursti (the golden-bristled), a personification of the sun. The radiant bristles of this animal were considered symbolical either of the solar rays, of the golden grain, which at his bidding waved over the harvest fields of Midgard, or of agriculture; for the boar (by tearing up the ground with his sharp tusk) was supposed to have first taught mankind how to plough.

> "There was Frey, and sat
> On the gold-bristled boar, who first, they say,
> Plowed the brown earth, and made it green for Frey."
> *Lovers of Gudrun (William Morris).*

Frey sometimes rode astride of this marvellous boar, whose speed was very great, and at other times harnessed him to his golden chariot, which was said to contain the fruits and flowers which he lavishly scattered abroad over the face of the earth.

Frey was, moreover, the proud possessor not only of the dauntless steed Blodug-hofi, which would dash through fire and water at his command, but also of the magic ship Skidbladnir, a personification of the clouds. This vessel, sailing over land and sea, was always wafted along by favourable winds, and was so elastic that, while it could assume large enough proportions to carry the gods, their steeds, and all their equipments, it could also be folded up like a napkin and thrust into a pocket.

> "Ivaldi's sons
> Went in days of old
> Skidbladnir to form,
> Of ships the best,
> For the bright Frey,
> Niörd's benign son."
> *Lay of Grimnir (Thorpe's tr.).*

Frey   118
Jacques Reich

The Wooing of Gerda

It is related in one of the lays of the Edda that Frey
once ventured to ascend Odin's throne Hlidskialf, from
which exalted seat his gaze ranged over the wide earth.
Looking towards the frozen North, he saw a beautiful
young maiden enter the house of the frost giant Gymir,
and as she raised her hand to lift the latch her radiant
beauty illuminated sea and sky.

A moment later, this lovely creature, whose name
was Gerda, and who is considered as a personification
of the flashing Northern lights, vanished within her
father's house, and Frey pensively wended his way back
to Alfheim, his heart oppressed with longing to make
this fair maiden his wife. Being deeply in love, he
was melancholy and absent-minded in the extreme, and
began to behave so strangely that his father, Niörd, became greatly alarmed about his health, and bade his
favourite servant, Skirnir, discover the cause of this
sudden change. After much persuasion, Skirnir finally
won from Frey an account of his ascent of Hlidskialf,
and of the fair vision he had seen. He confessed his
love and also his utter despair, for as Gerda was the
daughter of Gymir and Angur-boda, and a relative of
the murdered giant Thiassi, he feared she would
never view his suit with favour.

> " In Gymer's court I saw her move,
> The maid who fires my breast with love ;
> Her snow-white arms and bosom fair
> Shone lovely, kindling sea and air.
> Dear is she to my wishes, more
> Than e'er was maid to youth before ;
> But gods and elves, I wot it well,
> Forbid that we together dwell."
> *Skirner's Lay (Herbert's tr.).*

Skirnir, however, replied consolingly that he could

see no reason why his master should take a despondent view of the case, and he offered to go and woo the maiden in his name, providing Frey would lend him his steed for the journey, and give him his glittering sword for reward.

Overjoyed at the prospect of winning the beautiful Gerda, Frey willingly handed Skirnir the flashing sword, and gave him permission to use his horse. But he quickly relapsed into the state of reverie which had become usual with him since falling in love, and thus he did not notice that Skirnir was still hovering near him, nor did he perceive him cunningly steal the reflection of his face from the surface of the brook near which he was seated, and imprison it in his drinking horn, with intent " to pour it out in Gerda's cup, and by its beauty win the heart of the giantess for the lord " for whom he was about to go a-wooing. Provided with this portrait, with eleven golden apples, and with the magic ring Draupnir, Skirnir now rode off to Jötun-heim, to fulfil his embassy. As he came near Gymir's dwelling he heard the loud and persistent howling of his watch-dogs, which were personifications of the wintry winds. A shepherd, guarding his flock in the vicinity, told him, in answer to his inquiry, that it would be impossible to approach the house, on account of the flaming barrier which surrounded it; but Skirnir, knowing that Blodug-hofi would dash through any fire, merely set spurs to his steed, and, riding up unscathed to the giant's door, was soon ushered into the presence of the lovely Gerda.

To induce the fair maiden to lend a favourable ear to his master's proposals, Skirnir showed her the stolen portrait, and proffered the golden apples and magic ring, which, however, she haughtily refused to accept, declaring that her father had gold enough and to spare.

THE WOOING OF GERDA

"I take not, I, that wondrous ring,
   Though it from Balder's pile you bring
   Gold lack not I, in Gymer's bower;
   Enough for me my father's dower."
                    Skirner's Lay (*Herbert's tr.*).

Indignant at her scorn, Skirnir now threatened to
decapitate her with his magic sword, but as this did not
in the least frighten the maiden, and she calmly defied
him, he had recourse to magic arts. Cutting runes in
his stick, he told her that unless she yielded ere the spell
was ended, she would be condemned either to eternal
celibacy, or to marry some aged frost giant whom she
could never love.

Terrified into submission by the frightful description
of her cheerless future in case she persisted in her
refusal, Gerda finally consented to become Frey's wife,
and dismissed Skirnir, promising to meet her future
spouse on the ninth night, in the land of Buri, the
green grove, where she would dispel his sadness and
make him happy.

"Burri is hight the seat of love ;
   'Nine nights elapsed, in that known grove
   Shall brave Niorder's gallant boy
   From Gerda take the kiss of joy."
                    Skirner's Lay (*Herbert's tr.*).

Delighted with his success, Skirnir hurried back to
Alf-heim, where Frey came eagerly to learn the result
of his journey. When he learned that Gerda had consented to become his wife, his face grew radiant with
joy ; but when Skirnir informed him that he would
have to wait nine nights ere he could behold his
promised bride, he turned sadly away, declaring the
time would appear interminable.

> " Long is one night, and longer twain ;
> But how for three endure my pain ?
> A month of rapture sooner flies
> Than half one night of wishful sighs."
>
> *Skirner's Lay (Herbert's tr.).*

In spite of this loverlike despondency, however, the time of waiting came to an end, and Frey joyfully hastened to the green grove, where, true to her appointment, he found Gerda, and she became his happy wife, and proudly sat upon his throne beside him.

> " Frey to wife had Gerd ;
> She was Gymir's daughter,
> From Jötuns sprung."
>
> *Sæmund's Edda (Thorpe's tr.).*

According to some mythologists, Gerda is not a personification of the aurora borealis, but of the earth, which, hard, cold, and unyielding, resists the spring-god's proffers of adornment and fruitfulness (the apples and ring), defies the flashing sunbeams (Frey's sword), and only consents to receive his kiss when it learns that it will else be doomed to perpetual barrenness, or given over entirely into the power of the giants (ice and snow). The nine nights of waiting are typical of the nine winter months, at the end of which the earth becomes the bride of the sun, in the groves where the trees are budding forth into leaf and blossom.

Frey and Gerda, we are told, became the parents of a son called Fiolnir, whose birth consoled Gerda for the loss of her brother Beli. The latter had attacked Frey and had been slain by him, although the sun-god, deprived of his matchless sword, had been obliged to defend himself with a stag horn which he hastily snatched from the wall of his dwelling.

Besides the faithful Skirnir, Frey had two other

attendants, a married couple, Beyggvir and Beyla, the personifications of mill refuse and manure, which two ingredients, being used in agriculture for fertilising purposes, were therefore considered Frey's faithful servants, in spite of their unpleasant qualities.

The historical Frey

Snorro-Sturleson, in his "Heimskringla," or chronicle of the ancient kings of Norway, state that Frey was an historical personage who bore the name of Ingvi-Frey, and ruled in Upsala after the death of the semi-historical Odin and Niörd. Under his rule the people enjoyed such prosperity and peace that they declared their king must be a god. They therefore began to invoke him as such, carrying their enthusiastic admiration to such lengths that when he died the priests, not daring to reveal the fact, laid him in a great mound instead of burning his body, as had been customary until then. They then informed the people that Frey—whose name was the Northern synonym for " master "—had " gone into the mound," an expression which eventually became the Northman's phrase for death.

Not until three years later did the people, who had continued paying their taxes to the king by pouring gold, silver, and copper coin into the mound through three different openings, discover that Frey was dead. As their peace and prosperity had remained undisturbed, they decreed that his corpse should never be burned, and they thus inaugurated the custom of mound-burial, which in due time supplanted the funeral pyre in many places. One of the three mounds near Gamla Upsala still bears this god's name. His statues were placed in the great temple there, and his name was duly mentioned in all solemn oaths, of which the usual formula was, " So help me Frey, Niörd, and the Almighty Asa " (Odin).

Worship of Frey

No weapons were ever admitted in Frey's temples, the most celebrated of which were at Throndhjeim in Norway, and at Thvera in Iceland. In these temples oxen or horses were offered in sacrifice to him, a heavy gold ring being dipped in the victim's blood ere the above-mentioned oath was solemnly taken upon it.

Frey's statues, like those of all the other Northern divinities, were roughly hewn blocks of wood, and the last of these sacred images seems to have been destroyed by Olaf the Saint, who, as we have seen, forcibly converted many of his subjects. Besides being god of sunshine, fruitfulness, peace, and prosperity, Frey was considered the patron of horses and horsemen, and the deliverer of all captives.

> " Frey is the best
> Of all the chiefs
> Among the gods.
> He causes not tears
> To maids or mothers :
> His desire is to loosen the fetters
> Of those enchained."
> *Norse Mythology* (*R. B. Anderson*).

The Yule Feast

One month of every year, the Yule month, or Thor's month, was considered sacred to Frey as well as to Thor, and began on the longest night of the year, which bore the name of Mother Night. This month was a time of feasting and rejoicing, for it heralded the return of the sun. The festival was called Yule (wheel) because the sun was supposed to resemble a wheel rapidly revolving across the sky. This resemblance gave rise to a singular custom in England, Germany, and along the banks of the Moselle. Until within late years, the

124

people were wont to assemble yearly upon a mountain, to set fire to a huge wooden wheel, twined with straw, which, all ablaze, was then sent rolling down the hill, to plunge with a hiss into the water.

> " Some others get a rotten Wheele, all worn and cast aside,
> Which, covered round about with strawe and tow, they closely hide;
> And caryed to some mountaines top, being all with fire light,
> They hurle it down with violence, when darke appears the night ;
> Resembling much the sunne, that from the Heavens down should fal,
> A strange and monstrous sight it seemes, and fearful to them all ;
> But they suppose their mischiefs are all likewise throwne to hell,
> And that, from harmes and dangers now, in safetie here they dwell."
>
> *Naogeorgus.*

All the Northern races considered the Yule feast the greatest of the year, and were wont to celebrate it with dancing, feasting, and drinking, each god being pledged by name. The first Christian missionaries, perceiving the extreme popularity of this feast, thought it best to encourage drinking to the health of the Lord and his twelve apostles when they first began to convert the Northern heathens. In honour of Frey, boar's flesh was eaten on this occasion. Crowned with laurel and rosemary, the animal's head was brought into the banqueting-hall with much ceremony—a custom long after observed, as the following lines will show :

> " Caput Apri defero
> Reddens laudes Domino.
> The boar's head in hand bring I,
> With garlands gay and rosemary ;
> I pray you all sing merrily,
> Qui estis in convivio."
>
> *Queen's College Carol, Oxford.*

The father of the family laid his hand on the sacred dish, which was called " the boar of atonement," swearing he would be faithful to his family, and would

125

fulfil all his obligations—an example which was followed by all present, from the highest to the lowest. This dish could be carved only by a man of unblemished reputation and tried courage, for the boar's head was a sacred emblem which was supposed to inspire every one with fear. For that reason a boar's head was frequently used as ornament for the helmets of Northern kings and heroes whose bravery was unquestioned.

As Frey's name of Fro is phonetically the same as the word used in German for gladness, he was considered the patron of every joy, and was invariably invoked by married couples who wished to live in harmony. Those who succeeded in doing so for a certain length of time were publicly rewarded by the gift of a piece of boar's flesh, for which in later times, the English and Viennese substituted a flitch of bacon or a ham.

> " You shall swear, by custom of confession,
> If ever you made nuptial transgression,
> Be you either married man or wife :
> If you have brawls or contentious strife ;
> Or otherwise, at bed or at board,
> Offended each other in deed or word ;
> Or, since the parish clerk said Amen,
> You wish'd yourselves unmarried again ;
> Or, in a twelvemonth and a day
> Repented not in thought any way,
> But continued true in thought and desire,
> As when you join'd hands in the quire.
> If to these conditions, with all feare,
> Of your own accord you will freely sweare,
> A whole gammon of bacon you shall receive,
> And bear it hence with love and good leave :
> For this our custom at Dunmow well known—
> Though the pleasure be ours, the bacon's your own."
>
> *Brand's Popular Antiquities.*

At the village of Dunmow in Essex, the ancient custom is still observed. In Vienna the ham or flitch of bacon was hung over the city gate, whence the successful candidate was expected to bring it down, after he had satisfied the judges that he lived in peace with his wife, but was not under petticoat rule. It is said that in Vienna this ham remained for a long time unclaimed until at last a worthy burgher presented himself before the judges, bearing his wife's written affidavit that they had been married twelve years and had never disagreed—a statement which was confirmed by all their neighbours. The judges, satisfied with the proofs laid before them, told the candidate that the prize was his, and that he only need climb the ladder placed beneath it and bring it down. Rejoicing at having secured such a fine ham, the man speedily mounted the ladder ; but as he was about to reach for the prize he noticed that the ham, exposed to the noonday sun, was beginning to melt, and that a drop of fat threatened to fall upon his Sunday coat. Hastily beating a retreat, he pulled off his coat, jocosely remarking that his wife would scold him roundly were he to stain it, a confession which made the bystanders roar with laughter, and which cost him his ham.

Another Yuletide custom was the burning of a huge log, which had to last through the night, otherwise it was considered a very bad omen indeed. The charred remains of this log were carefully collected, and treasured up for the purpose of setting fire to the log of the following year.

> " With the last yeeres brand
>   Light the new block, and
> For good successe in his spending,
>   On your psaltries play,
>   That sweet luck may
> Come while the log is a-tending."
>
> *Hesperides* (*Herrick*).

This festival was so popular in Scandinavia, where it was celebrated in January, that King Olaf, seeing how dear it was to the Northern heart, transferred most of its observances to Christmas day, thereby doing much to reconcile the ignorant people to their change of religion.

As god of peace and prosperity, Frey is supposed to have reappeared upon earth many times, and to have ruled the Swedes under the name of Ingvi-Frey, whence his descendants were called Inglings. He also governed the Danes under the name of Fridleef. In Denmark he is said to have married the beautiful maiden Frey-gerda, whom he had rescued from a dragon. By her he had a son named Frodi, who, in due time, succeeded him as king.

Frodi ruled Denmark in the days when there was "peace throughout the world," that is say, just at the time when Christ was born in Bethlehem of Judea; and because all his subjects lived in amity, he was generally known as Peace Frodi.

How the Sea became salt

It is related that Frodi once received from Hengi-kiaptr a pair of magic millstones, called Grotti, which were so ponderous that none of his servants nor even his strongest warriors could turn them. The king was aware that the mill was enchanted and would grind anything he wished, so he was very anxious indeed to set it to work, and, during a visit to Sweden, he saw and purchased as slaves the two giantesses Menia and Fenia, whose powerful muscles and frames had attracted his attention.

On his return home, Peace Frodi led his new servants to the mill, and bade them turn the grindstones and grind out gold, peace, and prosperity, and they immediately fulfilled his wishes. Cheerfully the women worked on, hour after hour, until the king's coffers were overflowing with gold, and prosperity and peace were rife throughout his land.

> " Let us grind riches to Frothi!
> Let us grind him, happy
> In plenty of substance,
> On our gladdening Quern."
>
> *Grotta-Savngr* (*Longfellow's tr.*).

But when Menia and Fenia would fain have rested awhile, the king, whose greed had been excited, bade them work on. In spite of their entreaties he forced them to labour hour after hour, allowing them only as much time to rest as was required for the singing of a verse in a song, until exasperated by his cruelty, the giantesses resolved at length to have revenge. One night while Frodi slept they changed their song, and, instead of prosperity and peace, they grimly began to grind an armed host, whereby they induced the Viking Mysinger to land with a large body of troops. While the spell was working the Danes continued in slumber, and thus they were completely surprised by the Viking host, who slew them all.

> " An army must come
> Hither forthwith,
> And burn the town
> For the prince."
>
> *Grotta Savngr* (*Longfellow's tr.*).

Mysinger took the magic millstones Grotti and the two slaves and put them on board his vessel, bidding the women grind salt, which was a very valuable staple of commerce at that time. The women obeyed, and their millstones went round, grinding salt in abundance ; but the Viking, as cruel as Frodi, would give the poor women no rest, wherefore a heavy punishment overtook him and his followers. Such an immense quantity of salt was ground by the magic millstones that in the end its weight sunk the ship and all on board.

The ponderous stones sank into the sea in the Pentland Firth, or off the north-western coast of Norway, making a deep round hole, and the waters, rushing into the vortex and gurgling in the holes in the centre of the stones, produced the great whirlpool which is known as the Maelstrom. As for the salt it soon melted; but such was the immense quantity ground by the giantesses that it permeated all the waters of the sea, which have ever since been very salt.

CHAPTER X: FREYA

The Goddess of Love

FREYA, the fair Northern goddess of beauty and love, was the sister of Frey and the daughter of Niörd and Nerthus, or Skadi. She was the most beautiful and best beloved of all the goddesses, and while in Germany she was identified with Frigga, in Norway, Sweden, Denmark, and Iceland she was considered a separate divinity. Freya, having been born in Vanaheim, was also known as Vanadis, the goddess of the Vanas, or as Vanabride.

When she reached Asgard, the gods were so charmed by her beauty and grace that they bestowed upon her the realm of Folkvang and the great hall Sessrymnir (the roomy-seated), where they assured her she could easily accommodate all her guests.

> " Folkvang 'tis called,
> Where Freyja has right
> To dispose of the hall-seats.
> Every day of the slain
> She chooses the half,
> And leaves half to Odin."
>
> *Norse Mythology* (*R. B. Anderson*).

Queen of the Valkyrs

Although goddess of love, Freya was not soft and pleasure-loving only, for the ancient Northern races believed that she had very martial tastes, and that as Valfreya she often led the Valkyrs down to the battle-fields, choosing and claiming one half the heroes slain. She was therefore often represented with corselet and helmet, shield and spear, the lower part of her body only being clad in the usual flowing feminine garb.

Freya transported the chosen slain to Folkvang, where they were duly entertained. There also she welcomed all pure maidens and faithful wives, that they might enjoy the company of their lovers and husbands after death. The joys of her abode were so enticing to the heroic Northern women that they often rushed into battle when their loved ones were slain, hoping to meet with the same fate; or they fell upon their swords, or were voluntarily burned on the same funeral pyre as the remains of their beloved.

As Freya was believed to lend a favourable ear to lovers' prayers, she was often invoked by them, and it was customary to compose in her honour love-songs, which were sung on all festive occasions, her very name in Germany being used as the verb " to woo."

Freya and Odur

Freya, the golden-haired and blue-eyed goddess, was also, at times, considered as a personification of the earth. As such she married Odur, a symbol of the summer sun, whom she dearly loved, and by whom she had two daughters, Hnoss and Gersemi. These maidens were so beautiful that all things lovely and precious were called by their names.

While Odur lingered contentedly at her side, Freya was smiling and perfectly happy; but, alas! the god was a rover at heart, and, wearying of his wife's company, he suddenly left home and wandered far out into the wide world. Freya, sad and forsaken, wept abundantly, and her tears fell upon the hard rocks, which softened at their contact. We are told even that they trickled down to the very centre of the stones, where they were transformed to gold. Some tears fell into the sea and were changed into translucent amber.

Weary of her widowed condition, and longing to clasp her beloved in her arms once more, Freya finally started out in search of him, passing through many

132

Freya

N. J. O. Blommér

lands, where she became known by different names, such as Mardel, Horn, Gefn, Syr, Skialf, and Thrung, inquiring of all she met whether her husband had passed that way, and shedding everywhere so many tears that gold is to be found in all parts of the earth.

> "And Freya next came nigh, with golden tears ;
> The loveliest Goddess she in Heaven, by all
> Most honour'd after Frea, Odin's wife.
> Her long ago the wandering Oder took
> To mate, but left her to roam distant lands ;
> Since then she seeks him, and weeps tears of gold.
> Names hath she many ; Vanadis on earth
> They call her, Freya is her name in Heaven."
>
> *Balder Dead (Matthew Arnold).*

Far away in the sunny South, under the flowering myrtle-trees, Freya found Odur at last, and her love being restored to her, she was happy and smiling once again, and as radiant as a bride. It is perhaps because Freya found her husband beneath the flowering myrtle, that Northern brides, to this day, wear myrtle in preference to the conventional orange wreath of other climes.

Hand in hand, Odur and Freya now gently wended their way home once more, and in the light of their happiness the grass grew green, the flowers bloomed, and the birds sang, for all Nature sympathised as heartily with Freya's joy as it had mourned with her when she was in sorrow.

> " Out of the morning land,
> Over the snowdrifts,
> Beautiful Freya came
> Tripping to Scoring.
> White were the moorlands,
> And frozen before her;
> Green were the moorlands,
> And blooming behind her.
> Out of her gold locks

Shaking the spring flowers,
Out of her garments
Shaking the south wind,
Around in the birches
Awaking the throstles,
And making chaste housewives all
Long for their heroes home,
Loving and love-giving,
Came she to Scoring."
    The Longbeards' Saga (*Charles Kingsley*).

The prettiest plants and flowers in the North were called Freya's hair or Freya's eye dew, while the butterfly was called Freya's hen. This goddess was also supposed to have a special affection for the fairies, whom she loved to watch dancing in the moonbeams, and for whom she reserved her daintiest flowers and sweetest honey. Odur, Freya's husband, besides being considered a personification of the sun, was also regarded as an emblem of passion, or of the intoxicating pleasures of love; so the ancients declared that it was no wonder his wife could not be happy without him.

Freya's Necklace

Being goddess of beauty, Freya, naturally, was very fond of the toilet, of glittering adornments, and of precious jewels. One day, while she was in Svart-alfaheim, the underground kingdom, she saw four dwarfs fashioning the most wonderful necklace she had ever seen. Almost beside herself with longing to possess this treasure, which was called Brisinga-men, and was an emblem of the stars, or of the fruitfulness of the earth, Freya implored the dwarfs to give it to her; but they obstinately refused to do so unless she would promise to grant them her favour. Having secured the necklace at this price, Freya hastened to put it on, and its beauty so enhanced her charms that she wore it night

134

and day, and only occasionally could be persuaded to lend it to the other divinities. Thor, however, wore this necklace when he personated Freya in Jötun-heim, and Loki coveted and would have stolen it, had it not been for the watchfulness of Heimdall.

Freya was also the proud possessor of a falcon garb, or falcon plumes, which enabled the wearer to flit through the air as a bird; and this garment was so invaluable that it was twice borrowed by Loki, and was used by Freya herself when she went in search of the missing Odur.

> " Freya one day
> Falcon wings took, and through space hied away ;
> Northward and southward she sought her
> Dearly-loved Odur."
>
> *Frithiof Saga, Tegnér (Stephens's tr.)*

As Freya was also considered the goddess of fruitfulness, she was sometimes represented as riding about with her brother Frey in the chariot drawn by the golden-bristled boar, scattering, with lavish hands, fruits and flowers to gladden the hearts of mankind. She had a chariot of her own, however, in which she generally travelled. This was drawn by cats, her favourite animals, the emblems of caressing fondness and sensuality, or the personifications of fecundity.

> " Then came dark-bearded Niörd, and after him
> Freyia, thin robed, about her ankles slim
> The gray cats playing."
>
> *Lovers of Gudrun (William Morris).*

Frey and Freya were held in such high honour throughout the North that their names, in modified forms, are still used for " master " and " mistress," and one day of the week is called Freya's day, or Friday, by the English-speaking race. Freya's temples were very numerous indeed, and were long maintained by her

135

votaries, the last, in Magdeburg, Germany, being destroyed by order of Charlemagne.

Story of Ottar and Angantyr

The Northern people were wont to invoke Freya not only for success in love, prosperity, and increase, but also, at times, for aid and protection. This she vouchsafed to all who served her truly, as appeared in the story of Ottar and Angantyr, two men who, after disputing for some time concerning their rights to a certain piece of property, laid their quarrel before the Thing. That popular assembly decreed that the man who could prove that he had the longest line of noble ancestors should be declared the winner, and a special day was appointed to investigate the genealogy of each claimant.

Ottar, unable to remember the names of more than a few of his progenitors, offered sacrifices to Freya, entreating her aid. The goddess graciously heard his prayer, and appearing before him, she changed him into a boar, and rode off upon his back to the dwelling of the sorceress Hyndla, a most renowned witch. By threats and entreaties, Freya compelled the old woman to trace Ottar's genealogy back to Odin, and to name every individual in turn, with a synopsis of his achievements. Then, fearing lest her votary's memory should be unable to retain so many details, Freya further compelled Hyndla to brew a potion of remembrance, which she gave him to drink.

> "He shall drink
> Delicious draughts.
> All the gods I pray
> To favour Ottar."
>
> *Sæmund's Edda (Thorpe's tr.).*

WORSHIP OF FREYA

Thus prepared, Ottar presented himself before the Thing on the appointed day, and glibly reciting his pedigree, he named so many more ancestors than Angantyr could recollect, that he was easily awarded possession of the property he coveted.

> " A duty 'tis to act
> So that the young prince
> His paternal heritage may have
> After his kindred."
> *Sæmund's Edda* (*Thorpe's tr.*).

The Husbands of Freya

Freya was so beautiful that all the gods, giants, and dwarfs longed for her love and in turn tried to secure her as wife. But Freya scorned the ugly giants and refused even Thrym, when urged to accept him by Loki and Thor. She was not so obdurate where the gods themselves were concerned, if the various mythologists are to be believed, for as the personification of the earth she is said to have wedded Odin (the sky), Frey (the fruitful rain), Odur (the sunshine), &c., until it seems as if she deserved the accusation hurled against her by the arch-fiend Loki, of having loved and wedded all the gods in turn.

Worship of Freya

It was customary on solemn occasions to drink Freya's health with that of the other gods, and when Christianity was introduced in the North this toast was transferred to the Virgin or to St. Gertrude ; Freya herself, like all the heathen divinities, was declared a demon or witch, and banished to the mountain peaks of Norway, Sweden, or Germany, where the Brocken is pointed out as her special abode, and the general trysting-place of her demon train on Valpurgisnacht.

MYTHS OF THE NORSEMEN

Chorus of Witches.

"On to the Brocken the witches are flocking—
Merry meet—merry part—how they gallop and drive,
Yellow stubble and stalk are rocking,
And young green corn is merry alive,
With the shapes and shadows swimming by.
To the highest heights they fly,
Where Sir Urian sits on high—
Throughout and about,
With clamour and shout,
Drives the maddening rout,
Over stock, over stone ;
Shriek, laughter, and moan,
Before them are blown."
                        Goethe's Faust (*Anster's tr.*).

As the swallow, cuckoo, and cat were held sacred to
Freya in heathen times, these creatures were supposed
to have demoniacal attributes, and to this day witches
are always depicted with coal-black cats beside them.

CHAPTER XI: ULLER

The God of Winter

ULLER, the winter-god, was the son of Sif, and the stepson of Thor. His father, who is never mentioned in the Northern sagas, must have been one of the dreaded frost giants, for Uller loved the cold and delighted in travelling over the country on his broad snowshoes or glittering skates. This god also delighted in the chase, and pursued his game through the Northern forests, caring but little for ice and snow, against which he was well protected by the thick furs in which he was always clad.

As god of hunting and archery, he is represented with a quiver full of arrows and a huge bow, and as the yew furnishes the best wood for the manufacture of these weapons, it is said to have been his favourite tree. To have a supply of suitable wood ever at hand ready for use, Uller took up his abode at Ydalir, the vale of yews, where it was always very damp.

> " Ydalir it is called,
> Where Ullr has
> Himself a dwelling made."
> *Sæmund's Edda (Thorpe's tr.)*.

As winter-god, Uller, or Oller, as he was also called, was considered second only to Odin, whose place he usurped during his absence in the winter months of the year. During this period he exercised full sway over Asgard and Midgard, and even, according to some authorities, took possession of Frigga, Odin's wife, as related in the myth of Vili and Ve. But as Uller was very parsimonious, and never bestowed any gifts upon mankind, they gladly hailed the return of Odin, who drove his supplanter away, forcing him to take refuge either in the frozen North or on the tops of the Alps. Here, if we are to believe the poets, he had built a summer house into which he retreated until, knowing Odin had departed once more, he again dared appear in the valleys.

Uller was also considered god of death, and was supposed to ride in the Wild Hunt, and at times even to lead it. He is specially noted for his rapidity of motion, and as the snowshoes used in Northern regions are sometimes made of bone, and turned up in front like the prow of a ship, it was commonly reported that Uller had spoken magic runes over a piece of bone, changing it into a vessel, which bore him over land or sea at will.

As snowshoes are shaped like a shield, and as the ice with which he yearly enveloped the earth acts as a shield to protect it from harm during the winter, Uller was surnamed the shield-god, and he was specially invoked by all persons about to engage in a duel or in a desperate fight.

In Christian times, his place in popular worship was taken by St. Hubert, the hunter, who, also, was made patron of the first month of the year, which began on November 22, and was dedicated to him as the sun passed through the constellation of Sagittarius, the bowman.

In Anglo-Saxon, Uller was known as Vulder ; but in some parts of Germany he was called Holler and considered to be the husband of the fair goddess Holda, whose fields he covered with a thick mantle of snow, to make them more fruitful when the spring came.

By the Scandinavians, Uller was said to have married Skadi, Niörd's divorced wife, the female personification of winter and cold, and their tastes were so congenial that they lived in perfect harmony together.

Worship of Uller

Numerous temples were dedicated to Uller in the North, and on his altars, as well as on those of all the other gods, lay a sacred ring upon which oaths were sworn. This ring was said to have the power of shrinking so violently as to sever the finger of any premeditated perjurer. The people visited Uller's shrine, especially during the months of November and December, to entreat him to send a thick covering of snow over their lands, as earnest of a good harvest; and as he was supposed to send out the glorious flashes of the aurora borealis, which illumine the Northern sky during its long night, he was considered nearly akin to Balder, the personification of light.

According to other authorities, Uller was Balder's special friend, principally because he too spent part of the year in the dismal depths of Nifl-heim, with Hel, the goddess of death. Uller was supposed to endure a yearly banishment thither, during the summer months, when he was forced to resign his sway over the earth to Odin, the summer god, and there Balder came to join him at Midsummer, the date of his disappearance from Asgard, for then the days began to grow shorter, and the rule of light (Balder) gradually yielded to the ever encroaching power of darkness (Hodur).

CHAPTER XII: FORSETI

The God of Justice and Truth

SON of Balder, god of light, and of Nanna, goddess of immaculate purity, Forseti was the wisest, most eloquent, and most gentle of all the gods. When his presence in Asgard became known, the gods awarded him a seat in the council hall, decreed that he should be patron of justice and righteousness, and gave him as abode the radiant palace Glitnir. This dwelling had a silver roof, supported on pillars of gold, and it shone so brightly that it could be seen from a great distance.

> " Glitner is the tenth ;
> It is on gold sustained,
> And also with silver decked.
> There Forseti dwells
> Throughout all time,
> And every strife allays."
> *Sæmund's Edda* (*Thorpe's tr.*).

Here, upon an exalted throne, Forseti, the lawgiver, sat day after day, settling the differences of gods and men, patiently listening to both sides of every question, and finally pronouncing sentences so equitable that none ever found fault with his decrees. Such were this god's eloquence and power of persuasion that he always succeeded in touching his hearers' hearts, and never failed to reconcile even the most bitter foes. All who left his presence were thereafter sure to live in peace, for none dared break a vow once made to him, lest they should incur his just anger and be smitten immediately unto death.

> " Forsete, Balder's high-born son,
> Hath heard mine oath ;
> Strike dead, Forset', if e'er I'm won
> To break my troth."
> *Viking Tales of the North* (*R. B. Anderson*).

THE STORY OF HELIGOLAND

As god of justice and eternal law, Forseti was supposed to preside over every judicial assembly; he was invariably appealed to by all who were about to undergo a trial, and it was said that he rarely failed to help the deserving.

The Story of Heligoland

In order to facilitate the administration of justice throughout their land it is related that the Frisians commissioned twelve of their wisest men, the Asegeir, or elders, to collect the laws of the various families and tribes composing their nation, and to compile from them a code which should be the basis of uniform laws. The elders, having painstakingly finished their task of collecting this miscellaneous information, embarked upon a small vessel, to seek some secluded spot where they might conduct their deliberations in peace. But no sooner had they pushed away from shore than a tempest arose, which drove their vessel far out to sea, first on this course and then on that, until they entirely lost their bearings. In their distress the twelve jurists called upon Forseti, begging him to help them to reach land once again, and the prayer was scarcely ended when they perceived, to their utter surprise, that the vessel contained a thirteenth passenger.

Seizing the rudder, the newcomer silently brought the vessel round, steering it towards the place where the waves dashed highest, and in an incredibly short space of time they came to an island, where the steersman motioned them to disembark. In awestruck silence the twelve men obeyed; and their surprise was further excited when they saw the stranger fling his battle-axe, and a limpid spring gush forth from the spot on the greensward where it fell. Imitating the stranger, all drank of this water without a word; then they sat down in a circle, marvelling because the newcomer resembled each one of them in some particular, but yet was very different from any one of them in general aspect and mien.

Suddenly the silence was broken, and the stranger began to speak in low tones, which grew firmer and louder as he proceeded to expound a code of laws which combined all the good points of the various existing regulations which the Asegeir had collected. His speech being finished, the speaker vanished as suddenly and mysteriously as he had appeared, and the twelve jurists, recovering power of speech, simultaneously exclaimed that Forseti himself had been among them, and had delivered the code of laws by which the Frisians should henceforth be judged. In commemoration of the god's appearance they declared the island upon which they stood to be holy, and they pronounced a solemn curse upon any who might dare to desecrate its sanctity by quarrel or bloodshed. Accordingly this island, known as Forseti's land or Heligoland (holy land), was greatly respected by all the Northern nations, and even the boldest vikings refrained from raiding its shores, lest they should suffer shipwreck or meet a shameful death in punishment for their crime.

Solemn judicial assemblies were frequently held upon this sacred isle, the jurists always drawing water and drinking it in silence, in memory of Forseti's visit. The waters of his spring were, moreover, considered to be so holy that all who drank of them were held to be sacred, and even the cattle who had tasted of them might not be slain. As Forseti was said to hold his assizes in spring, summer, and autumn, but never in winter, it became customary, in all the Northern countries, to dispense justice in those seasons, the people declaring that it was only when the light shone clearly in the heavens that right could become apparent to all, and that it would be utterly impossible to render an equitable verdict during the dark winter season. Forseti is seldom mentioned except in connection with Balder. He apparently had no share in the closing battle in which all the other gods played such prominent parts.

CHAPTER XIII: HEIMDALL

The Watchman of the Gods

IN the course of a walk along the sea-shore Odin once beheld nine beautiful giantesses, the wave maidens, Gialp, Greip, Egia, Augeia, Ulfrun, Aurgiafa, Sindur, Atla, and Iarnsaxa, sound asleep on the white sand. The god of the sky was so charmed with these beautiful creatures that, as the Eddas relate, he wedded all nine of them, and they combined, at the same moment, to bring forth a son, who received the name of Heimdall.

> "Born was I of mothers nine,
> Son I am of sisters nine."
> *Sæmund's Edda* (*Thorpe's tr.*).

The nine mothers proceeded to nourish their babe on the strength of the earth, the moisture of the sea, and the heat of the sun, which singular diet proved so strengthening that the new god acquired his full growth in a remarkably short space of time, and hastened to join his father in Asgard. He found the gods proudly contemplating the rainbow bridge Bifröst, which they had just constructed out of fire, air, and water, the three materials which can still plainly be seen in its long arch, where glow the three primary colours : the red representing the fire, the blue the air, and the green the cool depths of the sea.

The Guardian of the Rainbow

This bridge connected heaven and earth, and ended under the shade of the mighty world-tree Yggdrasil, close beside the fountain where Mimir kept guard, and the only drawback to prevent the complete enjoyment of the glorious spectacle, was the fear lest the frost-

The Rainbow Bridge

H. Heudrich

By Permission of the "Illustrirte Zeitung" (J. J Weber, Leipzig

giants should make their way over it and so gain entrance into Asgard.

The gods had been debating the advisability of appointing a trustworthy guardian, and they hailed the new recruit as one well-fitted to fulfil the onerous duties of the office.

Heimdall gladly undertook the responsibility and henceforth, night and day, he kept vigilant watch over the rainbow highway into Asgard.

> " Bifröst i' th' east shone forth in brightest green ;
> On its top, in snow-white sheen,
> Heimdal at his post was seen."
> *Oehlenschläger* (*Pigott's tr.*).

To enable their watchman to detect the approach of any enemy from afar, the assembled gods bestowed upon him senses so keen that he is said to have been able to hear the grass grow on the hillside, and the wool on the sheep's back ; to see one hundred miles off as plainly by night as by day ; and with all this he required less sleep than a bird.

> " 'Mongst shivering giants wider known
> Than him who sits unmoved on high,
> The guard of heaven, with sleepless eye."
> *Lay of Skirner* (*Herbert's tr.*).

Heimdall was provided further with a flashing sword and a marvellous trumpet, called Giallar-horn, which the gods bade him blow whenever he saw their enemies approach, declaring that its sound would rouse all creatures in heaven, earth, and Nifl-heim. Its last dread blast would announce the arrival of that day when the final battle would be fought.

"To battle the gods are called
By the ancient
Gjallar-horn.
Loud blows Heimdall,
His sound is in the air."
Sæmund's Edda (Thorpe's tr.).

To keep this instrument, which was a symbol of the crescent moon, ever at hand, Heimdall either hung it on a branch of Yggdrasil above his head or sank it in the waters of Mimir's well. In the latter it lay side by side with Odin's eye, which was an emblem of the moon at its full.

Heimdall's palace, called Himinbiorg, was situated on the highest point of the bridge, and here the gods often visited him to quaff the delicious mead which he set before them.

"'Tis Himminbjorg called
Where Heimdal, they say,
Hath dwelling and rule.
There the gods' warder drinks,
In peaceful old halls,
Gladsome the good mead."
Norse Mythology (R. B. Anderson).

Heimdall was always depicted in resplendent white armour, and he was therefore called the bright god. He was also known as the light, innocent, and graceful god, all of which names he fully deserved, for he was as good as he was beautiful, and all the gods loved him. Connected on his mothers' side with the sea, he was sometimes included with the Vanas ; and as the ancient Northmen, especially the Icelanders, to whom the surrounding sea appeared the most important element, fancied that all things had risen out of it, they attributed to him an all-embracing knowledge and imagined him particularly wise.

148

Heimdall
Dorothy Hardy

LOKI AND FREYA

"Of Æsir the brightest—
He well foresaw
Like other Vanir."
Sæmund's Edda (Thorpe's tr.).

Heimdall was further distinguished by his golden teeth, which flashed when he smiled, and won for him the surname of Gullintani (golden-toothed). He was also the proud possessor of a swift, golden-maned steed called Gull-top, which bore him to and fro over the quivering rainbow bridge. This he crossed many times a day, but particularly in the early morn, at which time, as herald of the day, he bore the name of Heim-dellinger.

"Early up Bifröst
Ran Ulfrun's son,
The mighty hornblower
Of Himinbiörg."
Sæmund's Edda (Thorpe's tr.).

Loki and Freya

His extreme acuteness of hearing caused Heimdall to be disturbed one night by the sound of soft, catlike footsteps in the direction of Freya's palace, Folkvang. Projecting his eagle gaze through the darkness, Heimdall perceived that the sound was produced by Loki, who, having stealthily entered the palace as a fly, had approached Freya's bedside, and was trying to steal her shining golden necklace, Brisinga-men, the emblem of the fruitfulness of the earth.

Heimdall saw that the goddess was resting in her sleep in such a way that no one could possibly unclasp the necklace without awaking her. Loki stood hesitatingly by the bedside for a few moments, and then began rapidly to mutter the runes which enabled the gods to change their form at will. As he did this,

149

Heimdall saw him shrivel up until he was changed to the size and form of a flea, when he crept under the bed-clothes and bit Freya's side, thus causing her to change her position without being roused from sleep.

The clasp was now in view, and Loki, cautiously un-fastening it, secured the coveted treasure, and forthwith proceeded to steal away with it. Heimdall immedi-ately started out in pursuit of the midnight thief, and quickly overtaking him, he drew his sword from its scabbard, with intent to cut off his head, when the god transformed himself into a flickering blue flame. Quick as thought, Heimdall changed himself into a cloud and sent down a deluge of rain to quench the fire ; but Loki as promptly altered his form to that of a huge polar bear, and opened wide his jaws to swallow the water. Heimdall, nothing daunted, then likewise assumed the form of a bear, and attacked fiercely ; but the combat threatening to end disastrously for Loki, the latter changed himself into a seal, and, Heimdall imitating him, a last struggle took place, which ended in Loki being forced to give up the necklace, which was duly restored to Freya.

In this myth, Loki is an emblem of drought, or of the baleful effects of the too ardent heat of the sun, which comes to rob the earth (Freya) of its most cherished ornament (Brisinga-men). Heimdall is a personification of the gentle rain and dew, which after struggling for a while with his foe, the drought, even-tually conquers him and forces him to relinquish his prize.

Heimdall's Names

Heimdall has several other names, among which we find those of Hallinskide and Irmin, for at times he takes Odin's place and is identified with that god, as well as with the other sword-gods, Er, Heru, Cheru and Tyr, who are all noted for their shining weapons. He, however, is most generally known as warder of the rainbow, and god of heaven, and of the fruitful rains and dews which bring refreshment to the earth.

Heimdall also shared with Bragi the honour of welcoming heroes to Valhalla, and, under the name of Riger, was considered the divine sire of the various classes which compose the human race, as appears in the following story :

The Story of Riger

"Sacred children,
Great and small,
Sons of Heimdall ! "
Sæmund's Edda (Thorpe's tr.).

Heimdall left his place in Asgard one day to wander upon the earth, as the gods were wont to do. He had not gone far ere he came to a poor hut on the seashore, where he found Ai (great grandfather) and Edda (great grandmother), a poor but worthy couple, who hospitably invited him to share their meagre meal of porridge. Heimdall, who gave his name as Riger, gladly accepted this invitation, and remained with the couple three whole days, teaching them many things. At the end of that time he left to resume his journey. Some time after his visit, Edda bore a dark-skinned thick-set boy, whom she called Thrall.

Thrall soon showed uncommon physical strength and a great aptitude for all heavy work ; and when he had grown up he took to wife Thyr, a heavily built girl with sunburnt hands and flat feet, who, like her husband, laboured early and late. Many children were born to this couple and from them all the serfs or thralls of the Northland were descended.

151

"They had children
Lived and were happy;

They laid fences,
Enriched the plow-land,
Tended swine,
Herded goats,
Dug peat."
Rigsmál (Du Chaillu's version).

After leaving the poor hut on the barren seacoast Riger had pushed inland, where ere long he came to cultivated fields and a thrifty farmhouse. Entering this comfortable dwelling, he found Afi (grandfather) and Amma (grandmother), who hospitably invited him to sit down with them and share the plain but bountiful fare which was prepared for their meal.

Riger accepted the invitation and he remained three days with his hosts, imparting the while all manner of useful knowledge to them. After his departure from their house, Amma gave birth to a blue-eyed sturdy boy, whom she called Karl. As he grew up he exhibited great skill in agricultural pursuits, and in due course he married a buxom and thrifty wife named Snor, who bore him many children, from whom the race of husbandmen is descended.

"He did grow
And thrive well;
He broke oxen,
Made plows;
Timbered houses,
Made barns,
Made carts,
And drove the plow."
Rigsmál (Du Chaillu's version).

Leaving the house of this second couple, Riger continued his journey until he came to a hill, upon which was perched a stately castle. Here he was received by

Jarl

Albert Edelfelt

THE STORY OF RIGER

Fadir (father) and Modir (mother), who, delicately nurtured and luxuriously clad, received him cordially, and set before him dainty meats and rich wines.

Riger tarried three days with this couple, afterwards returning to Himinbiorg to resume his post as guardian of Asa-bridge; and ere long the lady of the castle bore a handsome, slenderly built little son, whom she called Jarl. This child early showed a great taste for the hunt and all manner of martial exercises, learned to understand runes, and lived to do great deeds of valour which made his name distinguished and added glory to his race. Having attained manhood, Jarl married Erna, an aristocratic, slender-waisted maiden, who ruled his household wisely and bore him many children, all destined to rule, the youngest of whom, Konur, became the first king of Denmark. This myth well illustrates the marked sense of class among the Northern races.

> " Up grew
> The sons of Jarl ;
> They brake horses,
> Bent shields,
> Smoothed shafts,
> Shook ash spears
> But Kon, the young,
> Knew runes,
> Everlasting runes
> And life runes."
>
> *Rigsmál (Du Chaillu's version).*

CHAPTER XIV : HERMOD

The Nimble God

ANOTHER of Odin's sons was Hermod, his special attendant, a bright and beautiful young god, who was gifted with great rapidity of motion and was therefore designated as the swift or nimble god.

> " But there was one, the first of all the gods
> For speed, and Hermod was his name in Heaven ;
> Most fleet he was."
>
> *Balder Dead (Matthew Arnold).*

On account of this important attribute Hermod was usually employed by the gods as messenger, and at a mere sign from Odin he was always ready to speed to any part of creation. As a special mark of favour, Allfather gave him a magnificent corselet and helmet, which he often donned when he prepared to take part in war, and sometimes Odin entrusted to his care the precious spear Gungnir, bidding him cast it over the heads of combatants about to engage in battle, that their ardour might be kindled into murderous fury.

> " Let us Odin pray
> Into our minds to enter ;
> He gives and grants
> Gold to the deserving.
> He gave to Hermod
> A helm and corselet."
>
> *Sæmund's Edda (Thorpe's tr.).*

Hermod delighted in battle, and was often called " the valiant in battle," and confounded with the god of the universe, Irmin. It is said that he sometimes accompanied the Valkyrs on their ride to earth, and

154

frequently escorted the warriors to Valhalla, wherefore he was considered the leader of the heroic dead.

> "To him spake Hermoder and Brage :
>   'We meet thee and greet thee from all,
>   To the gods thou art known by thy valour,
>   And they bid thee a guest to their hall.'"
>   *Owen Meredith.*

Hermod's distinctive attribute, besides his corselet and helm, was a wand or staff called Gambantein, the emblem of his office, which he carried with him wherever he went.

Hermod and the Soothsayer

Once, oppressed by shadowy fears for the future, and unable to obtain from the Norns satisfactory answers to his questions, Odin bade Hermod don his armour and saddle Sleipnir, which he alone, besides Odin, was allowed to ride, and hasten off to the land of the Finns. This people, who lived in the frozen regions of the pole, besides being able to call up the cold storms which swept down from the North, bringing much ice and snow in their train, were supposed to have great occult powers.

The most noted of these Finnish magicians was Rossthiof (the horse thief) who was wont to entice travellers into his realm by magic arts, that he might rob and slay them ; and he had power to predict the future, although he was always very reluctant to do so.

Hermod, "the swift," rode rapidly northward, with directions to seek this Finn, and instead of his own wand, he carried Odin's runic staff, which Allfather had given him for the purpose of dispelling any obstacles that Rossthiof might conjure up to hinder his advance. In spite, therefore, of phantom-like monsters and of

155

invisible snares and pitfalls, Hermod was enabled safely to reach the magician's abode, and upon the giant attacking him, he was able to master him with ease, and he bound him hand and foot, declaring that he would not set him free until he promised to reveal all that he wished to know.

Rossthiof, seeing that there was no hope of escape, pledged himself to do as his captor wished, and upon being set at liberty, he began forthwith to mutter incantations, at the mere sound of which the sun hid behind the clouds, the earth trembled and quivered, and the storm winds howled like a pack of hungry wolves.

Pointing to the horizon, the magician bade Hermod look, and the swift god saw in the distance a great stream of blood reddening the ground. While he gazed wonderingly at this stream, a beautiful woman suddenly appeared, and a moment later a little boy stood beside her. To the god's amazement, this child grew with such marvellous rapidity that he soon attained his full growth, and Hermod further noticed that he fiercely brandished a bow and arrows.

Rossthiof now began to explain the omens which his art had conjured up, and he declared that the stream of blood portended the murder of one of Odin's sons, but that if the father of the gods should woo and win Rinda, in the land of the Ruthenes (Russia), she would bear him a son who would attain his full growth in a few hours and would avenge his brother's death.

> " Rind a son shall bear,
> In the western halls :
> He shall slay Odin's son,
> When one night old."
> *Sæmund's Edda* (*Thorpe's tr.*).

Hermod listened attentively to the words of Rossthiof

and upon his return to Asgard he reported all he had seen and heard to Odin, whose fears were confirmed and who thus definitely ascertained that he was doomed to lose a son by violent death. He consoled himself, however, with the thought that another of his descendants would avenge the crime and thereby obtain the satisfaction which a true Northman ever required.

CHAPTER XV: VIDAR

The Silent God

IT is related that Odin once loved the beautiful giantess Grid, who dwelt in a cave in the desert, and that, wooing her, he prevailed upon her to become his wife. The offspring of this union between Odin (mind) and Grid (matter) was Vidar, a son as strong as he was taciturn, whom the ancients considered a personification of the primæval forest or of the imperishable forces of Nature.

As the gods, through Heimdall, were intimately connected with the sea, they were also bound by close ties to the forests and Nature in general through Vidar, surnamed " the silent," who was destined to survive their destruction and rule over a regenerated earth. This god had his habitation in Landvidi (the wide land), a palace decorated with green boughs and fresh flowers, situated in the midst of an impenetrable primæval forest where reigned the deep silence and solitude which he loved.

> " Grown over with shrubs
> And with high grass
> In Vidar's wide land."
> *Norse Mythology* (*R. B. Anderson*).

This old Scandinavian conception of the silent Vidar is indeed very grand and poetical, and was inspired by the rugged Northern scenery. " Who has ever wandered through such forests, in a length of many miles, in a boundless expanse, without a path, without a goal, amid their monstrous shadows, their sacred gloom, without being filled with deep reverence for the sublime greatness of Nature above all human agency, without feeling the grandeur of the idea which forms the basis of Vidar's essence ? "

THE NORN'S PROPHECY

Vidar's Shoe

Vidar is depicted as tall, well-made, and handsome, clad in armour, girded with a broad-bladed sword, and shod with a great iron or leather shoe. According to some mythologists, he owed this peculiar footgear to his mother Grid, who, knowing that he would be called upon to fight against fire on the last day, designed it as a protection against the fiery element, as her iron gauntlet had shielded Thor in his encounter with Geirrod. But other authorities state that this shoe was made of the leather scraps which Northern cobblers had either given or thrown away. As it was essential that the shoe should be large and strong enough to resist the Fenris wolf's sharp teeth at the last day, it was a matter of religious observance among Northern shoemakers to give away as many odds and ends of leather as possible.

The Norn's Prophecy

When Vidar joined his peers in Valhalla, they welcomed him gaily, for they knew that his great strength would serve them well in their time of need. After they had lovingly regaled him with the golden mead, Allfather bade him follow to the Urdar fountain, where the Norns were ever busy weaving their web. Questioned by Odin concerning his future and Vidar's destiny, the three sisters answered oracularly ; each uttering a sentence :

" *Early begun.*"

" *Further spun.*"

" *One day done.*"

To these their mother, Wyrd, the primitive goddess of fate, added : " *With joy once more won.*" These mysterious answers would have remained totally unintelligible had the goddess not gone on to explain that

159

time progresses, that all must change, but that even if the father fell in the last battle, his son Vidar would be his avenger, and would live to rule over a regenerated world, after having conquered all his enemies.

> " There sits Odin's
> Son on the horse's back ;
> He will avenge his father."
>> *Norse Mythology* (*R. B. Anderson*).

As Wyrd spoke, the leaves of the world tree fluttered as if agitated by a breeze, the eagle on its topmost bough flapped its wings, and the serpent Nidhug for a moment suspended its work of destruction at the roots of the tree. Grid, joining the father and son, rejoiced with Odin when she heard that their son was destined to survive the older gods and to rule over the new heaven and earth.

> " There dwell Vidar and Vale
> In the gods' holy seats,
> When the fire of Surt is slaked."
>> *Norse Mythology* (*R. B. Anderson*).

Vidar, however, uttered not a word, but slowly wended his way back to his palace Landvidi, in the heart of the primæval forest, and there, sitting upon his throne, he pondered long about eternity, futurity, and infinity. If he fathomed their secrets he never revealed them, for the ancients averred that he was " as silent as the grave "—a silence which indicated that no man knows what awaits him in the life to come.

Vidar was not only a personification of the imperishability of Nature, but he was also a symbol of resurrection and renewal, exhibiting the eternal truth that new shoots and blossoms will spring forth to replace those which have fallen into decay.

The shoe he wore was to be his defence against the

wolf Fenris, who, having destroyed Odin, would direct his wrath against him, and open wide his terrible jaws to devour him. But the old Northmen declared that Vidar would brace the foot thus protected against the monster's lower jaw, and, seizing the upper, would struggle with him until he had rent him in twain.

As one shoe only is mentioned in the Vidar myths, some mythologists suppose that he had but one leg, and was the personification of a waterspout, which would rise suddenly on the last day to quench the wild fire personified by the terrible wolf Fenris.

CHAPTER XVI : VALI

The Wooing of Rinda

BILLING, king of the Ruthenes, was sorely dismayed when he heard that a great force was about to invade his kingdom, for he was too old to fight as of yore, and his only child, a daughter named Rinda, although she was of marriageable age, obstinately refused to choose a husband from among her many suitors, and thus give her father the help which he so sadly needed.

While Billing was musing disconsolately in his hall, a stranger suddenly entered his palace. Looking up, the king beheld a middle-aged man wrapped in a wide cloak, with a broad-brimmed hat drawn down over his forehead to conceal the fact that he had but one eye. The stranger courteously enquired the cause of his evident depression, and as there was that in his bearing that compelled confidence, the king told him all, and at the end of the relation he volunteered to command the army of the Ruthenes against their foe.

His services being joyfully accepted, it was not long ere Odin—for it was he—won a signal victory, and, returning in triumph, he asked permission to woo the king's daughter Rinda for his wife. Despite the suitor's advancing years, Billing hoped that his daughter would lend a favourable ear to a wooer who appeared to be very distinguished, and he immediately signified his consent. So Odin, still unknown, presented himself before the princess, but she scornfully rejected his proposal, and rudely boxed his ears when he attempted to kiss her.

Forced to withdraw, Odin nevertheless did not relinquish his purpose to make Rinda his wife, for he knew, thanks to Rossthiof's prophecy, that none but she could bring forth the destined avenger of his murdered son. His next step, therefore, was to assume the form of a smith, in which guise he came back to Billing's hall, and fashioning costly ornaments of silver and gold, he so artfully multiplied these precious trinkets that the king joyfully acquiesced when he inquired whether he might pay his addresses to the princess. The smith, Rosterus as he announced himself, was, however, as unceremoniously dismissed by Rinda as the successful general had been ; but although his ear once again tingled with the force of her blow, he was more determined than ever to make her his wife.

The next time Odin presented himself before the capricious damsel, he was disguised as a dashing warrior, for, thought he, a young soldier might perchance touch the maiden's heart ; but when he again attempted to kiss her, she pushed him back so suddenly that he stumbled and fell upon one knee.

> " Many a fair maiden
> When rightly known,
> Towards men is fickle ;
> That I experienced,
> When that discreet maiden I
> Strove to win ;
> Contumely of every kind
> That wily girl
> Heaped upon me ;
> Nor of that damsel gained I aught."
> *Sæmund's Edda (Thorpe's tr.)*.

This third insult so enraged Odin that he drew his magic rune stick out of his breast, pointed it at Rinda, and uttered such a terrible spell that she fell back into the arms of her attendants rigid and apparently lifeless.

When the princess came to life again, her suitor had disappeared, but the king discovered with great dismay that she had entirely lost her senses and was melancholy mad. In vain all the physicians were summoned and all their simples tried; the maiden remained passive and sad, and her distracted father had well-nigh abandoned hope when an old woman, who announced herself as Vecha, or Vak, appeared and offered to undertake the cure of the princess. The seeming old woman, who was Odin in disguise, first prescribed a foot-bath for the patient; but as this did not appear to have any very marked effect, she proposed to try a more drastic treatment. For this, Vecha declared, the patient must be entrusted to her exclusive care, securely bound so that she could not offer the least resistance. Billing, anxious to save his child, was ready to assent to anything; and having thus gained full power over Rinda, Odin compelled her to wed him, releasing her from bonds and spell only when she had faithfully promised to be his wife.

The Birth of Vali

The prophecy of Rossthiof was now fulfilled, for Rinda duly bore a son named Vali (Ali, Bous, or Beav), a personification of the lengthening days, who grew with such marvellous rapidity that in the course of a single day he attained his full stature. Without waiting even to wash his face or comb his hair, this young god hastened to Asgard, bow and arrow in hand, to avenge the death of Balder upon his murderer, Hodur, the blind god of darkness.

> " But, see ! th' avenger, Vali, come,
> Sprung from the west, in Rinda's womb,
> True son of Odin ! one day's birth !
> He shall not stop nor stay on earth
> His locks to comb, his hands to lave,
> His frame to rest, should rest it crave,

WORSHIP OF VALI

Until his mission be complete,
And Balder's death find vengeance meet."
Valhalla (J. C. Jones).

In this myth, Rinda, a personification of the hard-frozen rind of the earth, resists the warm wooing of the sun, Odin, who vainly points out that spring is the time for warlike exploits, and offers the adornments of golden summer. She only yields when, after a shower (the footbath), a thaw sets in. Conquered then by the sun's irresistible might, the earth yields to his embrace, is freed from the spell (ice) which made her hard and cold, and brings forth Vali the nourisher, or Bous the peasant, who emerges from his dark hut when the pleasant days have come. The slaying of Hodur by Vali is therefore emblematical of "the breaking forth of new light after wintry darkness."

Vali, who ranked as one of the twelve deities occupying seats in the great hall of Glads-heim, shared with his father the dwelling called Valaskialf, and was destined, even before birth, to survive the last battle and twilight of the gods, and to reign with Vidar over the regenerated earth.

Worship of Vali

Vali is god of eternal light, as Vidar is of imperishable matter ; and as beams of light were often called arrows, he is always represented and worshipped as an archer. For that reason his month in Norwegian calendars is designated by the sign of the bow, and is called Lios-beri, the light-bringing. As it falls between the middle of January and of February, the early Christians dedicated this month to St. Valentine, who was also a skilful archer, and was said, like Vali, to be the harbinger of brighter days, the awakener of tender sentiments, and the patron of all lovers.

CHAPTER XVII : THE NORNS

The Three Fates

THE Northern goddesses of fate, who were called Norns, were in nowise subject to the other gods, who might neither question nor influence their decrees. They were three sisters, probably descendants of the giant Norvi, from whom sprang Nott (night). As soon as the Golden Age was ended, and sin began to steal even into the heavenly homes of Asgard, the Norns made their appearance under the great ash Yggdrasil, and took up their abode near the Urdar fountain. According to some mythologists, their mission was to warn the gods of future evil, to bid them make good use of the present, and to teach them wholesome lessons from the past.

These three sisters, whose names were Urd, Verdandi, and Skuld, were personifications of the past, present, and future. Their principal occupations were to weave the web of fate ; to sprinkle daily the sacred tree with water from the Urdar fountain, and to put fresh clay around its roots, that it might remain fresh and ever green.

> " Thence come the maids
> Who much do know;
> Three from the hall
> Beneath the tree;
> One they named *Was*,
> And *Being* next,
> The third *Shall be*."
> *The Völuspâ (Henderson's tr.)*.

Some authorities further state that the Norns kept watch over the golden apples which hung on the branches of the tree of life, experience, and knowledge, allowing none but Idun to pick the fruit, which was that with which the gods renewed their youth.

166

The Norns

C. Ehrenberg

THE NORNS' WEB

The Norns also fed and tenderly cared for two swans which swam over the mirror-like surface of the Urdar fountain, and from this pair of birds all the swans on earth are supposed to be descended. At times, it is said, the Norns clothed themselves with swan plumage to visit the earth, or sported like mermaids along the coast and in various lakes and rivers, appearing to mortals, from time to time, to foretell the future or give them sage advice.

The Norns' Web

The Norns sometimes wove webs so large that while one of the weavers stood on a high mountain in the extreme east, another waded far out into the western sea. The threads of their woof resembled cords, and varied greatly in hue, according to the nature of the events about to occur, and a black thread, tending from north to south, was invariably considered an omen of death. As these sisters flashed the shuttle to and fro, they chanted a solemn song. They did not seem to weave according to their own wishes, but blindly, as if reluctantly executing the wishes of Orlog, the eternal law of the universe, an older and superior power, who apparently had neither beginning nor end.

Two of the Norns, Urd and Verdandi, were considered to be very beneficent indeed, while the third, it is said, relentlessly undid their work, and often, when nearly finished, tore it angrily to shreds, scattering the remnants to the winds of heaven. As personifications of time, the Norns were represented as sisters of different ages and characters, Urd (Wurd, weird) appearing very old and decrepit, continually looking backward, as if absorbed in contemplating past events and people ; Verdandi, the second sister, young, active, and fearless, looked straight before her, while Skuld, the type of the

167

future, was generally represented as closely veiled, with head turned in the direction opposite to where Urd was gazing, and holding a book or scroll which had not yet been opened or unrolled.

These Norns were visited daily by the gods, who loved to consult them; and even Odin himself frequently rode down to the Urdar fountain to bespeak their aid, for they generally answered his questions, maintaining silence only about his own fate and that of his fellow gods.

> " Rode he long and rode he fast.
> First beneath the great Life Tree,
> At the sacred Spring sought he
> Urdar, Norna of the Past;
> But her backward seeing eye
> Could no knowledge now supply.
> Across Verdandi's page there fell
> Dark shades that ever woes foretell;
> The shadows which 'round Asgard hung
> Their baleful darkness o'er it flung;
> The secret was not written there
> Might save Valhal, the pure and fair.
> Last youngest of the sisters three,
> Skuld, Norna of Futurity,
> Implored to speak, stood silent by,—
> Averted was her tearful eye."
>
> *Valhalla (J. C. Jones).*

Other Guardian Spirits

Besides the three principal Norns there were many others, far less important, who seem to have been the guardian spirits of mankind, to whom they frequently appeared, lavishing all manner of gifts upon their favourites, and seldom failing to be present at births, marriages, and deaths.

> " Oh, manifold is their kindred, and who shall tell them all ?
> There are they that rule o'er men folk, and the stars that rise and fall."
>
> *Sigurd the Volsung (William Morris).*

THE STORY OF NORNAGESTA

The Story of Nornagesta

On one occasion the three sisters visited Denmark, and entered the dwelling of a nobleman as his first child came into the world. Entering the apartment where the mother lay, the first Norn promised that the child should be handsome and brave, and the second that he should be prosperous and a great scald—predictions which filled the parents' hearts with joy. Meantime news of what was taking place had gone abroad, and the neighbours came thronging the apartment to such a degree that the pressure of the curious crowd caused the third Norn to be pushed rudely from her chair.

Angry at this insult, Skuld proudly rose and declared that her sister's gifts should be of no avail, since she would decree that the child should live only as long as the taper then burning near the bedside. These ominous words filled the mother's heart with terror, and she tremblingly clasped her babe closer to her breast, for the taper was nearly burned out and its extinction could not be very long delayed. The eldest Norn, however, had no intention of seeing her prediction thus set at naught; but as she could not force her sister to retract her words, she quickly seized the taper, put out the light, and giving the smoking stump to the child's mother, bade her carefully treasure it, and never light it again until her son was weary of life.

> " In the mansion it was night:
> The Norns came,
> Who should the prince's
> Life determine."
> *Sæmund's Edda (Thorpe's tr.).*

The boy was named Nornagesta, in honour of the Norns, and grew up to be as beautiful, brave, and

169

talented as any mother could wish. When he was old enough to comprehend the gravity of the trust his mother told him the story of the Norns' visit, and placed in his hands the candle end, which he treasured for many a year, placing it for safe-keeping inside the frame of his harp. When his parents were dead, Nornagesta wandered from place to place, taking part and distinguishing himself in every battle, singing his heroic lays wherever he went. As he was of an enthusiastic and poetic temperament, he did not soon weary of life, and while other heroes grew wrinkled and old, he remained young at heart and vigorous in frame. He therefore witnessed the stirring deeds of the heroic ages, was the boon companion of the ancient warriors, and after living three hundred years, saw the belief in the old heathen gods gradually supplanted by the teachings of Christian missionaries. Finally Nornagesta came to the court of King Olaf Tryggvesson, who, according to his usual custom, converted him almost by force, and compelled him to receive baptism. Then, wishing to convince his people that the time for superstition was past, the king forced the aged scald to produce and light the taper which he had so carefully guarded for more than three centuries.

In spite of his recent conversion, Nornagesta anxiously watched the flame as it flickered, and when, finally, it went out, he sank lifeless to the ground, thus proving that in spite of the baptism just received, he still believed in the prediction of the Norns.

In the middle ages, and even later, the Norns figure in many a story or myth, appearing as fairies or witches, as, for instance, in the tale of "the Sleeping Beauty," and Shakespeare's tragedy of *Macbeth*.

> " 1st *Witch*. When shall we three meet again,
>   In thunder, lightning, or in rain ?

The Dises

Dorothy Hardy

THE VALA

2nd Witch. When the hurlyburly's done,
When the battle's lost and won :
3rd Witch. That will be ere the set of sun."

Macbeth (*Shakespeare*).

The Vala

Sometimes the Norns bore the name of Vala, or prophetesses, for they had the power of divination—a power which was held in great honour by all the Northern races, who believed that it was restricted to the female sex. The predictions of the Vala were never questioned, and it is said that the Roman general Drusus was so terrified by the appearance of Veleda, one of these prophetesses, who warned him not to cross the Elbe, that he actually beat a retreat. She foretold his approaching death, which indeed happened shortly after through a fall from his steed.

These prophetesses, who were also known as Idises, Dises, or Hagedises, officiated at the forest shrines and in the sacred groves, and always accompanied invading armies. Riding ahead, or in the midst of the host, they would vehemently urge the warriors on to victory, and when the battle was over they would often cut the bloody-eagle upon the bodies of the captives. The blood was collected into great tubs, wherein the Dises plunged their naked arms up to the shoulders, previous to joining in the wild dance with which the ceremony ended.

It is not to be wondered at that these women were greatly feared. Sacrifices were offered to propitiate them, and it was only in later times that they were degraded to the rank of witches, and sent to join the demon host on the Brocken, or Blocksberg, on Valpurgisnacht.

Besides the Norns or Dises, who were also regarded as protective deities, the Northmen ascribed to each human being a guardian spirit named Fylgie, which

171

attended him through life, either in human or brute shape, and was invisible except at the moment of death by all except the initiated few.

The allegorical meaning of the Norns and of their web of fate is too patent to need explanation ; still some mythologists have made them demons of the air, and state that their web was the woof of clouds, and that the bands of mists which they strung from rock to tree, and from mountain to mountain, were ruthlessly torn apart by the suddenly rising wind.   Some authorities, moreover, declare that Skuld, the third Norn, was at times a Valkyr, and at others personated the goddess of death, the terrible Hel.

CHAPTER XVIII : THE VALKYRS

The Battle Maidens

ODIN'S special attendants, the Valkyrs, or battle maidens, were either his daughters, like Brunhild, or the offspring of mortal kings, maidens who were privileged to remain immortal and invulnerable as long as they implicitly obeyed the god and remained virgins. They and their steeds were the personification of the clouds, their glittering weapons being the lightning flashes. The ancients imagined that they swept down to earth at Valfather's command, to choose among the slain in battle heroes worthy to taste the joys of Valhalla, and brave enough to lend aid to the gods when the great battle should be fought.

> " There through some battlefield, where men fall fast,
> Their horses fetlock-deep in blood, they ride,
> And pick the bravest warriors out for death,
> Whom they bring back with them at night to Heaven
> To glad the gods and feast in Odin's hall."
>
> *Balder Dead* (*Matthew Arnold*).

These maidens were pictured as young and beautiful, with dazzling white arms and flowing golden hair. They wore helmets of silver or gold, and bloodred corselets, and with spears and shields glittering, they boldly charged through the fray on their mettlesome white steeds. These horses galloped through the realms of air and over the quivering Bifröst, bearing not only their fair riders, but the heroes slain, who after having received the Valkyrs' kiss of death, were thus immediately transported to Valhalla.

The Cloud Steeds

As the Valkyrs' steeds were personifications of the clouds, it was natural to fancy that the hoar frost and dew dropped down upon earth from their glittering manes as they rapidly dashed to and fro through the air. They were therefore held in high honour and regard, for the people ascribed to their beneficent influence much of the fruitfulness of the earth, the sweetness of dale and mountain-slope, the glory of the pines, and the nourishment of the meadow-land.

Choosers of the Slain

The mission of the Valkyrs was not only to battle-fields upon earth, but they often rode over the sea, snatching the dying Vikings from their sinking dragon-ships. Sometimes they stood upon the strand to beckon them thither, an infallible warning that the coming struggle would be their last, and one which every Northland hero received with joy.

> " Slowly they moved to the billow side;
> And the forms, as they grew more clear,
> Seem'd each on a tall pale steed to ride,
> And a shadowy crest to rear,
> And to beckon with faint hand
> From the dark and rocky strand,
> And to point a gleaming spear.
>
> " Then a stillness on his spirit fell,
> Before th' unearthly train;
> For he knew Valhalla's daughters well,
> The chooser of the slain ! "
>
> *Valkyriur Song (Mrs. Hemans).*

Their Numbers and Duties

The numbers of the Valkyrs differ greatly according to various mythologists, ranging from three to sixteen, most authorities, however, naming only nine. The Valkyrs were considered as divinities of the air ; they were also called Norns, or wish maidens. It was said that Freya and Skuld led them on to the fray.

174

The Swan Maiden

Gertrude Demain Hammond, R.I.

WAYLAND AND THE VALKYRS

"She saw Valkyries
Come from afar,
Ready to ride
To the tribes of god;
Skuld held the shield,
Skaugul came next,
Gunnr, Hildr, Gaundul,
And Geir-skaugul.
Thus now are told
The Warrior's Norns."

Sæmund's Edda (Henderson's tr.).

The Valkyrs, as we have seen, had important duties in Valhalla, when, their bloody weapons laid aside, they poured out the heavenly mead for the Einheriar. This beverage delighted the souls of the new-comers, and they welcomed the fair maidens as warmly as when they had first seen them on the battlefield and realised that they had come to transport them where they fain would be.

"In the shade now tall forms are advancing,
And their wan hands like snowflakes in the moonlight are gleaming;
They beckon, they whisper, 'Oh! strong Armed in Valour,
The pale guests await thee—mead foams in Valhalla.'"

Finn's Saga (Hewitt).

Wayland and the Valkyrs

The Valkyrs were supposed to take frequent flights to earth in swan plumage, which they would throw off when they came to a secluded stream, that they might indulge in a bath. Any mortal surprising them thus, and securing their plumage, could prevent them from leaving the earth, and could even force these proud maidens to mate with him if such were his pleasure.

It is related that three of the Valkyrs, Olrun, Alvit, and Svanhvit, were once sporting in the waters, when suddenly the three brothers Egil, Slagfinn, and Völund, or Wayland the smith, came upon them, and securing

175

their swan plumage, the young men forced them to remain upon earth and become their wives. The Valkyrs, thus detained, remained with their husbands nine years, but at the end of that time, recovering their plumage, or the spell being broken in some other way, they effected their escape.

> " There they stayed
> Seven winters through;
> But all the eighth
> Were with longing seized;
> And in the ninth
> Fate parted them.
> The maidens yearned
> For the murky wood,
> The young Alvit,
> Fate to fulfil."
> Lay of Völund (Thorpe's tr.).

The brothers felt the loss of their wives extremely, and two of them, Egil and Slagfinn, putting on their snow shoes, went in search of their loved ones, disappearing in the cold and foggy regions of the North. The third brother, Völund, however, remained at home, knowing all search would be of no avail, and he found solace in the contemplation of a ring which Alvit had given him as a love-token, and he indulged the constant hope that she would return. As he was a very clever smith, and could manufacture the most dainty ornaments of silver and gold, as well as magic weapons which no blow could break, he now employed his leisure in making seven hundred rings exactly like the one which his wife had given him. These, when finished, he bound together ; but one night, on coming home from the hunt, he found that some one had carried away one ring, leaving the others behind, and his hopes received fresh inspiration, for he told himself that his wife had been there and would soon return for good.

176

The Ride of the Valkyrs
J. C. Dollman

By Arrangement with the Artist

THEIR NUMBERS AND DUTIES

That selfsame night, however, he was surprised in his sleep, and bound and made prisoner by Nidud, King of Sweden, who took possession of his sword, a choice weapon invested with magic powers, which he reserved for his own use, and of the love ring made of pure Rhine gold, which latter he gave to his only daughter, Bodvild. As for the unhappy Völund himself, he was led captive to a neighbouring island, where, after being hamstrung, in order that he should not escape, the king put him to the incessant task of forging weapons and ornaments for his use. He also compelled him to build an intricate labyrinth, and to this day a maze in Iceland is known as " Völund's house."

Völund's rage and despair increased with every new insult offered him by Nidud, and night and day he thought upon how he might obtain revenge. Nor did he forget to provide for his escape, and during the pauses of his labour he fashioned a pair of wings similar to those his wife had used as a Valkyr, which he intended to don as soon as his vengeance had been accomplished. One day the king came to visit his captive, and brought him the stolen sword that he might repair it; but Völund cleverly substituted another weapon so exactly like the magic sword as to deceive the king when he came again to claim it. A few days later, Völund enticed the king's sons into his smithy and slew them, after which he cunningly fashioned drinking vessels out of their skulls, and jewels out of their eyes and teeth, bestowing these upon their parents and sister.

> " But their skulls
> Beneath the hair
> He in silver set,
> And to Nidud gave ;
> And of their eyes
> Precious stones he formed,

Which to Nidud's
Wily wife he sent.
But of the teeth
Of the two
Breast ornaments he made,
And to Bödvild sent."

Lay of Völund (Thorpe's tr.).

The royal family did not suspect whence they came; and so these gifts were joyfully accepted. As for the poor youths, it was believed that they had drifted out to sea and had been drowned.

Some time after this, Bodvild, wishing to have her ring repaired, also visited the smith's hut, where, while waiting, she unsuspectingly partook of a magic drug, which sent her to sleep and left her in Völund's power. His last act of vengeance accomplished, Völund immediately donned the wings which he had made in readiness for this day, and grasping his sword and ring he rose slowly in the air. Directing his flight to the palace, he perched there out of reach, and proclaimed his crimes to Nidud. The king, beside himself with rage, summoned Egil, Völund's brother, who had also fallen into his power, and bade him use his marvellous skill as an archer to bring down the impudent bird. Obeying a signal from Völund, Egil aimed for a protuberance under his wing where a bladder full of the young princes' blood was concealed, and the smith flew triumphantly away without hurt, declaring that Odin would give his sword to Sigmund—a prediction which was duly fulfilled.

Völund then went to Alf-heim, where, if the legend is to be believed, he found his beloved wife, and lived happily again with her until the twilight of the gods.

But, even in Alf-heim, this clever smith continued to ply his craft, and various suits of impenetrable armour,

178

Brunhild and Siegmund   178
J. Wagrez
Photo, Braun, Clément & Co.

which he is said to have fashioned, are described in later heroic poems. Besides Balmung and Joyeuse, Sigmund's and Charlemagne's celebrated swords, he is reported to have fashioned Miming for his son Heime, and many other remarkable blades.

> " It is the mate of Miming
> Of all swerdes it is king,
> And Weland it wrought,
> Bitterfer it is hight."
> *Anglo-Saxon Poetry* (*Coneybeare's tr.*).

There are countless other tales of swan maidens or Valkyrs, who are said to have consorted with mortals ; but the most popular of all is that of Brunhild, the wife of Sigurd, a descendant of Sigmund and the most renowned of Northern heroes.

William Morris, in " The Land East of the Sun and West of the Moon," gives a fascinating version of another of these Norse legends. The story is amongst the most charming of the collection in " The Earthly Paradise."

Brunhild

The story of Brunhild is to be found in many forms. Some versions describe the heroine as the daughter of a king taken by Odin to serve in his Valkyr band, others as chief of the Valkyrs and daughter of Odin himself. In Richard Wagner's story, " The Ring of the Nibelung," the great musician presents a particularly attractive, albeit a more modern conception of the chief Battle-Maiden, and her disobedience to the command of Odin when sent to summon the youthful Siegmund from the side of his beloved Sieglinde to the Halls of the Blessed.

CHAPTER XIX : HEL

Loki's Offspring

HEL, goddess of death, was the daughter of Loki, god of evil, and of the giantess Angurboda, the portender of ill. She came into the world in a dark cave in Jötun-heim together with the serpent Iörmungandr and the terrible Fenris wolf, the trio being considered as the emblems of pain, sin, and death.

> "Now Loki comes, cause of all ill!
> Men and Æsir curse him still.
> Long shall the gods deplore,
> Even till Time be o'er,
> His base fraud on Asgard's hill.
> While, deep in Jotunheim, most fell,
> Are Fenrir, Serpent, and Dread Hel,
> Pain, Sin, and Death, his children three,
> Brought up and cherished; thro' them he
> Tormentor of the world shall be."
> *Valhalla* (*J. C. Jones*).

In due time Odin became aware of the terrible brood which Loki was cherishing, and resolved, as we have already seen, to banish them from the face of the earth. The serpent was therefore cast into the sea, where his writhing was supposed to cause the most terrible tempests; the wolf Fenris was secured in chains, thanks to the dauntless Tyr; and Hel or Hela, the goddess of death, was hurled into the depths of Niflheim, where Odin gave her power over nine worlds.

> "Hela into Niflheim thou threw'st,
> And gav'st her nine unlighted worlds to rule,
> A queen, and empire over all the dead."
> *Balder Dead* (*Matthew Arnold*).

Hel's Kingdom in Nifl-heim

This realm, which was supposed to be situated under

the earth, could only be entered after a painful journey over the roughest roads in the cold, dark regions of the extreme North. The gate was so far from all human abode that even Hermod the swift, mounted upon Sleipnir, had to journey nine long nights ere he reached the river Giöll. This formed the boundary of Nifl-heim, over which was thrown a bridge of crystal arched with gold, hung on a single hair, and constantly guarded by the grim skeleton Mödgud, who made every spirit pay a toll of blood ere she would allow it to pass.

> " The bridge of glass hung on a hair
> Thrown o'er the river terrible,—
> The Giöll, boundary of Hel.
> Now here the maiden Mödgud stood,
> Waiting to take the toll of blood,—
> A maiden horrible to sight,
> Fleshless, with shroud and pall bedight."
>
> *Valhalla* (*J. C. Jones*).

The spirits generally rode or drove across this bridge on the horses or in the waggons which had been burned upon the funeral pyre with the dead to serve that purpose, and the Northern races were very careful to bind upon the feet of the departed a specially strong pair of shoes, called Hel shoes, that they might not suffer during the long journey over rough roads. Soon after the Giallar bridge was passed, the spirit reached the Ironwood, where stood none but bare and iron-leafed trees, and, passing through it, reached Hel-gate, beside which the fierce, blood-stained dog Garm kept watch, cowering in a dark hole known as the Gnipa cave. This monster's rage could only be appeased by the offering of a Hel-cake, which never failed those who had ever given bread to the needy.

> " Loud bays Garm
> Before the Gnipa cave."
>
> *Sæmund's Edda* (*Thorpe's tr.*).

Within the gate, amid the intense cold and impenetrable darkness, was heard the seething of the great cauldron Hvergelmir, the rolling of the glaciers in the Elivagar and other streams of Hel, among which were the Leipter, by which solemn oaths were sworn, and the Slid, in whose turbid waters naked swords continually rolled.

Further on in this gruesome place was Elvidner (misery), the hall of the goddess Hel, whose dish was Hunger. Her knife was Greed. "Idleness was the name of her man, Sloth of her maid, Ruin of her threshold, Sorrow of her bed, and Conflagration of her curtains."

> " Elvidner was Hela's hall.
> Iron-barred, with massive wall;
> Horrible that palace tall !
> Hunger was her table bare;
> Waste, her knife; her bed, sharp Care;
> Burning Anguish spread her feast ;
> Bleached bones arrayed each guest;
> Plague and Famine sang their runes,
> Mingled with Despair's harsh tunes.
> Misery and Agony
> E'er in Hel's abode shall be ! "
>
> *Valhalla* (*J. C. Jones*).

This goddess had many different abodes for the guests who daily came to her, for she received not only perjurers and criminals of all kinds, but also those who were unfortunate enough to die without shedding blood. To her realm also were consigned those who died of old age or disease—a mode of decease which was contemptuously called " straw death," as the beds of the people were generally of that material.

> "Temper'd hard by frost,
> Tempest and toil their nerves, the sons of those
> Whose only terror was a bloodless death."
>
> *Thomson.*

The Road to Valhalla

Severin Nilsson

182

Ideas of the Future Life

Although the innocent were treated kindly by Hel, and enjoyed a state of negative bliss, it is no wonder that the inhabitants of the North shrank from the thought of visiting her cheerless abode. And while the men preferred to mark themselves with the spear point, to hurl themselves down from a precipice, or to be burned ere life was quite extinct, the women did not shrink from equally heroic measures. In the extremity of their sorrow, they did not hesitate to fling themselves down a mountain side, or fall upon the swords which were given them at their marriage, so that their bodies might be burned with those whom they loved, and their spirits released to join them in the bright home of the gods.

Further horrors, however, awaited those whose lives had been criminal or impure, these spirits being banished to Nastrond, the strand of corpses, where they waded in ice-cold streams of venom, through a cave made of wattled serpents, whose poisonous fangs were turned towards them. After suffering untold agonies there, they were washed down into the cauldron Hvergelmir, where the serpent Nidhug ceased for a moment gnawing the root of the tree Yggdrasil to feed upon their bones.

> " A hall standing
> Far from the sun
> In Nåströnd;
> Its doors are northward turned,
> Venom-drops fall
> In through its apertures;
> Entwined is that hall
> With serpents' backs.
> She there saw wading
> The sluggish streams

Bloodthirsty men
And perjurers,
And him who the ear beguiles
Of another's wife.
There Nidhog sucks
The corpses of the dead."

Sæmund's Edda (Thorpe's tr.).

Pestilence and Famine

Hel herself was supposed occasionally to leave her dismal abode to range the earth upon her three-legged white horse, and in times of pestilence or famine, if a part of the inhabitants of a district escaped, she was said to use a rake, and when whole villages and provinces were depopulated, as in the case of the historical epidemic of the Black Death, it was said that she had ridden with a broom.

The Northern races further fancied that the spirits of the dead were sometimes allowed to revisit the earth and appear to their relatives, whose sorrow or joy affected them even after death, as is related in the Danish ballad of Aager and Else, where a dead lover bids his sweetheart smile, so that his coffin may be filled with roses instead of the clotted blood drops produced by her tears.

> " ' Listen now, my good Sir Aager !
>   Dearest bridegroom, all I crave
> Is to know how it goes with thee
>   In that lonely place, the grave.'
>
> " ' Every time that thou rejoicest,
>   And art happy in thy mind,
> Are my lonely grave's recesses
>   All with leaves of roses lined.
>
> " ' Every time that, love, thou grievest,
>   And dost shed the briny flood,
> Are my lonely grave's recesses
>   Filled with black and loathsome blood.' "

Ballad of Aager and Else (Longfellow's tr.).

CHAPTER XX : ÆGIR

The God of the Sea

BESIDES Niörd and Mimir, who were both ocean divinities, the one representing the sea near the coast and the other the primæval ocean whence all things were supposed to have sprung, the Northern races recognised another sea-ruler, called Ægir or Hler, who dwelt either in the cool depths of his liquid realm or had his abode on the Island of Lessoe, in the Cattegat, or Hlesey.

> " Beneath the watery dome,
>   With crystalline splendour,
>   In radiant grandeur,
> Upreared the sea-god's home.
> More dazzling than foam of the waves
> E'er glimmered and gleamed thro' deep caves
> The glistening sands of its floor,
> Like some placid lake rippled o'er."
>
> *Valhalla (J. C. Jones).*

Ægir (the sea), like his brothers Kari (the air) and Loki (fire), is supposed to have belonged to an older dynasty of the gods, for he ranked neither with the Æsir, the Vanas, the giants, dwarfs, or elves, but was considered omnipotent within his realm.

He was supposed to occasion and quiet the great tempests which swept over the deep, and was generally represented as a gaunt old man, with long white beard and hair, and clawlike fingers ever clutching convulsively, as though he longed to have all things within his grasp. Whenever he appeared above the waves, it was only to pursue and overturn vessels, and to greedily drag them to the bottom of the sea, a vocation in which he was thought to take fiendish delight.

The Goddess Ran

Ægir was mated with his sister, the goddess Ran, whose name means " robber," and who was as cruel, greedy, and insatiable as her husband. Her favourite pastime was to lurk near dangerous rocks, whither she enticed mariners, and there spread her net, her most prized possession, when, having entangled the men in its meshes and broken their vessels on the jagged cliffs, she would calmly draw them down into her cheerless realm.

> " In the deep sea caves
>   By the sounding shore,
>   In the dashing waves
>   When the wild storms roar,
>   In her cold green bowers
>   In the Northern fiords,
>   She lurks and she glowers,
>   She grasps and she hoards,
>   And she spreads her strong net for her prey."
>   *Story of Siegfried* (*Baldwin*).

Ran was considered the goddess of death for all who perished at sea, and the Northern nations fancied that she entertained the drowned in her coral caves, where her couches were spread to receive them, and where the mead flowed freely as in Valhalla. The goddess was further supposed to have a great affection for gold, which was called the " flame of the sea," and was used to illuminate her halls. This belief originated with the sailors, and sprang from the striking phosphorescent gleam of the waves. To win Ran's good graces, the Northmen were careful to hide some gold about them whenever any special danger threatened them on the sea.

> " Gold, on sweetheart ramblings,
>   Pow'rful is and pleasant;

Ægir

J. P. Molin

189

THE WAVES

Who goes empty-handed
Down to sea-blue Ran,
Cold her kisses strike, and
Fleeting her embrace is—
But we ocean's bride be-
Troth with purest gold."
Viking Tales of the North (R. B. Anderson).

The Waves

Ægir and Ran had nine beautiful daughters, the Waves, or billow-maidens, whose snowy arms and bosoms, long golden hair, deep-blue eyes, and willowy, sensuous forms were fascinating in the extreme. These maidens delighted in sporting over the surface of their father's vast domain, clad lightly in transparent blue, white, or green veils. They were very moody and capricious, however, varying from playful to sullen and apathetic moods, and at times exciting one another almost to madness, tearing their hair and veils, flinging themselves recklessly upon their hard beds, the rocks, chasing one another with frantic haste, and shrieking aloud with joy or despair. But they seldom came out to play unless their brother, the Wind, were abroad, and according to his mood they were gentle and playful, or rough and boisterous.

The Waves were generally supposed to go about in triplets, and were often said to play around the ships of vikings whom they favoured, smoothing away every obstacle from their course, and helping them to reach speedily their goals.

" And Æger's daughters, in blue veils dight,
The helm leap round, and urge it on its flight."
Viking Tales of the North (R. B. Anderson).

Ægir's Brewing Kettle

To the Anglo-Saxons the sea-god Ægir was known by

the name of Eagor, and whenever an unusually large wave
came thundering towards the shore, the sailors were
wont to cry, as the Trent boatmen still do, " Look out,
Eagor is coming ! " He was also known by the name
of Hler (the shelterer) among the Northern nations,
and of Gymir (the concealer), because he was always
ready to hide things in the depths of his realm, and
could be depended upon not to reveal the secrets
entrusted to his care. And, because the waters of the
sea were frequently said to seethe and hiss, the ocean
was often called Ægir's brewing kettle or vat.

The god's two principal servants were Elde and
Funfeng, emblems of the phosphorescence of the sea ;
they were noted for their quickness and they invariably
waited upon the guests whom he invited to his banquets
in the depths of the sea. Ægir sometimes left his realm
to visit the Æsir in Asgard, where he was always royally
entertained, and he delighted in Bragi's many tales of
the adventures and achievements of the gods. Excited
by these narratives, as also by the sparkling mead which
accompanied them, the god on one occasion ventured to
invite the Æsir to celebrate the harvest feast with him
in Hlesey, where he promised to entertain them in his
turn.

Thor and Hymir

Surprised at this invitation, one of the gods ventured
to remind Ægir that they were accustomed to dainty
fare ; whereupon the god of the sea declared that as far
as eating was concerned they need be in no anxiety, as
he was sure that he could cater for the most fastidious
appetites ; but he confessed that he was not so confident
about drink, as his brewing kettle was rather small.
Hearing this, Thor immediately volunteered to procure
a suitable kettle, and set out with Tyr to obtain it.

THOR AND HYMIR

The two gods journeyed east of the Elivagar in Thor's goat chariot, and leaving this at the house of the peasant Egil, Thialfi's father, they wended their way on foot to the dwelling of the giant Hymir, who was known to own a kettle one mile deep and proportionately wide.

> " There dwells eastward
> Of Elivagar
> The all-wise Hymir,
> At heaven's end.
> My sire, fierce of mood,
> A kettle owns,
> A capacious cauldron,
> A rast in depth."
>
> *Sæmund's Edda (Thorpe's tr.).*

Only the women were at home, however, and Tyr recognised in the elder—an ugly old hag with nine hundred heads—his own grandmother ; while the younger, a beautiful young giantess, was, it appeared, his mother, and she received her son and his companion hospitably, and gave them to drink.

After learning their errand, Tyr's mother bade the visitors hide under some huge kettles, which rested upon a beam at the end of the hall, for her husband Hymir was very hasty and often slew his would-be guests with a single baleful glance. The gods quickly followed her advice, and no sooner were they concealed than the old giant Hymir came in. When his wife told him that visitors had come, he frowned so portentously, and flashed such a wrathful look towards their hiding-place, that the rafter split and the kettles fell with a crash, and, except the largest, were all dashed to pieces.

> " In shivers flew the pillar
> At the Jötun's glance;
> The beam was first
> Broken in two.

Eight kettles fell,
But only one of them,
A hard-hammered cauldron,
Whole from the column."
Sæmund's Edda (*Thorpe's tr.*).

The giant's wife, however, prevailed upon her husband
to welcome Tyr and Thor, and he slew three oxen for
their refection ; but great was his dismay to see the
thunder-god eat two of these for his supper. Muttering that he would have to go fishing early the next
morning to secure a breakfast for so voracious a guest,
the giant retired to rest, and when at dawn the next
day he went down to the shore, he was joined by Thor,
who said that he had come to help him. The giant
bade him secure his own bait, whereupon Thor coolly
slew his host's largest ox, Himinbrioter (heaven-breaker),
and cutting off its head, he embarked with it and proceeded to row far out to sea. In vain Hymir protested
that his usual fishing-ground had been reached, and that
they might encounter the terrible Midgard snake were
they to venture any farther ; Thor persistently rowed
on, until he fancied they were directly above this
monster.

" On the dark bottom of the great salt lake,
Imprisoned lay the giant snake,
With naught his sullen sleep to break."
Thor's Fishing, Oehlenschläger (*Pigott's tr.*).

Baiting his powerful hook with the ox head, Thor
angled for Iörmungandr, while the giant meantime
drew up two whales, which seemed to him to be enough
for an early morning meal. He was about to propose
to return, therefore, when Thor suddenly felt a jerk,
and began pulling as hard as he could, for he knew by
the resistance of his prey, and the terrible storm created
by its frenzied writhings, that he had hooked the
190

Ran

M. E. Winge

Midgard snake. In his determined efforts to force the
snake to rise to the surface, Thor braced his feet so
strongly against the bottom of the boat that he went
through it and stood on the bed of the sea.

After an indescribable struggle, the monster's terrible
venom-breathing head appeared, and Thor, seizing his
hammer, was about to annihilate it when the giant,
frightened by the proximity of Iörmungandr, and fearing lest the boat should sink and he should become
the monster's prey, cut the fishing-line, and thus allowed
the snake to drop back like a stone to the bottom of
the sea.

> " The knife prevails: far down beneath the main
> The serpent, spent with toil and pain,
> To the bottom sank again."
> *Thor's Fishing*, Oehlenschläger (*Pigott's tr.*).

Angry with Hymir for his inopportune interference,
Thor dealt him a blow with his hammer which knocked
him overboard ; but Hymir, undismayed, waded ashore,
and met the god as he returned to the beach. Hymir
then took both whales, his spoil of the sea, upon his
back, to carry them to the house ; and Thor, wishing
also to show his strength, shouldered boat, oars, and
fishing tackle, and followed him.

Breakfast being disposed of, Hymir challenged Thor
to prove his strength by breaking his beaker ; but
although the thunder-god threw it with irresistible
force against stone pillars and walls, it remained whole
and was not even bent. In obedience to a whisper from
Tyr's mother, however, Thor suddenly hurled the
vessel against the giant's forehead, the only substance
tougher than itself, when it fell shattered to the ground.
Hymir, having thus tested the might of Thor, told him
he could have the kettle which the two gods had come
to seek, but Tyr tried to lift it in vain, and Thor could

191

raise it from the floor only after he had drawn his belt
of strength to the very last hole.

> " Tyr twice assayed
> To move the vessel,
> Yet at each time
> Stood the kettle fast.
> Then Môdi's father
> By the brim grasped it,
> And trod through
> The dwelling's floor."
>
> *Lay of Hymir* (*Thorpe's tr.*)

The wrench with which he finally pulled it up did great
damage to the giant's house and his feet broke through
the floor. As Tyr and Thor were departing, the latter
with the huge pot clapped on his head in place of a hat,
Hymir summoned his brother frost giants, and proposed
that they should pursue and slay their inveterate foe.
Turning round, Thor suddenly became aware of their
pursuit, and, hurling Miölnir repeatedly at the giants,
he slew them all ere they could overtake him. Tyr
and Thor then resumed their journey back to Ægir,
carrying the kettle in which he was to brew ale for the
harvest feast.

The physical explanation of this myth is, of course,
a thunder storm (Thor), in conflict with the raging
sea (the Midgard snake), and the breaking up of the
polar ice (Hymir's goblet and floor) in the heat of
summer.

The gods now arrayed themselves in festive attire
and proceeded joyfully to Ægir's feast, and ever after
they were wont to celebrate the harvest home in his
coral caves.

> " Then Vans and Æsir, mighty gods,
> Of earth and air, and Asgard, lords,—
> Advancing with each goddess fair,
> A brilliant retinue most rare,—

OTHER DIVINITIES OF THE SEA

Attending mighty Odin, swept
Up wave-worn aisle in radiant march."
Valhalla (J. C. Jones).

Unloved Divinities

Ægir, as we have seen, ruled the sea with the help of the treacherous Ran. Both of these divinities were considered cruel by the Northern nations, who had much to suffer from the sea, which, surrounding them on all sides, ran far into the heart of their countries through the numerous fiords, and often swallowed the ships of their vikings, with all their warrior crews.

Other Divinities of the Sea

Besides these principal divinities of the sea, the Northern nations believed in mermen and mermaids, and many stories are related of mermaids who divested themselves for a brief while of swan plumage or seal-garments, which they left upon the beach to be found by mortals who were thus able to compel the fair maidens to remain on land.

" She came through the waves when the fair moon shone
(Drift o' the wave and foam o' the sea) ;
She came where I walked on the sands alone,
With a heart as light as a heart may be."
L. E. R.

There were also malignant marine monsters known as Nicors, from whose name has been derived the proverbial Old Nick. Many of the lesser water divinities had fish tails; the females bore the name of Undines, and the males of Stromkarls, Nixies, Necks, or Neckar.

"Where in the marisches boometh the bittern,
Nicker the Soul-less sits with his ghittern,
Sits inconsolable, friendless and foeless,
Wailing his destiny, Nicker the Soul-less."
From Brother Fabian's Manuscript.

In the middle ages these water spirits were believed sometimes to leave their native streams, to appear at village dances, where they were recognised by the wet hem of their garments. They often sat beside the flowing brook or river, playing on a harp, or singing alluring songs while combing out their long golden or green hair.

> " The Neck here his harp in the glass castle plays,
> And mermaidens comb out their green hair always,
> And bleach here their shining white clothes."
> *Stagnelius* (*Keightley's tr.*).

The Nixies, Undines, and Stromkarls were particularly gentle and lovable beings, and were very anxious to obtain repeated assurances of their ultimate salvation.

Many stories are told of priests or children meeting them playing by a stream, and taunting them with future damnation, which threat never failed to turn the joyful music into pitiful wails. Often priest or children, discovering their mistake, and touched by the agony of their victims, would hasten back to the stream and assure the green-toothed water sprites of future redemption, when they invariably resumed their happy strains.

> " Know you the Nixies, gay and fair?
> Their eyes are black, and green their hair—
> They lurk in sedgy shores."
> *Mathisson.*

River Nymphs

Besides Elf or Elb, the water sprite who gave its name to the Elbe River in Germany, the Neck, from whom the Neckar derives its name, and old Father Rhine, with his numerous daughters (tributary streams), the most famous of all the lesser water divinities is the Lorelei, the siren maiden who sits upon the Lorelei

194

The Neckan

J. P. Molin

rock near St. Goar, on the Rhine, and whose alluring song has enticed many a mariner to death. The legends concerning this siren are very numerous indeed, one of the most ancient being as follows:

Legends of the Lorelei

Lorelei was an immortal, a water nymph, daughter of Father Rhine; during the day she dwelt in the cool depths of the river bed, but late at night she would appear in the moonlight, sitting aloft upon a pinnacle of rock, in full view of all who passed up or down the stream. At times, the evening breeze wafted some of the notes of her song to the boatmen's ears, when, forgetting time and place in listening to these enchanting melodies, they drifted upon the sharp and jagged rocks, where they invariably perished.

> "Above the maiden sitteth,
>   A wondrous form, and fair;
> With jewels bright she plaiteth
>   Her shining golden hair:
> With comb of gold prepares it,
>   The task with song beguiled;
> A fitful burden bears it—
>   That melody so wild.

> "The boatman on the river
>   Lists to the song, spell-bound;
> Oh! what shall him deliver
>   From danger threat'ning round?
> The waters deep have caught them,
>   Both boat and boatman brave;
> 'Tis Loreley's song hath brought them
>   Beneath the foaming wave."
>
> *Song, Heine* (*Selcher's tr.*).

One person only is said to have seen the Lorelei close by. This was a young fisherman from Oberwesel, who met her every evening by the riverside, and spent a few delightful hours with her, drinking in her beauty and listening to her entrancing song. Tradition had it that ere they parted the Lorelei pointed out the places where the youth should cast his nets on the morrow— instructions which he always obeyed, and which invariably brought him success.

One night the young fisherman was seen going towards the river, but as he never returned search was made for him. No clue to his whereabouts being found, the credulous Teutons finally reported that the Lorelei had dragged him down to her coral caves that she might enjoy his companionship for ever.

According to another version, the Lorelei, with her entrancing strains from the craggy rocks, lured so many fishermen to a grave in the depths of Rhine, that an armed force was once sent at nightfall to surround and seize her. But the water nymph laid such a powerful spell upon the captain and his men that they could move neither hand nor foot. While they stood motionless around her, the Lorelei divested herself of her ornaments, and cast them into the waves below ; then, chanting a spell, she lured the waters to the top of the crag upon which she was perched, and to the wonder of the soldiers the waves enclosed a sea-green chariot drawn by white-maned steeds, and the nymph sprang lightly into this and the magic equipage was instantly lost to view. A few moments later the Rhine subsided to its usual level, the spell was broken, and the men recovered power of motion, and retreated to tell how their efforts had been baffled. Since then, however, the Lorelei has not been seen, and the peasants declare that she still resents the insult offered her and will never again leave her coral caves.

CHAPTER XXI : BALDER

The Best Loved

TO Odin and Frigga, we are told, were born twin sons as dissimilar in character and physical appearance as it was possible for two children to be. Hodur, god of darkness, was sombre, taciturn, and blind, like the obscurity of sin, which he was supposed to symbolise, while his brother Balder, the beautiful, was worshipped as the pure and radiant god of innocence and light. From his snowy brow and golden locks seemed to radiate beams of sunshine which gladdened the hearts of gods and men, by whom he was equally beloved.

> " Of all the twelve round Odin's throne,
> Balder, the Beautiful, alone,
> The Sun-god, good, and pure, and bright,
> Was loved by all, as all love light."
>
> *Valhalla* (*J. C. Jones*).

The youthful Balder attained his full growth with marvellous rapidity, and was early admitted to the council of the gods. He took up his abode in the palace of Breidablik, whose silver roof rested upon golden pillars, and whose purity was such that nothing common or unclean was ever allowed within its precincts, and here he lived in perfect unity with his young wife Nanna (blossom), the daughter of Nip (bud), a beautiful and charming goddess.

The god of light was well versed in the science of runes, which were carved on his tongue ; he knew the various virtues of simples, one of which, the camomile, was called "Balder's brow," because its flower was as immaculately pure as his forehead. The only thing hidden from Balder's radiant eyes was the perception of his own ultimate fate.

197

MYTHS OF THE NORSEMEN

" His own house
Breidablik, on whose columns Balder graved
The enchantments that recall the dead to life.
For wise he was, and many curious arts,
Postures of runes, and healing herbs he knew ;
Unhappy ! but that art he did not know,
To keep his own life safe, and see the sun."

Balder Dead (Matthew Arnold).

Balder's Dream

As it was so natural for Balder the beautiful to be
smiling and happy, the gods were greatly troubled when
on a day they began to notice a change in his bearing.
Gradually the light died out of his blue eyes, a careworn
look came into his face, and his step grew heavy and slow.
Odin and Frigga, seeing their beloved son's evident depression, tenderly implored him to reveal the cause of
his silent grief.   Balder, yielding at last to their anxious
entreaties, confessed that his slumbers, instead of being
peaceful and restful as of yore, had been strangely
troubled of late by dark and oppressive dreams, which,
although he could not clearly remember them when he
awoke, constantly haunted him with a vague feeling of
fear.

" To that god his slumber
Was most afflicting ;
His auspicious dreams
Seemed departed."

Lay of Vegtam (Thorpe's tr.).

When Odin and Frigga heard this, they were very
uneasy, but declared that nothing would harm their
universally beloved son. Nevertheless, when the anxious
parents further talked the matter over, they confessed
that they also were oppressed by strange forebodings,
and, coming at last to believe that Balder's life was
really threatened, they proceeded to take measures to
avert the danger.

198

THE VALA'S PROPHECY

Frigga sent her servants in every direction, with strict charge to prevail upon all living creatures, all plants, metals, stones—in fact, every animate and inanimate thing—to register a solemn vow not to harm Balder. All creation readily took the oath, for there was nothing on earth which did not love the radiant god. So the servants returned to Frigga, telling her that all had been duly sworn save the mistletoe, growing upon the oak stem at the gate of Valhalla, and this, they added, was such a puny, inoffensive thing that no harm could be feared from it.

> "On a course they resolved :
> That they would send
> To every being,
> Assurance to solicit,
> Balder not to harm.
> All species swore
> Oaths to spare him ;
> Frigg received all
> Their vows and compacts."
> *Sæmund's Edda* (*Thorpe's tr.*).

Frigga now resumed her spinning in great content, for she felt assured that no harm could come to the child she loved above all.

The Vala's Prophecy

Odin, in the meantime, had resolved to consult one of the dead Vala or prophetesses. Mounted upon his eight-footed steed Sleipnir, he rode over the tremulous bridge Bifröst and over the weary road which leads to Giallar and the entrance of Nifl-heim, where, passing through the Helgate and by the dog Garm, he penetrated into Hel's dark abode.

> "Uprose the king of men with speed,
> And saddled straight his coal-black steed ;

Down the yawning steep he rode,
That leads to Hela's drear abode."
Descent of Odin (Gray).

Odin saw to his surprise that a feast was being spread in this dark realm, and that the couches had been covered with tapestry and rings of gold, as if some highly honoured guest were expected. But he hurried on without pausing, until he reached the spot where the Vala had rested undisturbed for many a year, when he began solemnly to chant a magic spell and to trace the runes which had the power of raising the dead.

"Thrice pronounc'd, in accents dread,
The thrilling verse that wakes the dead :
Till from out the hollow ground
Slowly breath'd a sullen sound."
Descent of Odin (Gray).

Suddenly the tomb opened, and the prophetess slowly rose, inquiring who had dared thus to trouble her long rest. Odin, not wishing her to know that he was the mighty father of gods and men, replied that he was Vegtam, son of Valtam, and that he had awakened her to inquire for whom Hel was spreading her couches and preparing a festive meal. In hollow tones, the prophetess confirmed all his fears by telling him that the expected guest was Balder, who was destined to be slain by Hodur, his brother, the blind god of darkness.

"Hodur will hither
His glorious brother send ;
He of Balder will
The slayer be,
And Odin's son
Of life bereave.
By compulsion I have spoken ;
Now I will be silent."
Sæmund's Edda (Thorpe's tr.).

Despite the Vala's evident reluctance to speak further,

Odin was not yet satisfied, and he prevailed upon her to tell him who would avenge the murdered god and call his slayer to account. For revenge and retaliation were considered as a sacred duty by the races of the North.

Then the prophetess told him, as Rossthiof had already predicted, that Rinda, the earth-goddess, would bear a son to Odin, and that Vali, as this child would be named, would neither wash his face nor comb his hair until he had avenged upon Hodur the death of Balder.

> " In the caverns of the west,
> By Odin's fierce embrace comprest,
> A wondrous boy shall Rinda bear,
> Who ne'er shall comb his raven hair,
> Nor wash his visage in the stream,
> Nor see the sun's departing beam,
> Till he on Hoder's corse shall smile
> Flaming on the fun'ral pile."
> *Descent of Odin (Gray).*

When the reluctant Vala had thus spoken, Odin next asked : "Who would refuse to weep at Balder's death ?" This incautious question showed a knowledge of the future which no mortal could possess, and immediately revealed to the Vala the identity of her visitor. Therefore, refusing to speak another word, she sank back into the silence of the tomb, declaring that none would be able to lure her out again until the end of the world was come.

> " Hie thee hence, and boast at home,
> That never shall inquirer come
> To break my iron sleep again,
> Till Lok has burst his tenfold chain;
> Never, till substantial Night
> Has reassum'd her ancient right :
> Till wrapt in flames, in ruin hurl'd,
> Sinks the fabric of the world."
> *Descent of Odin (Gray).*

Odin having learned the decrees of Orlog (fate), which he knew could not be set aside, now remounted his steed, and sadly wended his way back to Asgard, thinking of the time, not far distant, when his beloved son would no more be seen in the heavenly abodes, and when the light of his presence would have vanished for ever.

On entering Glads-heim, however, Odin was somewhat reassured by the intelligence, promptly conveyed to him by Frigga, that all things under the sun had promised that they would not harm Balder, and feeling convinced that if nothing would slay their beloved son he must surely continue to gladden gods and men with his presence, he cast care aside and resigned himself to the pleasures of the festive board.

The Gods at Play

The playground of the gods was situated on the green plain of Ida, and was called Idavold. Here the gods would resort when in sportive mood, and their favourite game was to throw their golden disks, which they could cast with great skill. They had returned to this wonted pastime with redoubled zest since the cloud which had oppressed their spirits had been dispersed by the precautions of Frigga. Wearied at last, however, of the accustomed sport, they bethought them of a new game. They had learned that Balder could not be harmed by any missile, and so they amused themselves by casting all manner of weapons, stones, etc., at him, certain that no matter how cleverly they tried, and how accurately they aimed, the objects, having sworn not to injure him, would either glance aside or fall short. This new amusement proved to be so fascinating that soon all the gods gathered around Balder, greeting each new failure to hurt him with prolonged shouts of laughter.

202

Loki and Hodur
C. G. Qvarnström

The Death of Balder

These bursts of merriment excited the curiosity of Frigga, who sat spinning in Fensalir ; and seeing an old woman pass by her dwelling, she bade her pause and tell what the gods were doing to provoke such great hilarity. The old woman was none other than Loki in disguise, and he answered Frigga that the gods were throwing stones and other missiles, blunt and sharp, at Balder, who stood smiling and unharmed in their midst, challenging them to touch him.

The goddess smiled, and resumed her work, saying that it was quite natural that nothing should harm Balder, as all things loved the light, of which he was the emblem, and had solemnly sworn not to injure him. Loki, the personification of fire, was greatly chagrined upon hearing this, for he was jealous of Balder, the sun, who so entirely eclipsed him and who was generally beloved, while he was feared and avoided as much as possible ; but he cleverly concealed his vexation, and inquired of Frigga whether she were quite sure that all objects had joined the league.

Frigga proudly answered that she had received the solemn oath of all things, a harmless little parasite, the mistletoe, which grew on the oak near Valhalla's gate, only excepted, and this was too small and weak to be feared. This information was all that Loki wanted, and bidding adieu to Frigga he hobbled off. As soon as he was safely out of sight, however, he resumed his wonted form and hastened to Valhalla, where, at the gate, he found the oak and mistletoe as indicated by Frigga. Then by the exercise of magic arts he imparted to the parasite a size and hardness quite unnatural to it.

From the wooden stem thus produced he deftly

fashioned a shaft with which he hastened back to
Idavold, where the gods were still hurling missiles at
Balder, Hodur alone leaning mournfully against a tree
the while, and taking no part in the game.   Carelessly
Loki approached the blind god, and assuming an
appearance of interest, he inquired the cause of his
melancholy, at the same time artfully insinuating that
pride and indifference prevented him from participating
in the sport.   In answer to these remarks, Hodur
pleaded that only his blindness deterred him from
taking part in the new game, and when Loki put the
mistletoe-shaft in his hand, and led him into the midst
of the circle, indicating the direction of the novel target,
Hodur threw his shaft boldly.   But to his dismay,
instead of the loud laughter which he expected, a
shuddering cry of horror fell upon his ear, for Balder
the beautiful had fallen to the ground, pierced by the
fatal mistletoe.

> " So on the floor lay Balder dead ; and round
> Lay thickly strewn swords, axes, darts, and spears,
> Which all the Gods in sport had idly thrown
> At Balder, whom no weapon pierced or clove ;
> But in his breast stood fixed the fatal bough
> Of mistletoe, which Lok, the Accuser, gave
> To Hoder, and unwitting Hoder threw—
> 'Gainst that alone had Balder's life no charm."
> *Balder Dead* (*Matthew Arnold*).

In dire anxiety the gods crowded around their beloved
companion, but alas ! life was quite extinct, and all
their efforts to revive the fallen sun-god were unavailing.   Inconsolable at their loss, they now turned angrily
upon Hodur, whom they would there and then have
slain had they not been restrained by the law of the
gods that no wilful deed of violence should desecrate
their peace-steads.   The sound of their loud lamentation

brought the goddesses in hot haste to the dreadful scene, and when Frigga saw that her darling was dead, she passionately implored the gods to go to Nifl-heim and entreat Hel to release her victim, for the earth could not exist happily without him.

Hermod's Errand

As the road was rough and painful in the extreme, none of the gods would volunteer at first to go ; but when Frigga promised that she and Odin would reward the messenger by loving him above all the Æsir, Hermod signified his readiness to execute the commission. To enable him to do so, Odin lent him Sleipnir, and the noble steed, who was not wont to allow any but Odin upon his back, set off without demur upon the dark road which his hoofs had beaten twice before.

Meantime, Odin caused the body of Balder to be removed to Breidablik, and he directed the gods to go to the forest and cut down huge pines wherewith to build a worthy pyre.

> " But when the Gods were to the forest gone,
> Hermod led Sleipnir from Valhalla forth
> And saddled him ; before that, Sleipnir brook'd
> No meaner hand than Odin's on his mane,
> On his broad back no lesser rider bore ;
> Yet docile now he stood at Hermod's side,
> Arching his neck, and glad to be bestrode,
> Knowing the God they went to seek, how dear.
> But Hermod mounted him, and sadly fared
> In silence up the dark untravell'd road
> Which branches from the north of Heaven, and went
> All day ; and daylight waned, and night came on.
> And all that night he rode, and journey'd so,
> Nine days, nine nights, toward the northern ice,
> Through valleys deep-engulph'd by roaring streams.
> And on the tenth morn he beheld the bridge
> Which spans with golden arches Giall's stream,

And on the bridge a damsel watching, arm'd,
In the straight passage, at the further end,
Where the road issues between walling rocks."
Balder Dead (*Matthew Arnold*).

The Funeral Pyre

While Hermod was speeding along the cheerless road which led to Nifl-heim, the gods hewed and carried down to the shore a vast amount of fuel, which they piled upon the deck of Balder's dragon-ship, Ringhorn, constructing an elaborate funeral pyre. According to custom, this was decorated with tapestry hangings, garlands of flowers, vessels and weapons of all kinds, golden rings, and countless objects of value, ere the immaculate corpse, richly attired, was brought and laid upon it.

One by one, the gods now drew near to take a last farewell of their beloved companion, and as Nanna bent over him, her loving heart broke, and she fell lifeless by his side. Seeing this, the gods reverently laid her beside her husband, that she might accompany him even in death; and after they had slain his horse and hounds and twined the pyre with thorns, the emblems of sleep, Odin, last of the gods, drew near.

In token of affection for the dead and of sorrow for his loss, all had lain their most precious possessions upon his pyre, and Odin, bending down, now added to the offerings his magic ring Draupnir. It was noted by the assembled gods that he was whispering in his dead son's ear, but none were near enough to hear what word he said.

These sad preliminaries ended, the gods now prepared to launch the ship, but found that the heavy load of fuel and treasures resisted their combined efforts and they could not make the vessel stir an inch. The mountain giants, witnessing the scene from afar, and

The Death of Balder
Dorothy Hardy

noticing their quandary, now drew near and said that they knew of a giantess called Hyrrokin, who dwelt in Jötun-heim, and was strong enough to launch the vessel without any other aid. The gods therefore bade one of the storm giants hasten off to summon Hyrrokin, and she soon appeared, mounted upon a gigantic wolf, which she guided by a bridle made of writhing snakes. Riding down to the shore, the giantess dismounted and haughtily signified her readiness to give the required aid, if in the meantime the gods would take charge of her steed. Odin immediately despatched four of his maddest Berserkers to hold the wolf; but, in spite of their phenomenal strength, they could not restrain the monstrous creature until the giantess had thrown it down and bound it fast.

Hyrrokin, seeing that now they would be able to manage her refractory steed, strode along the strand to where, high up from the water's edge, lay Balder's mighty ship Ringhorn.

> " Seventy ells and four extended
>   On the grass the vessel's keel;
> High above it, gilt and splendid,
> Rose the figure-head ferocious
>   With its crest of steel."
>   *The Saga of King Olaf* (*Longfellow*).

Setting her shoulder against its stern, with a supreme effort she sent it with a rush into the water. Such was the weight of the mass, however, and the rapidity with which it shot down into the sea, that the earth shook as if from an earthquake, and the rollers on which the ship glided caught fire from the friction. The unexpected shock almost caused the gods to lose their balance, and this so angered Thor that he raised his hammer and would have slain the giantess had he not been restrained by his companions. Easily appeased, as usual—for Thor's temper, although quickly roused, was evanescent—he now boarded the vessel once more to consecrate the funeral pyre with his sacred hammer. As he was performing this ceremony, the dwarf Lit provokingly stumbled into his way, whereupon Thor, who had not entirely recovered his equanimity, kicked him into the fire, which he had just kindled with a thorn, and the dwarf was burned to ashes with the bodies of the divine pair.

The great ship now drifted out to sea, and the flames from the pyre presented a magnificent spectacle, which assumed a greater glory with every passing moment, until, when the vessel neared the western horizon, it seemed as if sea and sky were on fire. Sadly the gods watched the glowing ship and its precious freight, until suddenly it plunged into the waves and disappeared ; nor did they turn aside and return to Asgard until the last spark of light had vanished, and the world, in token of mourning for Balder the good, was enveloped in a mantle of darkness.

> " Soon with a roaring rose the mighty fire,
>   And the pile crackled ; and between the logs
>   Sharp quivering tongues of flame shot out, and leapt
>   Curling and darting, higher, until they lick'd
>   The summit of the pile, the dead, the mast,
>   And ate the shrivelling sails ; but still the ship
>   Drove on, ablaze above her hull with fire.
>   And the gods stood upon the beach, and gazed ;
>   And while they gazed, the sun went lurid down
>   Into the smoke-wrapt sea, and night came on.
>   Then the wind fell with night, and there was calm ;
>   But through the dark they watch'd the burning ship
>   Still carried o'er the distant waters, on
>   Farther and farther, like an eye of fire.
>   So show'd in the far darkness, Balder's pile ;
>   But fainter, as the stars rose high, it flared ;
>   The bodies were consumed, ash choked the pile.
>   And as, in a decaying winter fire,

HERMOD'S QUEST

A charr'd log, falling, makes a shower of sparks—
So, with a shower of sparks, the pile fell in,
Reddening the sea around ; and all was dark."
Balder Dead (Matthew Arnold).

Hermod's Quest

Sadly the gods entered Asgard, where no sounds of merriment or feasting greeted the ear, for all hearts were filled with anxious concern for the end of all things which was felt to be imminent. And truly the thought of the terrible Fimbul-winter, which was to herald their death, was one well calculated to disquiet the gods.

Frigga alone cherished hope, and she watched anxiously for the return of her messenger, Hermod the swift, who, meanwhile, had ridden over the tremulous bridge, and along the dark Hel-way, until, on the tenth night, he had crossed the rushing tide of the river Giöll. Here he was challenged by Mödgud, who inquired why the Giallar-bridge trembled more beneath his horse's tread than when a whole army passed, and asked why he, a living rider, was attempting to penetrate into the dreaded realm of Hel.

" Who art thou on thy black and fiery horse,
Under whose hoofs the bridge o'er Giall's stream
Rumbles and shakes ? Tell me thy race and home.
But yestermorn five troops of dead pass'd by,
Bound on their way below to Hela's realm,
Nor shook the bridge so much as thou alone.
And thou hast flesh and colour on thy cheeks,
Like men who live, and draw the vital air ;
Nor look'st thou pale and wan, like man deceased,
Souls bound below, my daily passers here."
Balder Dead (Matthew Arnold).

Hermod explained to Mödgud the reason of his coming, and, having ascertained that Balder and Nanna

o   209

had ridden over the bridge before him, he hastened on, until he came to the gate, which rose forbiddingly before him.

Nothing daunted by this barrier, Hermod dismounted on the smooth ice, and tightening the girths of his saddle, remounted, and burying his spurs deep into Sleipnir's sleek sides, he put him to a prodigious leap, which landed them safely on the other side of Hel-gate.

> " Thence on he journey'd o'er the fields of ice
> Still north, until he met a stretching wall
> Barring his way, and in the wall a grate.
> Then he dismounted, and drew tight the girths,
> On the smooth ice, of Sleipnir, Odin's horse,
> And made him leap the grate, and came within."
> *Balder Dead (Matthew Arnold).*

Riding onward, Hermod came at last to Hel's banqueting-hall, where he found Balder, pale and dejected, lying upon a couch, his wife Nanna beside him, gazing fixedly at a beaker of mead, which apparently he had no heart to quaff.

The Condition of Balder's Release

In vain Hermod informed his brother that he had come to redeem him ; Balder shook his head sadly, saying that he knew he must remain in his cheerless abode until the last day should come, but he implored Hermod to take Nanna back with him, as the home of the shades was no place for such a bright and beautiful creature. But when Nanna heard this request she clung more closely to her husband's side, vowing that nothing would ever induce her to part from him, and that she would stay with him for ever, even in Nifl-heim.

The long night was spent in close conversation, ere Hermod sought Hel and implored her to release Balder. The churlish goddess listened in silence to his request,

Hermod before Hela

J. C. Dollman

and declared finally that she would allow her victim to depart provided that all things animate and inanimate would show their sorrow for his loss by shedding tears.

"Come then ! if Balder was so dear beloved,
And this is true, and such a loss is Heaven's—
Hear, how to Heaven may Balder be restored.
Show me through all the world the signs of grief !
Fails but one thing to grieve, here Balder stops !
Let all that lives and moves upon the earth
Weep him, and all that is without life weep ;
Let Gods, men, brutes, beweep him ; plants and stones.
So shall I know the lost was dear indeed,
And bend my heart, and give him back to Heaven."
Balder Dead (Matthew Arnold).

This answer was full of encouragement, for all Nature mourned the loss of Balder, and surely there was nothing in all creation which would withhold the tribute of a tear. So Hermod cheerfully made his way out of Hel's dark realm, carrying with him the ring Draupnir, which Balder sent back to Odin, an embroidered carpet from Nanna for Frigga, and a ring for Fulla.

The Return of Hermod

The assembled gods crowded anxiously round Hermod as soon as he returned, and when he had delivered his messages and gifts, the Æsir sent heralds to every part of the world to bid all things animate and inanimate weep for Balder.

"Go quickly forth through all the world, and pray
All living and unliving things to weep
Balder, if haply he may thus be won ! "
Balder Dead (Matthew Arnold).

North, South, East and West rode the heralds, and as they passed tears fell from every plant and tree, so that the ground was saturated with moisture, and metals and stones, despite their hard hearts, wept too.

The way at last led back to Asgard, and by the roadside was a dark cave, in which the messengers saw, crouching, the form of a giantess named Thok, whom some mythologists suppose to have been Loki in disguise. When she was called upon to shed a tear, she mocked the heralds, and fleeing into the dark recesses of her cave, she declared that no tear should fall from her eyes, and that, for all she cared, Hel might retain her prey for ever.

> " Thok she weepeth
> With dry tears
> For Balder's death—
> Neither in life, nor yet in death,
> Gave he me gladness.
> Let Hel keep her prey."
>
> *Elder Edda* (*Howitt's version*).

As soon as the returning messengers arrived in Asgard, the gods crowded round them to learn the result of their mission ; but their faces, all aglow with the joy of anticipation, grew dark with despair when they heard that one creature had refused the tribute of tears, wherefore they would behold Balder in Asgard no more.

> " Balder, the Beautiful, shall ne'er
> From Hel return to upper air !
> Betrayed by Loki, *twice* betrayed,
> The prisoner of Death is made ;
> Ne'er shall he 'scape the place of doom
> Till fatal Ragnarok be come ! "
>
> *Valhalla* (*J. C. Jones*).

Vali the Avenger

The decrees of fate had not yet been fully consummated, and the final act of the tragedy remains to be briefly stated.

212

THE SIGNIFICATION OF THE STORY

We have already seen how Odin succeeded after many rebuffs in securing the consent of Rinda to their union, and that the son born of this marriage was destined to avenge the death of Balder. The advent of this wondrous infant now took place, and Vali the Avenger, as he was called, entered Asgard on the day of his birth, and on that very same day he slew Hodur with an arrow from a bundle which he seems to have carried for the purpose. Thus the murderer of Balder, unwitting instrument though he was, atoned for the crime with his blood, according to the code of the true Norseman.

The Signification of the Story

The physical explanation of this myth is to be found either in the daily setting of the sun (Balder), which sinks beneath the western waves, driven away by darkness (Hodur), or in the ending of the short Northern summer and the long reign of the winter season. " Balder represents the bright and clear summer, when twilight and daylight kiss each other and go hand in hand in these Northern latitudes."

> " Balder's pyre, of the sun a mark,
> Holy hearth red staineth ;
> Yet, soon dies its last faint spark,
> Darkly then Hoder reigneth."
> *Viking Tales of the North* (*R. B. Anderson*).

" His death by Hodur is the victory of darkness over light, the darkness of winter over the light of summer ; and the revenge by Vali is the breaking forth of new light after the wintry darkness."

Loki, the fire, is jealous of Balder, the pure light of heaven, who alone among the Northern gods never fought, but was always ready with words of conciliation and peace.

MYTHS OF THE NORSEMEN

" But from thy lips, O Balder, night or day,
Heard no one ever an injurious word
To God or Hero, but thou keptest back
The others, labouring to compose their brawls."
Balder Dead (Matthew Arnold).

The tears shed by all things for the beloved god are symbolical of the spring thaw, setting in after the hardness and cold of winter, when every tree and twig, and even the stones drip with moisture ; Thok (coal) alone shows no sign of tenderness, as she is buried deep within the dark earth and needs not the light of the sun.

" And as in winter, when the frost breaks up,
At winter's end, before the spring begins,
And a warm west wind blows, and thaw sets in—
After an hour a dripping sound is heard
In all the forests, and the soft-strewn snow
Under the trees is dibbled thick with holes,
And from the boughs the snow loads shuffle down ;
And, in fields sloping to the south, dark plots
Of grass peep out amid surrounding snow,
And widen, and the peasant's heart is glad—
So through the world was heard a dripping noise
Of all things weeping to bring Balder back ;
And there fell joy upon the Gods to hear."
Balder Dead (Matthew Arnold).

From the depths of their underground prison, the sun (Balder) and vegetation (Nanna) try to cheer heaven (Odin) and earth (Frigga) by sending them the ring Draupnir, the emblem of fertility, and the flowery tapestry, symbolical of the carpet of verdure which will again deck the earth and enhance her charms with its beauty.

The ethical signification of the myth is no less beautiful, for Balder and Hodur are symbols of the conflicting forces of good and evil, while Loki impersonates the tempter.

THE WORSHIP OF BALDER

" But in each human soul we find
That night's dark Hoder, Balder's brother blind,
Is born and waxeth strong as he ;
For blind is ev'ry evil born, as bear cubs be,
Night is the cloak of evil ; but all good
Hath ever clad in shining garments stood.
The busy Loke, tempter from of old,
Still forward treads incessant, and doth hold
The blind one's murder hand, whose quick-launch'd spear
Pierceth young Balder's breast, that sun of Valhal's sphere ! "
Viking Tales of the North (*R. B. Anderson*).

The Worship of Balder

One of the most important festivals was held at the summer solstice, or midsummer's eve, in honour of Balder the good, for it was considered the anniversary of his death and of his descent into the lower world. On that day, the longest in the year, the people congregated out of doors, made great bonfires, and watched the sun, which in extreme Northern latitudes barely dips beneath the horizon ere it rises upon a new day. From midsummer, the days gradually grow shorter, and the sun's rays less warm, until the winter solstice, which was called the " Mother night," as it was the longest night in the year. Midsummer's eve, once celebrated in honour of Balder, is now called St. John's day, that saint having entirely supplanted Balder the good.

CHAPTER XXII : LOKI

The Spirit of Evil

BESIDES the hideous giant Utgard-Loki, the personification of mischief and evil, whom Thor and his companions visited in Jötun-heim, the ancient Northern nations had another type of sin, whom they called Loki also, and whom we have already seen under many different aspects.

In the beginning, Loki was merely the personification of the hearth fire and of the spirit of life. At first a god, he gradually becomes "god and devil combined," and ends in being held in general detestation as an exact counterpart of the mediæval Lucifer, the prince of lies, "the originator of deceit, and the backbiter" of the Æsir.

By some authorities Loki was said to be the brother of Odin, but others assert that the two were not related, but had merely gone through the form of swearing blood brotherhood common in the North.

> " Odin ! dost thou remember
> When we in early days
> Blended our blood together ?
> When to taste beer
> Thou did'st constantly refuse
> Unless to both 'twas offered ? "
> *Sæmund's Edda (Thorpe's tr.).*

Loki's Character

While Thor is the embodiment of Northern activity, Loki represents recreation, and the close companionship early established between these two gods shows very plainly how soon our ancestors realised that both were necessary to the welfare of mankind. Thor is ever busy and ever in earnest, but Loki makes fun of

216

everything, until at last his love of mischief leads him entirely astray, and he loses all love for goodness and becomes utterly selfish and malevolent.

He represents evil in the seductive and seemingly beautiful form in which it parades through the world. Because of this deceptive appearance the gods did not at first avoid him, but treated him as one of themselves in all good-fellowship, taking him with them wherever they went, and admitting him not only to their merrymakings, but also to their council hall, where, unfortunately, they too often listened to his advice.

As we have already seen, Loki played a prominent part in the creation of man, endowing him with the power of motion, and causing the blood to circulate freely through his veins, whereby he was inspired with passions. As personification of fire as well as of mischief, Loki (lightning) is often seen with Thor (thunder), whom he accompanies to Jötun-heim to recover his hammer, to Utgard-Loki's castle, and to Geirrod's house. It is he who steals Freya's necklace and Sif's hair, and betrays Idun into the power of Thiassi; and although he sometimes gives the gods good advice and affords them real help, it is only to extricate them from some predicament into which he has rashly inveigled them.

Some authorities declare that, instead of making part of the creative trilogy (Odin, Hoenir, and Lodur or Loki), this god originally belonged to a pre-Odinic race of deities, and was the son of the great giant Fornjotnr (Ymir), his brothers being Kari (air) and Hler (water), and his sister Ran, the terrible goddess of the sea. Other mythologists, however, make him the son of the giant Farbauti, who has been identified with Bergelmir, the sole survivor of the deluge, and of Laufeia (leafy isle) or Nal (vessel), his mother, thus stating that his connection with Odin was only that of the Northern oath of good-fellowship.

Loki (fire) first married Glut (glow), who bore him two daughters, Eisa (embers) and Einmyria (ashes) ; it is therefore very evident that Norsemen considered him emblematic of the hearth-fire, and when the flaming wood crackles on the hearth the goodwives in the North are still wont to say that Loki is beating his children. Besides this wife, Loki is also said to have wedded the giantess Angur-boda (the anguish-boding), who dwelt in Jötun-heim, and who, as we have already seen, bore him the three monsters: Hel, goddess of death, the Midgard snake Iörmungandr, and the grim wolf Fenris.

> " Loki begat the wolf
> With Angur-boda."
>
> Sæmund's Edda (Thorpe's tr.).

Sigyn

Loki's third marriage was with Sigyn, who proved a most loving and devoted wife, and bore him two sons, Narve and Vali, the latter a namesake of the god who avenged Balder. Sigyn was always faithful to her husband, and did not forsake him even after he had definitely been cast out of Asgard and confined in the bowels of the earth.

As Loki was the embodiment of evil in the minds of the Northern races, they entertained nothing but fear of him, built no temples to his honour, offered no sacrifices to him, and designated the most noxious weeds by his name. The quivering, overheated atmosphere of summer was supposed to betoken his presence, for the people were then wont to remark that Loki was sowing his wild oats, and when the sun appeared to be drawing water they said Loki was drinking.

The story of Loki is so inextricably woven with that

218

of the other gods that most of the myths relating to him have already been told, and there remain but two episodes of his life to relate, one showing his better side before he had degenerated into the arch deceiver, and the other illustrating how he finally induced the gods to defile their peace-steads by wilful murder.

Skrymsli and the Peasant's Child

A giant and a peasant were playing a game together one day (probably a game of chess, which was a favourite winter pastime with the Northern vikings). They of course had determined to play for certain stakes, and the giant, being victorious, won the peasant's only son, whom he said he would come and claim on the morrow unless the parents could hide him so cleverly that he could not be found.

Knowing that such a feat would be impossible for them to perform, the parents fervently prayed to Odin to help them, and in answer to their entreaties the god came down to earth, and changed the boy into a tiny grain of wheat, which he hid in an ear of grain in the midst of a large field, declaring that the giant would not be able to find him. The giant Skrymsli, however, possessed wisdom far beyond what Odin imagined, and, failing to find the child at home, he strode off immediately to the field with his scythe, and mowing the wheat he selected the particular ear where the boy was hidden. Counting over the grains of wheat he was about to lay his hand upon the right one when Odin, hearing the child's cry of distress, snatched the kernel out of the giant's hand, and restored the boy to his parents, telling them that he had done all in his power to help them. But as the giant vowed he had been cheated, and would again claim the boy on the morrow unless the parents could outwit him, the unfortunate

219

peasants now turned to Hoenir for aid. The god heard them graciously and changed the boy into a fluff of down, which he hid in the breast of a swan swimming in a pond close by. Now when, a few minutes later, Skrymsli came up, he guessed what had occurred, and seizing the swan, he bit off its neck, and would have swallowed the down had not Hoenir wafted it away from his lips and out of reach, restoring the boy safe and sound to his parents, but telling them that he could not further aid them.

Skrymsli warned the parents that he would make a third attempt to secure the child, whereupon they applied in their despair to Loki, who carried the boy out to sea, and concealed him, as a tiny egg, in the roe of a flounder. Returning from his expedition, Loki encountered the giant near the shore, and seeing that he was bent upon a fishing excursion, he insisted upon accompanying him. He felt somewhat uneasy lest the terrible giant should have seen through his device, and therefore thought it would be well for him to be on the spot in case of need. Skrymsli baited his hook, and was more or less successful in his angling, when suddenly he drew up the identical flounder in which Loki had concealed his little charge. Opening the fish upon his knee, the giant proceeded to minutely examine the roe, until he found the egg which he was seeking.

The plight of the boy was certainly perilous, but Loki, watching his chance, snatched the egg out of the giant's grasp, and transforming it again into the child, he instructed him secretly to run home, passing through the boathouse on his way and closing the door behind him. The terrified boy did as he was told immediately he found himself on land, and the giant, quick to observe his flight, dashed after him into the boathouse. Now Loki had cunningly placed a sharp spike in such a position that the great head of the giant ran full tilt against it, and he sank to the ground with a groan, whereupon Loki, seeing him helpless, cut off one of his legs. Imagine the god's dismay, however, when he saw the pieces join and immediately knit together. But Loki was a master of guile, and recognising this as the work of magic, he cut off the other leg, promptly throwing flint and steel between the severed limb and trunk, and thereby hindering any further sorcery. The peasants were immensely relieved to find that their enemy was slain, and ever after they considered Loki the mightiest of all the heavenly council, for he had delivered them effectually from their foe, while the other gods had lent only temporary aid.

The Giant Architect

Notwithstanding their wonderful bridge Bifröst, the tremulous way, and the watchfulness of Heimdall, the gods could not feel entirely secure in Asgard, and were often fearful lest the frost giants should make their way into Asgard. To obviate this possibility, they finally decided to build an impregnable fortress ; and while they were planning how this could be done, an un-known architect came with an offer to undertake the construction, provided the gods would give him sun, moon, and Freya, goddess of youth and beauty, as reward. The gods were wroth at so presumptuous an offer, but when they would have indignantly driven the stranger from their presence, Loki urged them to make a bargain which it would be impossible for the stranger to keep, and so they finally told the architect that the guerdon should be his, provided the fortress were finished in the course of a single winter, and that he accomplished the work with no other assistance than that of his horse Svadilfare.

"To Asgard came an architect,
And castle offered to erect,—
A castle high
Which should defy
Deep Jotun guile and giant raid;
And this most wily compact made:
Fair Freya, with the Moon and Sun,
As price the fortress being done."
                              Valhalla (*J. C. Jones*).

The unknown architect agreed to these seemingly impossible conditions, and immediately set to work, hauling ponderous blocks of stone by night, building during the day, and progressing so rapidly that the gods began to feel somewhat anxious. Ere long they noticed that more than half the labour was accomplished by the wonderful steed Svadilfare, and when they saw, near the end of winter, that the work was finished save only one portal, which they knew the architect could easily erect during the night :

"Horror and fear the gods beset;
Finished almost the castle stood !
In three days more
The work be o'er;
Then must they make their contract good,
And pay the awful debt."
                              Valhalla (*J. C. Jones*).

Terrified lest they should be called upon to part, not only with the sun and moon, but also with Freya, the personification of the youth and beauty of the world, the gods turned upon Loki, and threatened to kill him unless he devised some means of hindering the architect from finishing the work within the specified time.

Loki's cunning proved once more equal to the situation. He waited until nightfall of the final day, when, as Svadilfare passed the fringe of a forest, painfully dragging one of the great blocks of stone required for

222

.

Loki and Svadilfari
Dorothy Hardy

the termination of the work, he rushed out from a dark glade in the guise of a mare, and neighed so invitingly that, in a trice, the horse kicked himself free of his harness and ran after the mare, closely pursued by his angry master. The mare galloped swiftly on, artfully luring horse and master deeper and deeper into the forest shades, until the night was nearly gone, and it was no longer possible to finish the work. The architect was none other than a redoubtable Hrim-thurs, in disguise, and he now returned to Asgard in a towering rage at the fraud which had been practised upon him. Assuming his wonted proportions, he would have annihilated the gods had not Thor suddenly returned from a journey and slain him with his magic hammer Miölnir, which he hurled with terrific force full in his face.

The gods had saved themselves on this occasion only by fraud and by the violent deed of Thor, and these were destined to bring great sorrow upon them, and eventually to secure their downfall, and to hasten the coming of Ragnarok. Loki, however, felt no remorse for his part, and in due time, it is said, he became the parent of an eight-footed steed called Sleipnir, which, as we have seen, was Odin's favourite mount.

> " But Sleipnir he begat
> With Svadilfari."
>
> *Lay of Hyndla* (*Thorpe's tr.*).

Loki performed so many evil deeds during his career that he richly deserved the title of " arch deceiver " which was given him. He was generally hated for his subtle malicious ways, and for an inveterate habit of prevarication which won for him also the title of " prince of lies."

Loki's last Crime

Loki's last crime, and the one which filled his measure

of iniquity, was to induce Hodur to throw the fatal mistletoe at Balder, whom he hated merely on account of his immaculate purity. Perhaps even this crime might have been condoned had it not been for his obduracy when, in the disguise of the old woman Thok, he was called upon to shed a tear for Balder. His action on this occasion convinced the gods that nothing but evil remained within him, and they pronounced unanimously upon him the sentence of perpetual banishment from Asgard.

Ægir's Banquet

To divert the gods' sadness and make them, for a short time, forget the treachery of Loki and the loss of Balder, Ægir, god of the sea, invited them to partake of a banquet in his coral caves at the bottom of the sea.

> " Now, to assuage the high gods' grief
> And bring their mourning some relief,
>   From coral caves
>   'Neath ocean waves,
>   Mighty King Ægir
>   Invited the Æsir
>   To festival
>   In Hlesey's hall ;
> That, tho' for Baldur every guest
>   Was grieving yet,
>   He might forget
> Awhile his woe in friendly feast."
>
> Valhalla (J. C. Jones)

The gods gladly accepted the invitation, and clad in their richest garb, and with festive smiles, they appeared in the coral caves at the appointed time. None were absent save the radiant Balder, for whom many a regretful sigh was heaved, and the evil Loki, whom none could regret. In the course of the feast, however, this last-named god appeared in their midst like a dark shadow, and when bidden to depart, he gave vent to his evil passions in a torrent of invective against the gods.

> " Of the Æsir and the Alfar
> That are here within
> Not one has a friendly word for thee."
> *Ægir's Compotation, or Loki's Altercation (Thorpe's tr.).*

Then, jealous of the praises which Funfeng, Ægir's servant, had won for the dexterity with which he waited upon his master's guests, Loki suddenly turned upon him and slew him. At this wanton crime, the gods in fierce wrath drove Loki away once more, threatening him with dire punishment should he ever appear before them again.

Scarcely had the Æsir recovered from this disagreeable interruption to their feast, and resumed their places at the board, when Loki came creeping in once more, resuming his slanders with venomous tongue, and taunting the gods with their weaknesses or shortcomings, dwelling maliciously upon their physical imperfections, and deriding them for their mistakes. In vain the gods tried to stem his abuse ; his voice rose louder and louder, and he was just giving utterance to some base slander about Sif, when he was suddenly cut short by the sight of Thor's hammer, angrily brandished by an arm whose power he knew full well, and he fled incontinently.

> " Silence, thou impure being !
> My mighty hammer, Miöllnir,
> Shall stop thy prating.
> I will thy head
> From thy neck strike ;
> Then will thy life be ended."
> *Ægir's Compotation, or Loki's Altercation (Thorpe's tr.).*

The Pursuit of Loki

Knowing that he could now have no hope of being

admitted into Asgard again, and that sooner or later the gods, seeing the effect of his evil deeds, would regret having permitted him to roam the world, and would try either to bind or slay him, Loki withdrew to the mountains, where he built himself a hut, with four doors which he always left wide open to permit of a hasty escape. Carefully laying his plans, he decided that if the gods should come in search of him he would rush down to the neighbouring cataract, according to tradition the Fraananger force or stream, and, changing himself into a salmon, would thus evade his pursuers. He reasoned, however, that although he could easily avoid any hook, it might be difficult for him to effect his escape if the gods should fashion a net like that of the sea-goddess Ran.

Haunted by this fear, he decided to test the possibility of making such a mesh, and started to make one out of twine. He was still engaged upon the task when Odin, Kvasir, and Thor suddenly appeared in the distance ; and knowing that they had discovered his retreat, Loki threw his half-finished net into the fire, and, rushing through one of his ever-open doors, he leaped into the waterfall, where, in the shape of a salmon, he hid among some stones in the bed of the stream.

The gods, finding the hut empty, were about to depart, when Kvasir perceived the remains of the burnt net on the hearth. After some thought an inspiration came to him, and he advised the gods to weave a similar implement and use it in searching for their foe in the neighbouring stream, since it would be like Loki to choose such a method of baffling their pursuit. This advice seemed good and was immediately followed, and, the net finished, the gods proceeded to drag the stream. Loki eluded the net at its first cast

226

by hiding at the bottom of the river between two stones; and when the gods weighted the mesh and tried a second time, he effected his escape by jumping up stream. A third attempt to secure him proved successful, however, for, as he once more tried to get away by a sudden leap, Thor caught him in mid-air and held him so fast, that he could not escape. The salmon, whose slipperiness is proverbial in the North, is noted for its remarkably slim tail, and Norsemen attribute this to Thor's tight grasp upon his foe.

Loki's Punishment

Loki now sullenly resumed his wonted shape, and his captors dragged him down into a cavern, where they made him fast, using as bonds the entrails of his son Narve, who had been torn to pieces by Vali, his brother, whom the gods had changed into a wolf for the purpose. One of these fetters was passed under Loki's shoulders, and one under his loins, thereby securing him firmly hand and foot; but the gods, not feeling quite satisfied that the strips, tough and enduring though they were, would not give way, changed them into adamant or iron.

> " Thee, on a rock's point,
> With the entrails of thy ice-cold son,
> The gods will bind."
> *Sæmund's Edda* (*Thorpe's tr.*).

Skadi, the giantess, a personification of the cold mountain stream, who had joyfully watched the fettering of her foe (subterranean fire), now fastened a serpent directly over his head, so that its venom would fall, drop by drop, upon his upturned face. But Sigyn, Loki's faithful wife, hurried with a cup to his side, and until the day of Ragnarok she remained by him, catching the drops as they fell, and never leaving her post except when her vessel was full, and she was obliged to empty it. Only during her short absences could the drops of venom fall upon Loki's face, and then they caused such intense pain that he writhed with anguish, his efforts to get free shaking the earth and producing the earthquakes which so frighten mortals.

> " Ere they left him in his anguish,
> O'er his treacherous brow, ungrateful,
> Skadi hung a serpent hateful,
> Venom drops for aye distilling,
> Every nerve with torment filling ;
> Thus shall he in horror languish.
> By him, still unwearied kneeling,
> Sigyn at his tortured side,—
> Faithful wife ! with beaker stealing
> Drops of venom as they fall,—
> Agonising poison all !
> Sleepless, changeless, ever dealing
> Comfort, will she still abide ;
> Only when the cup's o'erflowing
> Must fresh pain and smarting cause,
> Swift, to void the beaker going,
> Shall she in her watching pause.
> Then doth Loki
> Loudly cry ;
> Shrieks of terror,
> Groans of horror,
> Breaking forth in thunder peals
> With his writhings scared Earth reels.
> Trembling and quaking,
> E'en high Heav'n shaking !
> So wears he out his awful doom,
> Until dread Ragnarok be come."
>
> *Valhalla* (*J. C. Jones*).

In this painful position Loki was destined to remain until the twilight of the gods, when his bonds would be loosed, and he would take part in the fatal conflict on the battlefield of Vigrid, falling at last by the hand of Heimdall, who would be slain at the same time.

228

Loki and Sigyn

M. E. Winge

228

LOKI'S DAY

As we have seen, the venom-dropping snake in this myth is the cold mountain stream, whose waters, falling from time to time upon subterranean fire, evaporate in steam, which escapes through fissures, and causes earthquakes and geysers, phenomena with which the inhabitants of Iceland, for instance, were very familiar.

Loki's Day

When the gods were reduced to the rank of demons by the introduction of Christianity, Loki was confounded with Saturn, who had also been shorn of his divine attributes, and both were considered the prototypes of Satan. The last day of the week, which was held sacred to Loki, was known in the Norse as Laugardag, or wash-day, but in English it was changed to Saturday, and was said to owe its name not to Saturn but to Sataere, the thief in ambush, and the Teutonic god of agriculture, who is supposed to be merely another personification of Loki.

CHAPTER XXIII : THE GIANTS

Jötun-heim

AS we have already seen, the Northern races imagined that the giants were the first creatures who came to life among the icebergs which filled the vast abyss of Ginnunga-gap. These giants were from the very beginning the opponents and rivals of the gods, and as the latter were the personifications of all that is good and lovely, the former were representative of all that was ugly and evil.

> " He comes—he comes—the Frost Spirit comes ! on the rushing northern blast,
> And the dark Norwegian pines have bowed as his fearful breath went past.
> With an unscorched wing he has hurried on, where the fires on Hecla glow
> On the darkly beautiful sky above and the ancient ice below."
>
> *J. G. Whittier.*

When Ymir, the first giant, fell lifeless on the ice, slain by the gods, his progeny were drowned in his blood. One couple only, Bergelmir and his wife, effected their escape to Jötun-heim, where they took up their abode and became the parents of all the giant race. In the North the giants were called by various names, each having a particular meaning. Jötun, for instance, meant "the great eater," for the giants were noted for their enormous appetites as well as for their uncommon size. They were fond of drinking as well as of eating, wherefore they were also called Thurses, a word which some writers claim had the same meaning as thirst ; but others think they owed this name to the high towers ("turseis") which they were supposed to have built. As the giants were antagonistic to the gods, the latter always strove to force them to remain in Jötun-

230

Thor and the Giants
M. E. Winge

heim, which was situated in the cold regions of the Pole. The giants were almost invariably worsted in their encounters with the gods, for they were heavy and slow-witted, and had nothing but stone weapons to oppose to the Æsir's bronze. In spite of this inequality, however, they were sometimes greatly envied by the gods, for they were thoroughly conversant with all knowledge relating to the past. Even Odin was envious of this attribute, and no sooner had he secured it by a draught from Mimir's spring than he hastened to Jötun-heim to measure himself against Vafthrudnir, the most learned of the giant brood. But he might never have succeeded in defeating his antagonist in this strange encounter had he not ceased inquiring about the past and propounded a question relating to the future.

Of all the gods Thor was most feared by the Jötuns, for he was continually waging war against the frost and mountain giants, who would fain have bound the earth for ever in their rigid bands, thus preventing men from tilling the soil. In fighting against them, Thor, as we have already seen, generally had recourse to his terrible hammer Miölnir.

Origin of the Mountains

According to German legends the uneven surface of the earth was due to the giants, who marred its smoothness by treading upon it while it was still soft and newly created, while streams were formed from the copious tears shed by the giantesses upon seeing the valleys made by their husbands' huge footprints. As such was the Teutonic belief, the people imagined that the giants, who personified the mountains to them, were huge uncouth creatures, who could only move about in the darkness or fog, and were petrified as soon as the first rays of sunlight pierced through the gloom or scattered the clouds.

This belief led them to name one of their principal mountain chains the Riesengebirge (giant mountains). The Scandinavians also shared this belief, and to this day the Icelanders designate their highest mountain peaks by the name of Jokul, a modification of the word " Jötun." In Switzerland, where the everlasting snows rest upon the lofty mountain tops, the people still relate old stories of the time when the giants roamed abroad ; and when an avalanche came crashing down the mountain side, they say the giants have restlessly shaken off part of the icy burden from their brows and shoulders.

The First Gods

As the giants were also personifications of snow, ice, cold, stone, and subterranean fire, they were said to be descended from the primitive Fornjotnr, whom some authorities identify with Ymir. According to this version of the myth, Fornjotnr had three sons : Hler, the sea ; Kari, the air ; and Loki, fire. These three divinities, the first gods, formed the oldest trinity, and their respective descendants were the sea giants Mimir, Gymir, and Grendel, the storm giants Thiassi, Thrym, and Beli, and the giants of fire and death, such as the Fenris wolf and Hel.

As all the royal dynasties claimed descent from some mythical being, the Merovingians asserted that their first progenitor was a sea giant, who rose out of the waves in the form of an ox, and surprised the queen while she was walking alone on the seashore, compelling her to become his wife. She gave birth to a son named Meroveus, the founder of the first dynasty of Frankish kings.

THE GIANT IN LOVE

Many stories have already been told about the most important giants. They reappear in many of the later myths and fairy-tales, and manifest, after the introduction of Christianity, a peculiar dislike to the sound of church bells and the singing of monks and nuns.

The Giant in Love

The Scandinavians relate, in this connection, that in the days of Olaf the Saint a giant called Senjemand, dwelt on the Island of Senjen, and he was greatly incensed because a nun on the Island of Grypto daily sang her morning hymn. This giant fell in love with a beautiful maiden called Juterna-jesta, and it was long ere he could find courage to propose to her. When at last he made his halting request, the fair damsel scornfully rejected him, declaring that he was far too old and ugly for her taste.

> " Miserable Senjemand—ugly and grey !
> Thou win the maid of Kvedfiord !
> No—a churl thou art and shalt ever remain."
>
> *Ballad* (*Brace's tr.*).

In his anger at being thus scornfully refused, the giant swore vengeance, and soon after he shot a great flint arrow from his bow at the maiden, who dwelt eighty miles away. Another lover, Torge, also a giant, seeing her peril and wishing to protect her, flung his hat at the speeding arrow. This hat was a thousand feet high and proportionately broad and thick, nevertheless the arrow pierced the headgear, falling short, however, of its aim. Senjemand, seeing that he had failed, and fearing the wrath of Torge, mounted his steed and prepared to ride off as quickly as possible ; but the sun, rising just then above the

233

horizon, turned him into stone, together with the arrow and Torge's hat, the huge pile being known as the Torghatten mountain. The people still point to an obelisk which they say is the stone arrow; to a hole in the mountain, 289 feet high and 88 feet wide, which they say is the aperture made by the arrow in its flight through the hat; and to the horseman on Senjen Island, apparently riding a colossal steed and drawing the folds of his wide cavalry cloak closely about him. As for the nun whose singing had so disturbed Senjemand, she was petrified too, and never troubled any one with her psalmody again.

The Giant and the Church Bells

Another legend relates that one of the mountain giants, annoyed by the ringing of church bells more than fifty miles away, once caught up a huge rock, which he hurled at the sacred building. Fortunately it fell short and broke in two. Ever since then, the peasants say that the trolls come on Christmas Eve to raise the largest piece of stone upon golden pillars, and to dance and feast beneath it. A lady, wishing to know whether this tale were true, once sent her groom to the place. The trolls came forward and hospitably offered him a drink from a horn mounted in gold and ornamented with runes. Seizing the horn, the groom flung its contents away and dashed off with it at a mad gallop, closely pursued by the trolls, from whom he escaped only by passing through a stubble field and over running water. Some of their number visited the lady on the morrow to claim this horn, and when she refused to part with it they laid a curse upon her, declaring that her castle would be burned down every time the horn should be removed. The prediction has thrice been fulfilled, and now the family guard

234

Torghatten

From a photograph by S. J. Beckett, F.R.P.S.

the relic with superstitious care. A similar drinking vessel, obtained in much the same fashion by the Oldenburg family, is exhibited in the collection of the King of Denmark.

The giants were not supposed to remain stationary, but were said to move about in the darkness, sometimes transporting masses of earth and sand, which they dropped here and there. The sandhills in northern Germany and Denmark were supposed to have been thus formed.

The Giants' Ship

A North Frisian tradition relates that the giants possessed a colossal ship, called Mannigfual, which constantly cruised about in the Atlantic Ocean. Such was the size of this vessel that the captain was said to patrol the deck on horseback, while the rigging was so extensive and the masts so high that the sailors who went up as youths came down as gray-haired men, having rested and refreshed themselves in rooms fashioned and provisioned for that purpose in the huge blocks and pulleys.

By some mischance it happened that the pilot once directed the immense vessel into the North Sea, and wishing to return to the Atlantic as soon as possible, yet not daring to turn in such a small space, he steered into the English Channel. Imagine the dismay of all on board when they saw the passage growing narrower and narrower the farther they advanced. When they came to the narrowest spot, between Calais and Dover, it seemed barely possible that the vessel, drifting along with the current, could force its way through. The captain, with laudable presence of mind, promptly bade his men soap the sides of the ship, and to lay an extra-thick layer on the starboard, where the rugged cliffs of

Dover rose threateningly. These orders were no sooner carried out than the vessel entered the narrow space, and, thanks to the captain's precaution, it slipped safely through. The rocks of Dover scraped off so much soap, however, that ever since they have been particularly white, and the waves dashing against them still have an unusually foamy appearance.

This exciting experience was not the only one through which the Mannigfual passed, for we are told that it once, nobody knows how, penetrated into the Baltic Sea, where, the water not being deep enough to keep the vessel afloat, the captain ordered all the ballast to be thrown overboard. The material thus cast on either side of the vessel into the sea formed the two islands of Bornholm and Christiansoë.

Princess Ilse

In Thuringia and in the Black Forest the stories of the giants are legion, and one of the favourites with the peasants is that about Ilse, the lovely daughter of the giant of the Ilsenstein. She was so charming that far and wide she was known as the Beautiful Princess Ilse, and was wooed by many knights, of whom she preferred the Lord of Westerburg. But her father did not at all approve of her consorting with a mere mortal, and forbade her to see her lover. Princess Ilse was wilful, however, and in spite of her sire's prohibition she daily visited her lover. The giant, exasperated by her persistency and disobedience, finally stretched out his huge hands and, seizing the rocks, tore a great gap between the height where he dwelt and the castle of Westerburg. Upon this, Princess Ilse, going to the cleft which parted her from her lover, recklessly flung herself over the precipice into the raging flood beneath, and was there changed into a bewitching undine. She dwelt in the limpid waters for many a year, appearing from time to time to exercise her fascinations upon mortals, and even, it is said, captivating the affections of the Emperor Henry, who paid frequent visits to her cascade. Her last appearance, according to popular belief, was at Pentecost, a hundred years ago; and the natives have not yet ceased to look for the beautiful princess, who is said still to haunt the stream and to wave her white arms to entice travellers into the cool spray of the waterfall.

> "I am the Princess Ilse,
>   And I dwell at the Ilsenstein;
> Come with me to my castle,
>   And bliss shall be mine and thine.
>
> "With the cool of my glass-clear waters
>   Thy brow and thy locks I'll lave;
> And thou'lt think of thy sorrows no longer,
>   For all that thou look'st so grave.
>
> "With my white arms twined around thee,
>   And lapped on my breast so white,
> Thou shalt lie, and dream of elf-land—
>   Its loves and wild delight."
>
> *Heine (Martin's tr.).*

The Giantess's Plaything

The giants inhabited all the earth before it was given to mankind, and it was only with reluctance that they made way for the human race, and retreated into the waste and barren parts of the country, where they brought up their families in strict seclusion. Such was the ignorance of their offspring, that a young giantess, straying from home, once came to an inhabited valley, where for the first time in her life she saw a farmer ploughing on the hillside. Deeming him a pretty plaything, she caught him up with his team, and thrusting them into her apron, she gleefully carried them home to exhibit to her father. But the giant immediately bade her carry peasant and horses back to the place where she had found them, and when she had done so he sadly explained that the creatures whom she took for mere playthings, would eventually drive the giant folk away, and become masters of the earth.

CHAPTER XXIV : THE DWARFS

Little Men

IN the first chapter we saw how the black elves, dwarfs, or Svart-alfar, were bred like maggots in the flesh of the slain giant Ymir. The gods, perceiving these tiny, unformed creatures creeping in and out, gave them form and features, and they became known as dark elves, on account of their swarthy complexions. These small beings were so homely, with their dark skin, green eyes, large heads, short legs, and crow's feet, that they were enjoined to hide underground, being commanded never to show themselves during the daytime lest they should be turned into stone. Although less powerful than the gods, they were far more intelligent than men, and as their knowledge was boundless and extended even to the future, gods and men were equally anxious to question them.

The dwarfs were also known as trolls, kobolds, brownies, goblins, pucks, or Huldra folk, according to the country where they dwelt.

> "You are the grey, grey Troll,
> With the great green eyes,
> But I love you, grey, grey Troll—
> You are so wise !
>
> "Tell me this sweet morn,
> Tell me all you know—
> Tell me, was I born ?
> Tell me, did I grow ? "
> *The Legend of the Little Fay (Buchanan).*

The Tarnkappe

These little beings could transport themselves with marvellous celerity from one place to another, and they loved to conceal themselves behind rocks, when they would mischievously repeat the last words of conversations overheard from such hiding-places. Owing to this well-known trick, the echoes were called dwarfs' talk, and people fancied that the reason why the makers of such sounds were never seen was because each dwarf was the proud possessor of a tiny red cap which made the wearer invisible. This cap was called **Tarnkappe**, and without it the dwarfs dared not appear above the surface of the earth after sunrise for fear of being petrified. When wearing it they were safe from this peril.

> " Away ! let not the sun view me—
> I dare no longer stay ;
> An Elfin-child, thou wouldst me see,
> To stone turn at his ray."
>
> *La Motte-Fouqué.*

The Legend of Kallundborg

Helva, daughter of the Lord of Nesvek, was loved by Esbern Snare, whose suit, however, was rejected by the proud father with the scornful words : " When thou shalt build at Kallundborg a stately church, then will I give thee Helva to wife."

Now Esbern, although of low estate, was proud of heart, even as the lord, and he determined, come what might, to find a way to win his coveted bride. So off he strode to a troll in Ullshoi Hill, and effected a bargain whereby the troll undertook to build a fine church, on completion of which Esbern was to tell the builder's name or forfeit his eyes and heart.

Night and day the troll wrought on, and as the building took shape, sadder grew Esbern Snare. He listened at the crevices of the hill by night ; he watched during the day ; he wore himself to a shadow by anxious thought ; he besought the elves to aid him. All to no purpose. Not a sound did he hear, not a thing did he see, to suggest the name of the builder.

THE LEGEND OF KALLUNDBORG

Meantime, rumour was busy, and the fair Helva, hearing of the evil compact, prayed for the soul of the unhappy man.

Time passed until one day the church lacked only one pillar, and worn out by black despair, Esbern sank exhausted upon a bank, whence he heard the troll hammering the last stone in the quarry underground. "Fool that I am," he said bitterly, "I have builded my tomb."

Just then he heard a light footstep, and looking up, he beheld his beloved. "Would that I might die in thy stead," said she, through her tears, and with that Esbern confessed how that for love of her he had imperilled eyes and heart and soul.

Then fast as the troll hammered underground, Helva prayed beside her lover, and the prayers of the maiden prevailed over the spell of the troll, for suddenly Esbern caught the sound of a troll-wife singing to her infant, bidding it be comforted, for that, on the morrow, *Father Fine* would return bringing a mortal's eyes and heart.

Sure of his victim, the troll hurried to Kallundborg with the last stone. "Too late, Fine!" quoth Esbern, and at the word, the troll vanished with his stone, and it is said that the peasants heard at night the sobbing of a woman underground, and the voice of the troll loud with blame.

> "Of the Troll of the Church they sing the rune
> By the Northern Sea in the harvest moon;
> And the fishers of Zealand hear him still
> Scolding his wife in Ulshoi hill.

> "And seaward over its groves of birch
> Still looks the tower of Kallundborg church,
> Where, first at its altar, a wedded pair,
> Stood Helva of Nesvek and Esbern Snare!"

J. G. Whittier

The Magic of the Dwarfs

The dwarfs, as well as the elves, were ruled by a king, who, in various countries of northern Europe, was known as Andvari, Alberich, Elbegast, Gondemar, Laurin, or Oberon. He dwelt in a magnificent subterranean palace, studded with the gems which his subjects had mined from the bosom of the earth, and, besides untold riches and the Tarnkappe, he owned a magic ring, an invincible sword, and a belt of strength. At his command the little men, who were very clever smiths, would fashion marvellous jewels or weapons, which their ruler would bestow upon favourite mortals.

We have already seen how the dwarfs fashioned Sif's golden hair, the ship Skidbladnir, the point of Odin's spear Gungnir, the ring Draupnir, the golden-bristled boar Gullin-bursti, the hammer Miölnir, and Freya's golden necklace Brisinga-men. They are also said to have made the magic girdle which Spenser describes in his poem of the " Faerie Queene,"—a girdle which was said to have the power of revealing whether its wearer were virtuous or a hypocrite.

> " That girdle gave the virtue of chaste love
> And wifehood true to all that did it bear;
> But whosoever contrary doth prove
> Might not the same about her middle wear
> But it would loose, or else asunder tear."
>
> *Faerie Queene (Spenser).*

The dwarfs also manufactured the mythical sword Tyrfing, which could cut through iron and stone, and which they gave to Angantyr. This sword, like Frey's, fought of its own accord, and could not be sheathed, after it was once drawn, until it had tasted blood. Angantyr was so proud of this weapon that he had it buried with him ; but his daughter Hervor visited his tomb at midnight, recited magic spells, and forced him to rise from his grave to give her the precious blade. She wielded it bravely, and it eventually became the property of another of the Northern heroes.

Another famous weapon, which according to tradition was forged by the dwarfs in Eastern lands, was the sword Angurvadel which Frithiof received as a portion of his inheritance from his fathers. Its hilt was of hammered gold, and the blade was inscribed with runes which were dull until it was brandished in war, when they flamed red as the comb of the fighting-cock.

> " Quick lost was that hero
> Meeting in battle's night that blade high-flaming with runics.
> Widely renown'd was this sword, of swords most choice in the
> Northland."
>
> *Tegnér's Frithiof* (G. *Stephens's tr.*).

The Passing of the Dwarfs

The dwarfs were generally kind and helpful; sometimes they kneaded bread, ground flour, brewed beer, performed countless household tasks, and harvested and threshed the grain for the farmers. If ill-treated, however, or turned to ridicule, these little creatures would forsake the house and never come back again. When the old gods ceased to be worshipped in the Northlands, the dwarfs withdrew entirely from the country, and a ferryman related how he had been hired by a mysterious personage to ply his boat back and forth across the river one night, and at every trip his vessel was so heavily laden with invisible passengers that it nearly sank. When his night's work was over, he received a rich reward, and his employer informed him that he had carried the dwarfs across the river, as they were leaving the country for ever in consequence of the unbelief of the people.

243

Changelings

According to popular superstition, the dwarfs, in envy of man's taller stature, often tried to improve their race by winning human wives or by stealing unbaptized children, and substituting their own offspring for the human mother to nurse. These dwarf babies were known as changelings, and were recognisable by their puny and wizened forms. To recover possession of her own babe, and to rid herself of the changeling, a woman was obliged either to brew beer in egg-shells or to grease the soles of the child's feet and hold them so near the flames that, attracted by their offspring's distressed cries, the dwarf parents would hasten to claim their own and return the stolen child.

The troll women were said to have the power of changing themselves into Maras or nightmares, and of tormenting any one they pleased; but if the victim succeeded in stopping up the hole through which a Mara made her ingress into his room, she was entirely at his mercy, and he could even force her to wed him if he chose to do so. A wife thus obtained was sure to remain as long as the opening through which she had entered the house was closed, but if the plug were removed, either by accident or design, she immediately effected her escape and never returned.

The Peaks of the Trolls

Naturally, traditions of the little folk abound everywhere throughout the North, and many places are associated with their memory. The well-known Peaks of the Trolls (Trold-Tindterne) in Norway are said to be the scene of a conflict between two bands of trolls,

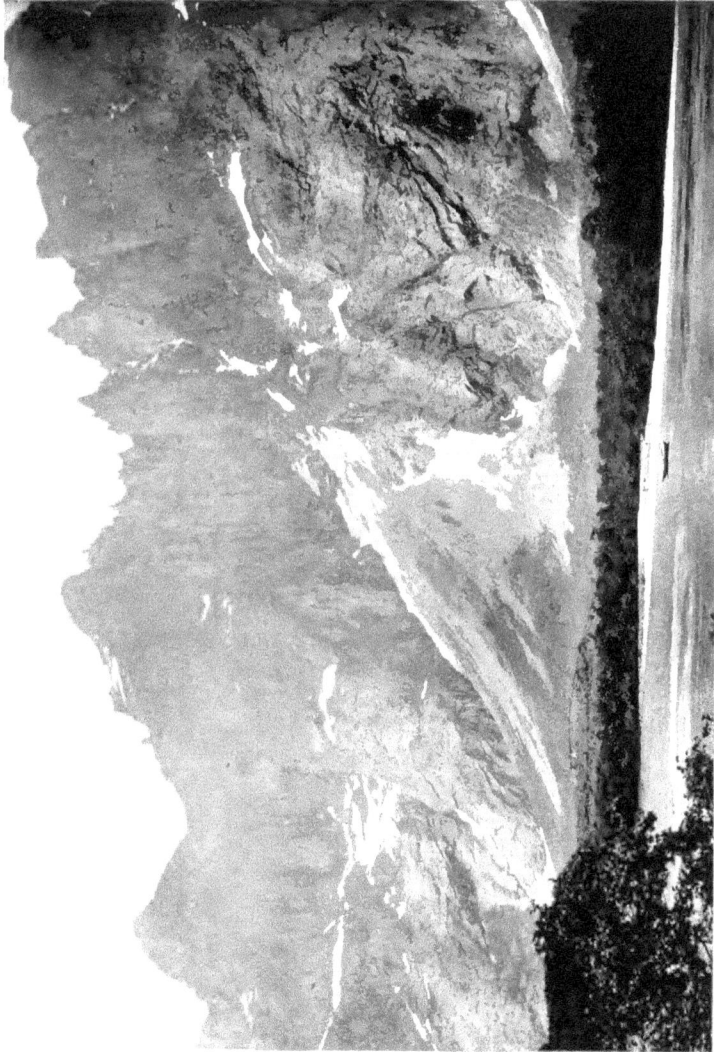

The Troldtinderne, Romsdal

From a photograph by S. J. Beckett, F.R.P.S.

who in the eagerness of combat omitted to note the approach of sunrise, with the result that they were changed into the small points of rock which stand up noticeably upon the crests of the mountain.

A Conjecture

Some writers have ventured a conjecture that the dwarfs so often mentioned in the ancient sagas and fairy-tales were real beings, probably the Phœnician miners, who, working the coal, iron, copper, gold, and tin mines of England, Norway, Sweden, etc., took advantage of the simplicity and credulity of the early inhabitants to make them believe that they belonged to a supernatural race and always dwelt underground, in a region which was called Svart-alfa-heim, or the home of the black elves.

CHAPTER XXV : THE ELVES

The Realm of Faery

BESIDES the dwarfs there was another numerous class of tiny creatures called Lios-alfar, light or white elves, who inhabited the realms of air between heaven and earth, and were gently governed by the genial god Frey from his palace in Alf-heim. They were lovely, beneficent beings, so pure and innocent that, according to some authorities, their name was derived from the same root as the Latin word " white " (*albus*), which, in a modified form, was given to the snow-covered Alps, and to Albion (England), because of her white chalk cliffs which could be seen afar.

The elves were so small that they could flit about unseen while they tended the flowers, birds, and butterflies ; and as they were passionately fond of dancing, they often glided down to earth on a moonbeam, to dance on the green. Holding one another by the hand, they would dance in circles, thereby making the " fairy rings," which were to be discerned by the deeper green and greater luxuriance of the grass which their little feet had pressed.

> " Merry elves, their morrice pacing
>   To aërial minstrelsy,
> Emerald rings on brown heath tracing,
>   Trip it deft and merrily."
>   *Sir Walter Scott.*

If any mortal stood in the middle of one of these fairy rings he could, according to popular belief in England, see the fairies and enjoy their favour ; but the Scandinavians and Teutons vowed that the unhappy man must die. In illustration of this superstition, a story is told of how Sir Olaf, riding off to his

246

The Elf-Dance
N. J. O. Blommér

wedding, was enticed by the fairies into their ring. On the morrow, instead of a merry marriage, his friends witnessed a triple funeral, for his mother and bride also died when they beheld his lifeless corpse.

> " Master Olof rode forth ere dawn of the day
> And came where the Elf-folk were dancing away.
>   The dance is so merry,
>   So merry in the greenwood.
>
> " And on the next morn, ere the daylight was red,
> In Master Olof's house lay three corpses dead.
>   The dance is so merry,
>   So merry in the greenwood.
>
> " First Master Olof, and next his young bride,
> And third his old mother—for sorrow she died.
>   The dance is so merry,
>   So merry in the greenwood."
>
>   *Master Olof at the Elfin Dance (Howitt's tr.).*

The Elf-dance

These elves, who in England were called fairies or fays, were also enthusiastic musicians, and delighted especially in a certain air known as the elf-dance, which was so irresistible that no one who heard it could refrain from dancing. If a mortal, overhearing the air, ventured to reproduce it, he suddenly found himself incapable of stopping and was forced to play on and on until he died of exhaustion, unless he were deft enough to play the tune backwards, or some one charitably cut the strings of his violin. His hearers, who were forced to dance as long as the tones continued, could only stop when they ceased.

The Will-o'-the-wisps

In mediæval times, the will-o'-the-wisps were known in the North as elf lights, for these tiny sprites were supposed to mislead travellers ; and popular superstition held that the Jack-o'-lanterns were the restless spirits of murderers forced against their will to return to the scene of their crimes. As they nightly walked thither, it is said that they doggedly repeated with every step, " It is right ; " but as they returned they sadly reiterated, " It is wrong."

Oberon and Titania

In later times the fairies or elves were said to be ruled by the king of the dwarfs, who, being an underground spirit, was considered a demon, and allowed to retain the magic power which the missionaries had wrested from the god Frey. In England and France the king of the fairies was known by the name of Oberon ; he governed fairyland with his queen Titania, and the highest revels on earth were held on Midsummer night. It was then that the fairies all congregated around him and danced most merrily.

> " Every elf and fairy sprite
> Hop as light as bird from brier ;
> And this ditty after me
> Sing, and dance it trippingly."
> *Midsummer-Night's Dream (Shakespeare).*

These elves, like the brownies, Huldra folk, kobolds, etc., were also supposed to visit human dwellings, and it was said that they took mischievous pleasure in tangling and knotting horses' manes and tails. These tangles were known as elf-locks, and whenever a farmer descried them he declared that his steeds had been elf-ridden during the night.

Alf-blot

In Scandinavia and Germany sacrifices were offered to the elves to make them propitious. These sacrifices

248

The White Elves   248
Chas. P. Sainton, R.I.

consisted of some small animal, or of a bowl of honey and milk, and were known as Alf-blot. They were quite common until the missionaries taught the people that the elves were mere demons, when they were transferred to the angels, who were long entreated to befriend mortals, and propitiated by the same gifts.

Many of the elves were supposed to live and die with the trees and plants which they tended, but these moss, wood, or tree maidens, while remarkably beautiful when seen in front, were hollow like a trough when viewed from behind. They appear in many of the popular tales, but almost always as benevolent and helpful spirits, for they were anxious to do good to mortals and to cultivate friendly relations with them.

Images on Doorposts

In Scandinavia the elves, both light and dark, were worshipped as household divinities, and their images were carved on the doorposts. The Norsemen, who were driven from home by the tyranny of Harald Harfager in 874, took their carved doorposts with them upon their ships. Similar carvings, including images of the gods and heroes, decorated the pillars of their high seats which they also carried away. The exiles showed their trust in their gods by throwing these wooden images overboard when they neared the Icelandic shores and settling where the waves carried the posts, even if the spot scarcely seemed the most desirable. "Thus they carried with them the religion, the poetry, and the laws of their race, and on this desolate volcanic island they kept these records unchanged for hundreds of years, while other Teutonic nations gradually became affected by their intercourse with Roman and Byzantine Christianity." These records, carefully collected by Sæmund the learned, form the

Elder Edda, the most precious relic of ancient Northern literature, without which we should know comparatively little of the religion of our forefathers.

The sagas relate that the first settlements in Greenland and Vinland were made in the same way,—the Norsemen piously landing wherever their household gods drifted ashore.

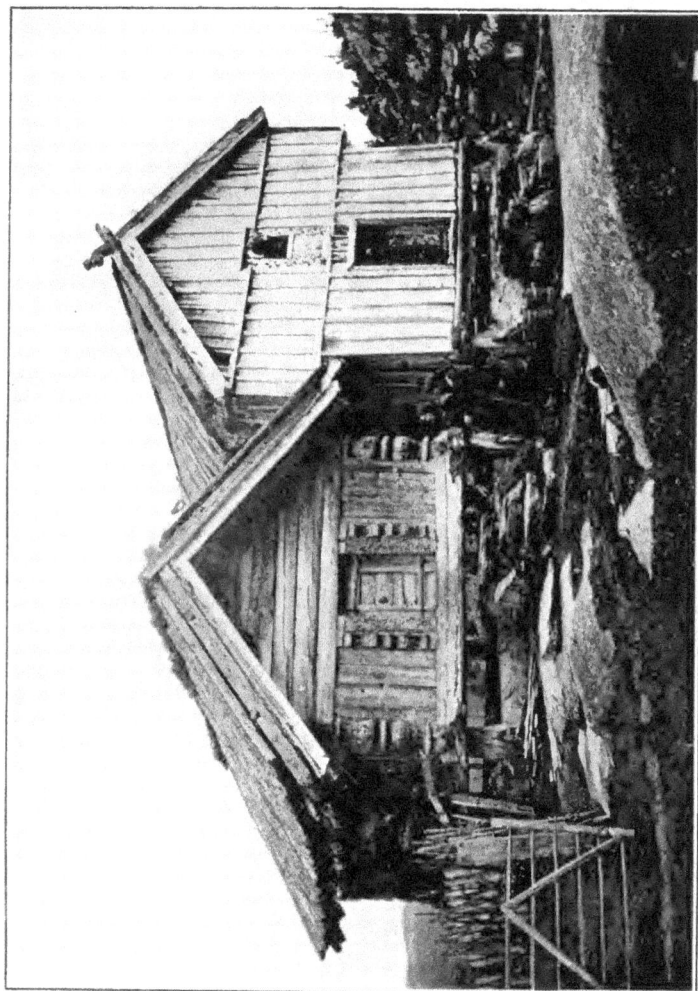

Old Houses with Carved Posts

CHAPTER XXVI : THE SIGURD SAGA

The Beginning of the Story

WHILE the first part of the Elder Edda con-
sists of a collection of alliterative poems
describing the creation of the world, the
adventures of the gods, their eventual downfall, and
gives a complete exposition of the Northern code of
ethics, the second part comprises a series of heroic lays
describing the exploits of the Volsung family, and
especially of their chief representative, Sigurd, the
favourite hero of the North.

The Volsunga Saga

These lays form the basis of the great Scandinavian
epic, the Volsunga Saga, and have supplied not only the
materials for the Nibelungenlied, the German epic, and
for countless folk tales, but also for Wagner's celebrated
operas, *The Rhinegold, Valkyr, Siegfried,* and *The Dusk
of the Gods.* In England, William Morris has given
them the form which they will probably retain in our
literature, and it is from his great epic poem, by the
courteous permission of his trustees, and of his pub-
lishers, Messrs. Longmans, Green and Co., that almost
all the quotations in this section are taken in preference to extracts from the Edda.

Sigi

The story of the Volsungs begins with Sigi, a son of
Odin, a powerful man, and generally respected, until
he killed a man from motives of jealousy, the latter
having slain more game when they were out hunting
together. In consequence of this crime, Sigi was driven
from his own land and declared an outlaw. But it
seems that he had not entirely forfeited Odin's favour,

for the god now provided him with a well-equipped vessel, together with a number of brave followers, and promised that victory should ever attend him.

Thus aided by Odin, the raids of Sigi became a terror to his foes, and in the end he won the glorious empire of the Huns and for many years reigned as a powerful monarch. But in extreme old age his fortune changed, Odin forsook him, his wife's kindred fell upon him, and he was slain in a treacherous encounter.

Rerir

His death was soon avenged, however, for Rerir, his son, returning from an expedition upon which he had been absent from the land at the time, put the murderers to death as his first act upon mounting the throne. The rule of Rerir was marked by every sign of prosperity, but his dearest wish, a son to succeed him, remained unfulfilled for many a year. Finally, however, Frigga decided to grant his constant prayer, and to vouchsafe the heir he longed for. She accordingly despatched her swift messenger Gna, or Liod, with a miraculous apple, which she dropped into his lap as he was sitting alone on the hillside. Glancing upward, Rerir recognised the emissary of the goddess, and joyfully hastened home to partake of the apple with his wife. The child who in due time was born under these favourable auspices was a handsome little lad. His parents called him Volsung, and while he was still a mere infant they both died, and the child became ruler of the land.

Volsung

Years passed and Volsung's wealth and power ever increased. He was the boldest leader, and rallied many brave warriors around him. Full oft did they drink his mead underneath the Branstock, a mighty oak, which, rising in the middle of his hall, pierced the roof and overshadowed the whole house.

"And as in all other matters 'twas all earthly houses' crown,
And the least of its wall-hung shields was a battle-world's renown,
So therein withal was a marvel and a glorious thing to see,
For amidst of its midmost hall-floor sprang up a mighty tree,
That reared its blessings roofward and wreathed the roof-tree dear
With the glory of the summer and the garland of the year."

Ten stalwart sons were born to Volsung, and one daughter, Signy, came to brighten his home. So lovely was this maiden that when she reached marriageable age many suitors asked for her hand, among whom was Siggeir, King of the Goths, who finally obtained Volsung's consent, although Signy had never seen him.

The Wedding of Signy

When the wedding-day came, and the bride beheld her destined husband she shrank in dismay, for his puny form and lowering glances contrasted sadly with her brothers' sturdy frames and open faces. But it was too late to withdraw—the family honour was at stake— and Signy so successfully concealed her dislike that none save her twin brother Sigmund suspected with what reluctance she became Siggeir's wife.

The Sword in the Branstock

While the wedding feast was in progress, and when the merry-making was at its height, the entrance to the hall was suddenly darkened by the tall form of a one-eyed man, closely enveloped in a mantle of cloudy blue. Without vouchsafing word or glance to any in the assembly, the stranger strode to the Branstock and

253

thrust a glittering sword up to the hilt in its great bole. Then, turning slowly round, he faced the awe-struck and silent assembly, and declared that the weapon would be for the warrior who could pull it out of its oaken sheath, and that it would assure him victory in every battle. The words ended, he then passed out as he had entered, and disappeared, leaving a conviction in the minds of all that Odin, king of the gods, had been in their midst.

" So sweet his speaking sounded, so wise his words did seem,
   That moveless all men sat there, as in a happy dream
   We stir not lest we waken ; but there his speech had end
   And slowly down the hall-floor, and outward did he wend ;
   And none would cast him a question or follow on his ways,
   For they knew that the gift was Odin's, a sword for the world to praise."

Volsung was the first to recover the power of speech, and, waiving his own right first to essay the feat, he invited Siggeir to make the first attempt to draw the divine weapon out of the tree-trunk. The bridegroom anxiously tugged and strained, but the sword remained firmly embedded in the oak and he resumed his seat, with an air of chagrin. Then Volsung tried, with the same result. The weapon was evidently not intended for either of them, and the young Volsung princes were next invited to try their strength.

" Sons I have gotten and cherished, now stand ye forth and try ;
   Lest Odin tell in God-home how from the way he strayed,
   And how to the man he would not he gave away his blade."

Sigmund

The nine eldest sons were equally unsuccessful ; but when Sigmund, the tenth and youngest, laid his firm young hand upon the hilt, the sword yielded easily to his touch, and he triumphantly drew it out as though it had merely been sheathed in its scabbard.

" At last by the side of the Branstock Sigmund the Volsung stood,
 And with right hand wise in battle the precious sword-hilt caught,
 Yet in a careless fashion, as he deemed it all for nought ;
 When, lo, from floor to rafter went up a shattering shout,
 For aloft in the hand of Sigmund the naked blade shone out
 As high o'er his head he shook it : for the sword had come away
 From the grip of the heart of the Branstock, as though all loose it
   lay."

Nearly all present were gratified at the success of the young prince ; but Siggeir's heart was filled with envy, and he coveted possession of the weapon. He offered to purchase it from his young brother-in-law, but Sigmund refused to part with it at any price, declaring that it was clear that the weapon had been intended for him to wear. This refusal so offended Siggeir that he secretly resolved to exterminate the proud Volsungs, and to secure the divine sword at the same time that he indulged his hatred towards his new kinsmen.

Concealing his chagrin, however, he turned to Volsung and cordially invited him to visit his court a month later, together with his sons and kinsmen. The invitation was immediately accepted, and although Signy, suspecting evil, secretly sought her father while her husband slept, and implored him to retract his promise and stay at home, he would not consent to withdraw his plighted word and so exhibit fear.

Siggeir's Treachery

A few weeks after the return of the bridal couple, therefore, Volsung's well-manned vessels arrived within sight of Siggeir's shores. Signy had been keeping anxious watch, and when she perceived them she hastened down to the beach to implore her kinsmen not to land, warning them that her husband had treacherously planned an ambush, whence they could not escape alive. But Volsung and his sons, whom no peril could daunt, calmly bade her return to her husband's palace, and donning their arms they boldly set foot ashore.

" Then sweetly Volsung kissed her: ' Woe am I for thy sake,
But Earth the word hath hearkened, that yet unborn I spake;
How I ne'er would turn me backward from the sword or fire of bale;
—I have held that word till to-day, and to-day shall I change the tale ?
And look on these thy brethren, how goodly and great are they,
Wouldst thou have the maidens mock them, when this pain hath passed away
And they sit at the feast hereafter, that they feared the deadly stroke ?
Let us do our day's work deftly for the praise and glory of folk ;
And if the Norns will have it that the Volsung kin shall fail,
Yet I know of the deed that dies not, and the name that shall ever avail.' "

It befell as Signy had said, for on their way to the palace the brave little troop fell into Siggeir's ambush, and, although they fought with heroic courage, they were so borne down by the superior number of their foes that Volsung was slain and all his sons were made captive. The young men were led bound into the presence of the cowardly Siggeir, who had taken no part in the fight, and Sigmund was forced to relinquish his precious sword, after which he and his brothers were condemned to death.

Signy, hearing the cruel sentence, vainly interceded for her brothers : all she could obtain by her prayers and entreaties was that they should be chained to a fallen oak in the forest, to perish of hunger and thirst if the wild beasts should spare them. Then, lest she should visit and succour her brothers, Siggeir confined his wife in the palace, where she was closely guarded night and day.

Every morning early Siggeir himself sent a messenger into the forest to see whether the Volsungs were still living, and every morning the man returned saying a monster had come during the night and had devoured one of the princes, leaving nothing but his bones. At last, when none but Sigmund remained alive, Signy thought of a plan, and she prevailed on one of her servants to carry some honey into the forest and smear it over her brother's face and mouth.

When the wild beast came that night, attracted by the smell of the honey, it licked Sigmund's face, and even thrust its tongue into his mouth. Clinching his teeth upon it, Sigmund, weak and wounded as he was, held on to the animal, and in its frantic struggles his bonds gave way, and he succeeded in slaying the prowling beast who had devoured his brothers. Then he vanished into the forest, where he remained concealed until the king's messenger had come as usual, and until Signy, released from captivity, came speeding to the forest to weep over her kinsmen's remains.

Seeing her intense grief, and knowing that she had not participated in Siggeir's cruelty, Sigmund stole out of his place of concealment and comforted her as best he could. Together they then buried the whitening bones, and Sigmund registered a solemn oath to avenge his family's wrongs. This vow was fully approved by Signy, who, however, bade her brother bide a favourable time, promising to send him aid. Then the brother and sister sadly parted, she to return to her distasteful palace home, and he to a remote part of the forest, where he built a tiny hut and plied the craft of a smith.

" And men say that Signy wept
When she left that last of her kindred: yet wept she never more
Amid the earls of Siggeir, and as lovely as before
Was her face to all men's deeming: nor aught it changed for ruth,
Nor for fear nor any longing ; and no man said for sooth
That she ever laughed thereafter till the day of her death was
     come."

Signy's Sons

Siggeir now took possession of the Volsung kingdom,
and during the next few years he proudly watched the
growth of his eldest son, whom Signy secretly sent to
her brother when he was ten years of age, that Sigmund
might train up the child to help him to obtain vengeance if he should prove worthy. Sigmund reluctantly
accepted the charge ; but as soon as he had tested the
boy he found him deficient in physical courage, so he
either sent him back to his mother, or, as some versions
relate, slew him.

Some time after this Signy's second son was sent
into the forest for the same purpose, but Sigmund
found him equally lacking in courage. Evidently
none but a pure-blooded Volsung would avail for the
grim work of revenge, and Signy, realising this, resolved
to commit a crime.

"And once in the dark she murmured : 'Where then was the
     ancient song
That the Gods were but twin-born once, and deemed it nothing
     wrong
To mingle for the world's sake, whence had the Æsir birth,
And the Vanir and the Dwarf-kind, and all the folk of earth ?' "

Her resolution taken, she summoned a beautiful
young witch, and exchanging forms with her, she
sought the depths of the dark forest and took shelter
in Sigmund's hut. The Volsung did not penetrate
his sister's disguise. He deemed her nought but the
258

gypsy she seemed, and being soon won by her coquetry, he made her his wife. Three days later she disappeared from the hut, and, returning to the palace, she resumed her own form, and when she next gave birth to a son, she rejoiced to see in his bold glance and strong frame the promise of a true Volsung hero.

Sinfiotli

When Sinfiotli, as the child was called, was ten years of age, she herself made a preliminary test of his courage by sewing his garment to his skin, and then suddenly snatching it off, and as the brave boy did not so much as wince, but laughed aloud, she confidently sent him to the forest hut. Sigmund speedily prepared his usual test, and ere leaving the hut one day he bade Sinfiotli take meal from a certain sack, and knead it and bake some bread. On returning home, Sigmund asked whether his orders had been carried out. The lad replied by showing the bread, and when closely questioned he artlessly confessed that he had been obliged to knead into the loaf a great adder which was hidden in the meal. Pleased to see that the boy, for whom he felt a strange affection, had successfully stood the test which had daunted his brothers, Sigmund bade him refrain from eating of the loaf, for although he was proof against the bite of a reptile, he could not, like his mentor, taste poison unharmed.

" For here, the tale of the elders doth men a marvel to wit,
That such was the shaping of Sigmund among all earthly kings,
That unhurt he handled adders and other deadly things,
And might drink unscathed of venom : but Sinfiotli was so wrought
That no sting of creeping creatures would harm his body aught."

The Werewolves

Sigmund now began patiently to teach Sinfiotli all

that a warrior of the North should know, and the two soon became inseparable companions. One day while ranging the forest together they came to a hut, where they found two men sound asleep. Near by hung two wolf-skins, which suggested immediately that the strangers were werewolves, whom a cruel spell prevented from bearing their natural form save for a short space at a time. Prompted by curiosity, Sigmund and Sinfiotli donned the wolf-skins, and they were soon, in the guise of wolves, rushing through the forest, slaying and devouring all that came in their way.

Such were their wolfish passions that soon they attacked each other, and after a fierce struggle Sinfiotli, the younger and weaker, fell dead. This catastrophe brought Sigmund to his senses, and he hung over his murdered companion in despair. While thus engaged he saw two weasels come out of the forest and attack each other fiercely until one lay dead. The victor then sprang into the thicket, to return with a leaf, which it laid upon its companion's breast. Then was seen a marvellous thing, for at the touch of the magic herb the dead beast came back to life. A moment later a raven flying overhead dropped a similar leaf at Sigmund's feet, and he, understanding that the gods wished to help him, laid it upon Sinfiotli, who was at once restored to life.

In dire fear lest they might work each other further mischief, Sigmund and Sinfiotli now crept home and patiently waited until the time of their release should come. To their great relief the skins dropped off on the ninth night, and they hastily flung them into the fire, where they were entirely consumed, and the spell was broken for ever.

The Were-wolves
J. C. Dollman

SIGMUND AND SINFIOTLI TAKEN

Sigmund and Sinfiotli taken by Siggeir

Sigmund now confided the story of his wrongs to Sinfiotli, who swore that, although Siggeir was his father (for neither he nor Sigmund knew the secret of his birth), he would aid him in his revenge. At nightfall, therefore, he accompanied Sigmund to the king's hall, and they entered unseen, concealing themselves in the cellar, behind the huge vats of beer. Here they were discovered by Signy's two youngest children, who, while playing with golden rings, which rolled into the cellar, came suddenly upon the men in ambush.

They loudly proclaimed their discovery to their father and his guests, but, before Siggeir and his men could take up arms, Signy took both children, and dragging them into the cellar bade her brother slay the little traitors. This Sigmund utterly refused to do, but Sinfiotli struck off their heads ere he turned to fight against the assailants, who were now closing in upon them.

In spite of all efforts Sigmund and his brave young companion soon fell into the hands of the Goths, whereupon Siggeir sentenced them to be buried alive in the same mound, with a stone partition between them so that they could neither see nor touch each other. The prisoners were accordingly confined in their living grave, and their foes were about to place the last stones on the roof, when Signy drew near, bearing a bundle of straw, which she was allowed to throw at Sinfiotli's feet, for the Goths fancied that it contained only a few provisions which would prolong his agony without helping him to escape.

When all was still, Sinfiotli undid the sheaf, and great was his joy when he found instead of bread the sword which Odin had given to Sigmund. Knowing that nothing could dull or break the keen edge of this fine weapon, Sinfiotli thrust it through the stone partition, and, aided by Sigmund, he succeeded in cutting an opening, and in the end both effected their escape through the roof.

> "Then in the grave-mound's darkness did Sigmund the king upstand,
>   And unto that saw of battle he set his naked hand ;
>   And hard the gift of Odin home to their breasts they drew ;
>   Sawed Sigmund, sawed Sinfiotli, till the stone was cleft atwo,
>   And they met and kissed together : then they hewed and heaved full hard
>   Till, lo, through the bursten rafters the winter heavens bestarred !
>   And they leap out merry-hearted ; nor is there need to say
>   A many words between them of whither was the way."

Sigmund's Vengeance

As soon as they were free, Sigmund and Sinfiotli returned to the king's hall, and piling combustible materials around it, they set fire to the mass. Then stationing themselves on either side of the entrance, they prevented all but the women from passing through. They loudly adjured Signy to escape ere it was too late, but she did not desire to live, and so coming to the entrance for a last embrace she found opportunity to whisper the secret of Sinfiotli's birth, after which she sprang back into the flames and perished with the rest.

> "And then King Siggeir's roof-tree upheaved for its utmost fall,
>   And its huge walls clashed together, and its mean and lowly things
>   The fire of death confounded with the tokens of the kings."

Helgi

The long-planned vengeance for the slaughter of the Volsungs having thus been carried out, Sigmund, feeling that nothing now detained him in the land of

the Goths, set sail with Sinfiotli and returned to Huna-
land, where he was warmly welcomed to the seat of
power under the shade of his ancestral tree, the mighty
Branstock.   When his authority was fully established,
Sigmund married Borghild, a beautiful princess, who
bore him two sons, Hamond and Helgi.   The latter
was visited by the Norns as he lay in his cradle, and
they promised him sumptuous entertainment in Valhalla
when his earthly career should be ended.

> " And the woman was fair and lovely and bore him sons of fame ;
>   Men called them Hamond and Helgi, and when Helgi first saw
>   light,   ·
>   There came the Norns to his cradle and gave him life full bright,
>   And called him Sunlit Hill, Sharp Sword, and Land of Rings,
>   And bade him be lovely and great, and a joy in the tale of kings."

Northern kings generally entrusted their sons' up-
bringing to a stranger, for they thought that so they
would be treated with less indulgence than at home.
Accordingly Helgi was fostered by Hagal, and under
his care the young prince became so fearless that at the
age of fifteen he ventured alone into the hall of Hunding, with whose race his family was at feud.   Passing
through the hall unmolested and unrecognised, he left
an insolent message, which so angered Hunding that
he immediately set out in pursuit of the bold young
prince, whom he followed to the dwelling of Hagal.
Helgi would then have been secured but that meanwhile he had disguised himself as a servant-maid, and
was busy grinding corn as if this were his wonted
occupation.   The invaders marvelled somewhat at the
maid's tall stature and brawny arms, nevertheless they
departed without suspecting that they had been so near
the hero whom they sought.

Having thus cleverly escaped, Helgi joined Sinfiotli,

and collecting an army, the two young men marched
boldly against the Hundings, with whom they fought
a great battle, over which the Valkyrs hovered, waiting
to convey the slain to Valhalla. Gudrun, one of the
battle-maidens, was so struck by the courage which
Helgi displayed, that she openly sought him and
promised to be his wife. Only one of the Hunding
race, Dag, remained alive, and he was allowed to go
free after promising not to endeavour to avenge his
kinsmen's death. This promise was not kept, however, and Dag, having obtained possession of Odin's
spear Gungnir, treacherously slew Helgi with it.
Gudrun, who in the meantime had fulfilled her promise
to become his wife, wept many tears at his death, and
laid a solemn curse upon his murderer; then, hearing
from one of her maids that her slain husband kept
calling for her from the depths of the tomb, she fear-
lessly entered the mound at night and tenderly inquired
why he called and why his wounds continued to bleed
after death. Helgi answered that he could not rest
happy because of her grief, and declared that for every
tear she shed a drop of his blood must flow.

> " Thou weepest, gold-adorned!
> Cruel tears,
> Sun-bright daughter of the south !
> Ere to sleep thou goest ;
> Each one falls bloody
> On the prince's breast,
> Wet, cold, and piercing,
> With sorrow big."
> *Sæmund's Edda* (*Thorpe's tr.*).

To appease the spirit of her beloved husband,
Gudrun from that time ceased to weep, but they did
not long remain separated ; for soon after the spirit of
Helgi had ridden over Bifröst and entered Valhalla,

A Hero's Farewell
M. E. Winge

to become leader of the Einheriar, he was joined by Gudrun who, as a Valkyr once more, resumed her loving tendance of him. When at Odin's command she left his side for scenes of human strife, it was to seek new recruits for the army which her lord was to lead into battle when Ragnarok, the twilight of the gods, should come.

The Death of Sinfiotli

Sinfiotli, Sigmund's eldest son, also met an early death; for, having slain in a quarrel the brother of Borghild, she determined to poison him. Twice Sinfiotli detected the attempt and told his father that there was poison in his cup. Twice Sigmund, whom no venom could injure, drained the bowl; and when Borghild made a third attempt, he bade Sinfiotli let the wine flow through his beard. Mistaking the meaning of his father's words, Sinfiotli forthwith drained the cup, and fell lifeless to the ground, for the poison was of the most deadly kind.

" He drank as he spake the word, and forthwith the venom ran
In a chill flood over his heart and down fell the mighty man
With never an uttered death-word and never a death-changed
    look,
And the floor of the hall of the Volsungs beneath his falling
    shook.
Then up rose the elder of days with a great and bitter cry,
And lifted the head of the fallen; and none durst come anigh
To hearken the words of his sorrow, if any words he said
But such as the Father of all men might speak over Baldur dead.
And again, as before the death-stroke, waxed the hall of the
    Volsungs dim,
And once more he seemed in the forest, where he spake with
    nought but him."

Speechless with grief, Sigmund tenderly raised his son's body in his arms, and strode out of the hall and down to the shore, where he deposited his precious burden in a skiff which an old one-eyed boatman brought at his call. He would fain have stepped aboard also, but ere he could do so the boatman pushed off and the frail craft was soon lost to sight. The bereaved father then slowly wended his way home, taking comfort from the thought that Odin himself had come to claim the young hero and had rowed away with him " out into the west."

Hiordis

Sigmund deposed Borghild as his wife and queen in punishment for this crime, and when he was very old he sued for the hand of Hiordis, a fair young princess, daughter of Eglimi, King of the Islands. This young maiden had many suitors, among others King Lygni of Hunding's race, but so great was Sigmund's fame that she gladly accepted him and became his wife. Lygni, the discarded suitor, was so angry at this decision, that he immediately collected a great army and marched against his successful rival, who, though overpowered by superior numbers, fought with the courage of despair.

From the depths of a thicket which commanded the field of battle, Hiordis and her maid anxiously watched the progress of the strife. They saw Sigmund pile the dead around him, for none could stand against him, until at last a tall, one-eyed warrior suddenly appeared, and the press of battle gave way before the terror of his presence.

Without a moment's pause the new champion aimed a fierce blow at Sigmund, which the old hero parried with his sword. The shock shattered the matchless blade, and although the strange assailant vanished as he had come, Sigmund was left defenceless and was soon wounded unto death by his foes.

HIORDIS

" But lo, through the hedge of the war-shafts, a mighty man there
 came,
One-eyed and seeming ancient, but his visage shone like flame :
Gleaming grey was his kirtle, and his hood was cloudy blue ;
And he bore a mighty twi-bill, as he waded the fight-sheaves
 through,
And stood face to face with Sigmund, and upheaved the bill to
 smite.
Once more round the head of the Volsung fierce glittered the
 Branstock's light,
The sword that came from Odin ; and Sigmund's cry once more
Rang out to the very heavens above the din of war.
Then clashed the meeting edges with Sigmund's latest stroke,
And in shivering shards fell earthward that fear of worldly folk.
But changed were the eyes of Sigmund, and the war-wrath left his
 face ;
For that grey-clad, mighty helper was gone, and in his place
Drave on the unbroken spear-wood 'gainst the Volsung's empty
 hands :
And there they smote down Sigmund, the wonder of all lands,
On the foemen, on the death-heap his deeds had piled that day."

As the battle was now won, and the Volsung family
all slain, Lygni hastened from the battlefield to take
possession of the kingdom and force the fair Hiordis
to become his wife. As soon as he had gone, however,
the beautiful young queen crept from her hiding-place
in the thicket, and sought the spot where Sigmund
lay all but dead. She caught the stricken hero to her
breast in a last passionate embrace, and then listened
tearfully while he bade her gather the fragments of his
sword and carefully treasure them for their son whom he
foretold was soon to be born, and who was destined to
avenge his father's death and to be far greater than he.

" ' I have wrought for the Volsungs truly, and yet have I known
 full well
That a better one than I am shall bear the tale to tell :
And for him shall these shards be smithied : and he shall be my son,
To remember what I have forgotten and to do what I left
 undone.' "

Elf, the Viking

While Hiordis was mourning over Sigmund's lifeless body, her handmaiden suddenly warned her of the approach of a band of vikings. Retreating into the thicket once more, the two women exchanged garments, after which Hiordis bade the maid walk first and personate the queen, and they went thus to meet the viking Elf (Helfrat or Helferich). Elf received the women graciously, and their story of the battle so excited his admiration for Sigmund that he caused the remains of the slain hero to be reverentially removed to a suitable spot, where they were interred with all due ceremony. He then offered the queen and her maid a safe asylum in his hall, and they gladly accompanied him over the seas.

As he had doubted their relative positions from the first, Elf took the first opportunity after arriving in his kingdom to ask a seemingly idle question in order to ascertain the truth. He asked the pretended queen how she knew the hour had come for rising when the winter days were short and there was no light to announce the coming of morn, and she replied that, as she was in the habit of drinking milk ere she fed the cows, she always awoke thirsty. When the same question was put to the real Hiordis, she answered, with as little reflection, that she knew it was morning because at that hour the golden ring which her father had given her grew cold on her hand.

The Birth of Sigurd

The suspicions of Elf having thus been confirmed, he offered marriage to the pretended handmaiden, Hiordis, promising to cherish her infant son, a promise which he nobly kept. When the child was born Elf

The Funeral Procession

H. Hendrich

By Permission of the "Illustrirte Zeitung" (J. J. Weber, Leipzig)

himself sprinkled him with water—a ceremony which
our pagan ancestors scrupulously observed—and bestowed upon him the name of Sigurd. As he grew
up he was treated as the king's own son, and his
education was entrusted to Regin, the wisest of men,
who knew all things, his own fate not even excepted,
for it had been revealed to him that he would fall by
the hand of a youth.

" Again in the house of the Helper there dwelt a certain man,
Beardless and low of stature, of visage pinched and wan :
So exceeding old was Regin, that no son of man could tell
In what year of the days passed over he came to that land to
    dwell :
But the youth of king Elf had he fostered, and the Helper's youth
    thereto,
Yea and his father's father's : the lore of all men he knew,
And was deft in every cunning, save the dealings of the sword :
So sweet was his tongue-speech fashioned, that men trowed · his
    every word ;
His hand with the harp-strings blended was the mingler of
    delight
With the latter days of sorrow ; all tales he told aright ;
The Master of the Masters in the smithying craft was he ;
And he dealt with the wind and the weather and the stilling of
    the sea ;
Nor might any learn him leech-craft, for before that race was
    made,
And that man-folk's generation, all their life-days had he
    weighed."

Under this tutor Sigurd grew daily in wisdom until
few could surpass him. He mastered the smith's
craft, and the art of carving all manner of runes ; he
learned languages, music, and eloquence ; and, last but
not least, he became a doughty warrior whom none
could subdue. When he had reached manhood Regin
prompted him to ask the king for a war-horse, a
request which was immediately granted, and Gripir,
the stud-keeper, was bidden to allow him to choose

from the royal stables the steed which he most fancied.

On his way to the meadow where the horses were at pasture, Sigurd met a one-eyed stranger, clad in grey and blue, who accosted the young man and bade him drive the horses into the river and select the one which could breast the tide with least difficulty.

Sigurd received the advice gladly, and upon reaching the meadow he drove the horses into the stream which flowed on one side. One of the number, after crossing, raced round the opposite meadow; and, plunging again into the river, returned to his former pasture without showing any signs of fatigue. Sigurd therefore did not hesitate to select this horse, and he gave him the name of Grane or Greyfell. The steed was a descendant of Odin's eight-footed horse Sleipnir, and besides being unusually strong and indefatigable, was as fearless as his master.

One winter day while Regin and his pupil were sitting by the fire, the old man struck his harp, and, after the manner of the Northern scalds, sang or recited in the following tale, the story of his life:

The Treasure of the Dwarf King

Hreidmar, king of the dwarf folk, was the father of three sons. Fafnir, the eldest, was gifted with a fearless soul and a powerful arm; Otter, the second, with snare and net, and the power of changing his form at will; and Regin, the youngest, with all wisdom and deftness of hand. To please the avaricious Hreidmar, this youngest son fashioned for him a house lined with glittering gold and flashing gems, and this was guarded by Fafnir, whose fierce glances and Ægis helmet none dared encounter.

270

THE TREASURE OF THE DWARF KING

Now it came to pass that Odin, Hoenir, and Loki once came in human guise, upon one of their wonted expeditions to test the hearts of men, unto the land where Hreidmar dwelt.

"And the three were the heart-wise Odin, the Father of the Slain,
And Loki, the World's Begrudger, who maketh all labour vain,
And Hænir, the Utter-Blameless, who wrought the hope of man,
And his heart and inmost yearnings, when first the work began ;—
The God that was aforetime, and hereafter yet shall be
When the new light yet undreamed of shall shine o'er earth and sea."

As the gods came near to Hreidmar's dwelling, Loki perceived an otter basking in the sun. This was none other than the dwarf king's second son, Otter, who now succumbed to Loki's usual love of destruction. Killing the unfortunate creature he flung its lifeless body over his shoulders, thinking it would furnish a good dish when meal time came.

Loki then hastened after his companions, and entering Hreidmar's house with them, he flung his burden down upon the floor. The moment the dwarf king's glance fell upon the seeming otter, he flew into a towering rage, and ere they could offer effective resistance the gods found themselves lying bound, and they heard Hreidmar declare that never should they recover their liberty until they could satisfy his thirst for gold by giving him of that precious substance enough to cover the skin of the otter inside and out.

" ' Now hearken the doom I shall speak ! Ye stranger-folk shall be free
When ye give me the Flame of the Waters, the gathered Gold of the Sea,
That Andvari hideth rejoicing in the wan realm pale as the grave ;
And the Master of Sleight shall fetch it, and the hand that never gave,

And the heart that begrudgeth for ever, shall gather and give and
    rue.
—Lo, this is the doom of the wise, and no doom shall be spoken
    anew.'"

As the otter-skin developed the property of stretch-
ing itself to a fabulous size, no ordinary treasure could
suffice to cover it, and the plight of the gods, therefore,
was a very bad one. The case, however, became a little
more hopeful when Hreidmar consented to liberate one
of their number. The emissary selected was Loki, who
lost no time in setting off to the waterfall where the
dwarf Andvari dwelt, in order that he might secure the
treasure there amassed.

"There is a desert of dread in the uttermost part of the world,
    Where over a wall of mountains is a mighty water hurled,
    Whose hidden head none knoweth, nor where it meeteth the sea ;
    And that force is the Force of Andvari, and an Elf of the Dark
        is he.
    In the cloud and the desert he dwelleth amid that land alone ;
    And his work is the storing of treasure within his house of stone."

In spite of diligent search, however, Loki could not
find the dwarf, until, perceiving a salmon sporting in
the foaming waters, it occurred to him that the dwarf
might have assumed this shape. Borrowing Ran's net
he soon caught the fish, and learned, as he had suspected,
that it was Andvari. Finding that there was nothing
else for it, the dwarf now reluctantly brought forth his
mighty treasure and surrendered it all, including the
Helmet of Dread and a hauberk of gold, reserving
only a ring which was gifted with miraculous powers,
and which, like a magnet, attracted the precious ore.
But the greedy Loki, catching sight of it, wrenched it
from off the dwarf's finger and departed laughing, while
his victim hurled angry curses after him, declaring that
the ring would ever prove its possessor's bane and would
cause the death of many.

THE TREASURE OF THE DWARF KING

"That gold
Which the dwarf possessed
Shall to two brothers
Be cause of death,
And to eight princes,
Of dissension.
From my wealth no one
Shall good derive."

Sæmund's Edda (Thorpe's tr.).

On arriving at Hreidmar's house, Loki found the mighty treasure none too great, for the skin became larger with every object placed upon it, and he was forced to throw in the ring Andvaranaut (Andvari's loom), which he had intended to retain, in order to secure the release of himself and his companions. Andvari's curse of the gold soon began to operate. Fafnir and Regin both coveted a share, while Hriedmar gloated over his treasure night and day, and would not part with an item of it. Fafnir the invincible, seeing at last that he could not otherwise gratify his lust, slew his father, and seized the whole of the treasure, then, when Regin came to claim a share he drove him scornfully away and bade him earn his own living.

Thus exiled, Regin took refuge among men, to whom he taught the arts of sowing and reaping. He showed them how to work metals, sail the seas, tame horses, yoke beasts of burden, build houses, spin, weave, and sew—in short, all the industries of civilised life, which had hitherto been unknown. Years elapsed, and Regin patiently bided his time, hoping that some day he would find a hero strong enough to avenge his wrongs upon Fafnir, whom years of gloating over his treasure had changed into a horrible dragon, the terror of Gnîtaheid (Glittering Heath), where he had taken up his abode.

His story finished, Regin turned suddenly to the attentive Sigurd, saying he knew that the young man could slay the dragon if he wished, and inquiring whether he were ready to aid him to avenge his wrongs.

> " And he spake: ' Hast thou hearkened, Sigurd ? Wilt thou help a man that is old
> To avenge him for his father ? Wilt thou win that treasure of Gold
> And be more than the Kings of the earth ? Wilt thou rid the earth of a wrong
> And heal the woe and the sorrow my heart hath endured o'er long ? ' "

Sigurd's Sword

Sigurd immediately assented, on the condition, however, that the curse should be assumed by Regin, who, also, in order to fitly equip the young man for the coming fight, should forge him a sword which no blow could break. Twice Regin fashioned a marvellous weapon, but twice Sigurd broke it to pieces on the anvil. Then Sigurd bethought him of the broken fragments of Sigmund's weapon which were treasured by his mother, and going to Hiordis he begged these from her ; and either he or Regin forged from them a blade so strong that it divided the great anvil in two without being dinted, and whose temper was such that it neatly severed some wool floating gently upon the stream.

Sigurd now went upon a farewell visit to Gripir, who, knowing the future, foretold every event in his coming career ; after which he took leave of his mother, and accompanied by Regin set sail for the land of his fathers, vowing to slay the dragon when he had fulfilled his first duty, which was to avenge the death of Sigmund.

274

Sigurd and Fafnir
K. Dielitz
By Permission of the Berlin Photographic Co., 133 New Bond St., W.

274

THE FIGHT WITH THE DRAGON

> " ' First wilt thou, prince,
> Avenge thy father,
> And for the wrongs of Eglymi
> Wilt retaliate.
> Thou wilt the cruel,
> The sons of Hunding,
> Boldly lay low :
> Thou wilt have victory.' "
>
> *Lay of Sigurd Fafnicide (Thorpe's tr.).*

On his way to the land of the Volsungs a most marvellous sight was seen, for there came a man walking on the waters. Sigurd straightway took him on board his dragon ship, and the stranger, who gave his name as Feng or Fiöllnir, promised favourable winds. Also he taught Sigurd how to distinguish auspicious omens. In reality the old man was Odin or Hnikar, the wave-stiller, but Sigurd did not suspect his identity.

The Fight with the Dragon

Sigurd was entirely successful in his descent upon Lygni, whom he slew, together with many of his followers. He then departed from his reconquered kingdom and returned with Regin to slay Fafnir. Together they rode through the mountains, which ever rose higher and higher before them, until they came to a great tract of desert which Regin said was the haunt of Fafnir. Sigurd now rode on alone until he met a one-eyed stranger, who bade him dig trenches in the middle of the track along which the dragon daily dragged his slimy length to the river to quench his thirst, and to lie in wait in one of these until the monster passed over him, when he could thrust his sword straight into its heart.

Sigurd gratefully followed this counsel, and was

275

rewarded with complete success, for as the monster's loathsome folds rolled overhead, he thrust his sword upward into its left breast, and as he sprang out of the trench the dragon lay gasping in the throes of death.

> "Then all sank into silence, and the son of Sigmund stood
> On the torn and furrowed desert by the pool of Fafnir's blood,
> And the Serpent lay before him, dead, chilly, dull, and grey ;
> And over the Glittering Heath fair shone the sun and the day,
> And a light wind followed the sun and breathed o'er the fateful place,
> As fresh as it furrows the sea-plain, or bows the acres' face."

Regin had prudently remained at a distance until all danger was past, but seeing that his foe was slain, he now came up. He was fearful lest the young hero should claim a reward, so he began to accuse him of having murdered his kin, but, with feigned magnanimity, he declared that instead of requiring life for life, in accordance with the custom of the North, he would consider it sufficient atonement if Sigurd would cut out the monster's heart and roast it for him on a spit.

> "Then Regin spake to Sigurd : 'Of this slaying wilt thou be free ?
> Then gather thou fire together and roast the heart for me,
> That I may eat it and live, and be thy master and more ;
> For therein was might and wisdom, and the grudged and hoarded lore :
> —Or, else depart on thy ways afraid from the Glittering Heath.'"

Sigurd was aware that a true warrior never refused satisfaction of some kind to the kindred of the slain, so he agreed to the seemingly small proposal, and immediately prepared to act as cook, while Regin dozed until the meat was ready. After an interval Sigurd touched the roast to ascertain whether it were tender, but burning his fingers severely, he instinctively thrust them into his mouth to allay the smart. No sooner had Fafnir's blood thus touched his lips than he discovered, to his utter surprise, that he could understand the songs of the birds, many of which were already gathering round the carrion. Listening attentively, he found that they were telling how Regin meditated mischief against him, and how he ought to slay the old man and take the gold, which was his by right of conquest, after which he ought to partake of the heart and blood of the dragon. As this coincided with his own wishes, he slew the evil old man with a thrust of his sword and proceeded to eat and drink as the birds had suggested, reserving a small portion of Fafnir's heart for future consumption. He then wandered off in search of the mighty hoard, and, after donning the Helmet of Dread, the hauberk of gold, and the ring Andvaranaut, and loading Greyfell with as much gold as he could carry, he sprang to the saddle and sat listening eagerly to the birds' songs to know what his future course should be.

The Sleeping Warrior Maiden

Soon he heard of a warrior maiden fast asleep on a mountain and surrounded by a glittering barrier of flames, through which only the bravest of men could pass to arouse her.

> "On the fell I know
> A warrior maid to sleep;
> Over her waves
> The linden's bane:
> Ygg whilom stuck
> A sleep-thorn in the robe
> Of the maid who
> Would heroes choose."
>
> *Lay of Fafnir* (*Thorpe's tr.*).

This adventure was the very thing for Sigurd, and he set off at once. The way lay through trackless regions, and the journey was long and cheerless, but at length he came to the Hindarfiall in Frankland, a tall mountain whose cloud-wreathed summit seemed circled by fiery flames.

> "Long Sigurd rideth the waste, when, lo, on a morning of day,
> From out of the tangled crag-walls, amidst the cloudland grey,
> Comes up a mighty mountain, and it is as though there burns
> A torch amidst of its cloud-wreath ; so thither Sigurd turns,
> For he deems indeed from its topmost to look on the best of the earth ;
> And Greyfell neigheth beneath him, and his heart is full of mirth."

Sigurd rode up the mountain side, and the light grew more and more vivid as he proceeded, until when he had neared the summit a barrier of lurid flames stood before him. The fire burned with a roar which would have daunted the heart of any other, but Sigurd remembered the words of the birds, and without a moment's hesitation he plunged bravely into its very midst.

> "Now Sigurd turns in his saddle, and the hilt of the Wrath he shifts,
> And draws a girth the tighter ; then the gathered reins he lifts,
> And crieth aloud to Greyfell, and rides at the wildfire's heart ;
> But the white wall wavers before him and the flame-flood rusheth apart,
> And high o'er his head it riseth, and wide and wild its roar
> As it beareth the mighty tidings to the very heavenly floor :
> But he rideth through its roaring as the warrior rides the rye,
> When it bows with the wind of the summer and the hid spears draw anigh ;
> The white flame licks his raiment and sweeps through Greyfell's mane,
> And bathes both hands of Sigurd and the hilt of Fafnir's bane,
> And winds about his war-helm and mingles with his hair,

Sigurd finds Brunhild

J. Wagrez

THE SLEEPING WARRIOR MAIDEN

But nought his raiment dusketh or dims his glittering gear;
Then it fails and fades and darkens till all seems left behind,
And dawn and the blaze is swallowed in mid-mirk stark and
    blind."

The threatening flames having now died away, Sigurd pursued his journey over a broad tract of white ashes, directing his course to a great castle, with shield-hung walls. The great gates stood wide open, and Sigurd rode through them unchallenged by warders or men at arms. Proceeding cautiously, for he feared some snare, he at last came to the centre of the court-yard, where he saw a recumbent form cased in armour. Sigurd dismounted from his steed and eagerly removed the helmet, when he started with surprise to behold, instead of a warrior, the face of a most beautiful maiden.

All his efforts to awaken the sleeper were vain, how-ever, until he had removed her armour, and she lay before him in pure-white linen garments, her long hair falling in golden waves around her. Then as the last fastening of her armour gave way, she opened wide her beautiful eyes, which met the rising sun, and first greeting with rapture the glorious spectacle, she turned to her deliverer, and the young hero and the maiden loved each other at first sight.

" Then she turned and gazed on Sigurd, and her eyes met the Vol-
    sung's eyes.
  And mighty and measureless now did the tide of his love arise,
  For their longing had met and mingled, and he knew of her heart
    that she loved,
  And she spake unto nothing but him and her lips with the speech-
    flood moved."

The maiden now proceeded to tell Sigurd her story. Her name was Brunhild, and according to some authorities she was the daughter of an earthly king whom Odin had raised to the rank of a Valkyr. She had served him faithfully for a long while, but once had ventured to set her own wishes above his, giving to a younger and therefore more attractive opponent the victory which Odin had commanded for another.

In punishment for this act of disobedience, she had been deprived of her office and banished to earth, where Allfather decreed she should wed like any other member of her sex. This sentence filled Brunhild's heart with dismay, for she greatly feared lest it might be her fate to mate with a coward, whom she would despise. To quiet these apprehensions, Odin took her to Hindarfiall or Hindfell, and touching her with the Thorn of Sleep, that she might await in unchanged youth and beauty the coming of her destined husband, he surrounded her with a barrier of flame which none but a hero would venture through.

From the top of Hindarfiall, Brunhild now pointed out to Sigurd her former home, at Lymdale or Huna-land, telling him he would find her there whenever he chose to come and claim her as his wife ; and then, while they stood on the lonely mountain top together, Sigurd placed the ring Andvaranaut upon her finger, in token of betrothal, swearing to love her alone as long as life endured.

"From his hand then draweth Sigurd Andvari's ancient Gold ;
There is nought but the sky above them as the ring together they hold,
The shapen ancient token, that hath no change nor end,
No change, and no beginning, no flaw for God to mend :
Then Sigurd cried : 'O Brynhild, now hearken while I swear,
That the sun shall die in the heavens and the day no more be fair,
If I seek not love in Lymdale and the house that fostered thee,

Odin and Brunhild

K. Dielitz

By Permission of the Berlin Photographic Co., New Bond St., W.

THE FOSTERING OF ASLAUG

And the land where thou awakedst 'twixt the woodland and the
   sea ! '
And she cried : 'O Sigurd, Sigurd, now hearken while I swear
That the day shall die for ever and the sun to blackness wear,
Ere I forget thee, Sigurd, as I lie 'twixt wood and sea
In the little land of Lymdale and the house that fostered me ! ' "

The Fostering of Aslaug

According to some authorities, the lovers parted
after thus plighting their troth ; but others say that
Sigurd soon sought out and wedded Brunhild, with
whom he lived for a while in perfect happiness. until
forced to leave her and his infant daughter Aslaug.
This child, left orphaned at three years of age, was
fostered by Brunhild's father, who, driven away from
home, concealed her in a cunningly fashioned harp,
until reaching a distant land he was murdered by a
peasant couple for the sake of the gold they supposed
it to contain. Their surprise and disappointment
were great indeed when, on breaking the instrument
open, they found a beautiful little girl, whom they
deemed mute, as she would not speak a word. Time
passed, and the child, whom they had trained as a
drudge, grew to be a beautiful maiden, and she won
the affection of a passing viking, Ragnar Lodbrog,
King of the Danes, to whom she told her tale. The
viking sailed away to other lands to fulfil the purposes of his voyage, but when a year had passed,
during which time he won much glory, he came back
and carried away Aslaug as his bride.

> " She heard a voice she deemed well known,
> Long waited through dull hours bygone
> And round her mighty arms were cast :
> But when her trembling red lips passed
> From out the heaven of that dear kiss,
> And eyes met eyes, she saw in his

Fresh pride, fresh hope, fresh love, and saw
The long sweet days still onward draw,
Themselves still going hand in hand,
As now they went adown the strand."
The Fostering of Aslaug (*William Morris*).

In continuation of the story of Sigurd and Brunhild, however, we are told that the young man went to seek adventures in the great world, where he had vowed, as a true hero, to right the wrong and defend the fatherless and oppressed.

The Niblungs

In the course of his wanderings, Sigurd came to the land of the Niblungs, the land of continual mist, where Giuki and Grimhild were king and queen. The latter was specially to be feared, as she was well versed in magic lore, and could weave spells and concoct marvellous potions which had power to steep the drinker in temporary forgetfulness and compel him to yield to her will.

The king and queen had three sons, Gunnar, Högni, and Guttorm, who were brave young men, and one daughter, Gudrun, the gentlest as well as the most beautiful of maidens. All welcomed Sigurd most warmly, and Giuki invited him to tarry awhile. The invitation was very agreeable after his long wanderings, and Sigurd was glad to stay and share the pleasures and occupations of the Niblungs. He accompanied them to war, and so distinguished himself by his valour, that he won the admiration of Grimhild and she resolved to secure him as her daughter's husband. One day, therefore, she brewed one of her magic potions, and when he had partaken of it at the hand of Gudrun, he utterly forgot Brunhild and his plighted troth, and all his love was diverted unto the queen's daughter.

282

Aslaug

Gertrude Demain Hammond, R.I.

THE NIBLUNGS

" But the heart was changed in Sigurd ; as though it ne'er had been
His love of Brynhild perished as he gazed on the Niblung Queen:
Brynhild's beloved body was e'en as a wasted hearth,
No more for bale or blessing, for plenty or for dearth."

Although there was not wanting a vague fear that
he had forgotten some event in the past which should
rule his conduct, Sigurd asked for and obtained
Gudrun's hand, and their wedding was celebrated
amid the rejoicings of the people, who loved the
young hero very dearly. Sigurd gave his bride some
of Fafnir's heart to eat, and the moment she had tasted
it her nature was changed, and she began to grow cold
and silent to all except him. To further cement his
alliance with the two eldest Giukings (as the sons of
Giuki were called) Sigurd entered the "doom ring" with
them, and the three young men cut a sod which was
placed upon a shield, beneath which they stood while
they bared and slightly cut their right arms, allowing their blood to mingle in the fresh earth. Then,
when they had sworn eternal friendship, the sod was
replaced.

But although Sigurd loved his wife and felt a true
fraternal affection for her brothers, he could not lose
his haunting sense of oppression, and was seldom seen
to smile as radiantly as of old. Giuki had now died,
and his eldest son, Gunnar, ruled in his stead. As the
young king was unwedded, Grimhild, his mother,
besought him to take a wife, suggesting that none
seemed more worthy to become Queen of the Niblungs
than Brunhild, who, it was reported, sat in a golden
hall surrounded by flames, whence she had declared
she would issue only to marry the warrior who would
dare brave the fire for her sake.

Gunnar's Stratagem

Gunnar immediately prepared to seek this maiden, and strengthened by one of his mother's magic potions, and encouraged by Sigurd, who accompanied him, he felt confident of success. But when on reaching the summit of the mountain he would have ridden into the fire, his steed drew back affrighted and he could not induce him to advance a step. Seeing that his companion's steed did not show signs of fear, he asked him of Sigurd; but although Greyfell allowed Gunnar to mount, he would not stir because his master was not on his back.

Now as Sigurd carried the Helmet of Dread, and Grimhild had given Gunnar a magic potion in case it should be needed, it was possible for the companions to exchange their forms and features, and seeing that Gunnar could not penetrate the flaming wall Sigurd proposed to assume the appearance of Gunnar and woo the bride for him. The king was greatly disappointed, but as no alternative offered he dismounted, and the necessary exchange was soon effected. Then Sigurd mounted Greyfell in the semblance of his companion, and this time the steed showed not the least hesitation, but leaped into the flames at the first touch on his bridle, and soon brought his rider to the castle, where, in the great hall, sat Brunhild. Neither recognised the other: Sigurd because of the magic spell cast over him by Grimhild; Brunhild because of the altered appearance of her lover.

The maiden shrank in disappointment from the dark-haired intruder, for she had deemed it impossible for any but Sigurd to ride through the flaming circle. But she advanced reluctantly to meet her visitor, and when he declared that he had come to woo her, she

Sigurd and Gunnar
J. C. Dollman

permitted him to take a husband's place at her side, for she was bound by solemn injunction to accept as her spouse him who should thus seek her through the flames.

Three days did Sigurd remain with Brunhild, and his bright sword lay bared between him and his bride. This singular behaviour aroused the curiosity of the maiden, wherefore Sigurd told her that the gods had bidden him celebrate his wedding thus.

> "There they went in one bed together ; but the foster-brother laid
> 'Twixt him and the body of Brynhild his bright blue battle-blade ;
> And she looked and heeded it nothing ; but, e'en as the dead folk lie,
> With folded hands she lay there, and let the night go by :
> And as still lay that Image of Gunnar as the dead of life forlorn,
> And hand on hand he folded as he waited for the morn.
> So oft in the moonlit minster your fathers may ye see
> By the side of the ancient mothers await the day to be."

When the fourth morning dawned, Sigurd drew the ring Andvaranaut from Brunhild's hand, and, replacing it by another, he received her solemn promise that in ten days' time she would appear at the Niblung court to take up her duties as queen and faithful wife.

> "'I thank thee, King, for thy goodwill, and thy pledge of love I take,
> Depart with my troth to thy people : but ere full ten days are o'er
> I shall come to the Sons of the Niblungs, and then shall we part no more
> Till the day of the change of our life-days, when Odin and Freya shall call.'"

The promise given, Sigurd again passed out of the palace, through the ashes, and joined Gunnar, with whom, after he had reported the success of his venture, he hastened to exchange forms once more. The warriors then turned their steeds homeward, and only to Gudrun did Sigurd reveal the secret of her brother's wooing, and he gave her the fatal ring, little suspecting the many woes which it was destined to occasion.

The Coming of Brunhild

True to her promise, Brunhild appeared ten days later, and solemnly blessing the house she was about to enter, she greeted Gunnar kindly, and allowed him to conduct her to the great hall, where sat Sigurd beside Gudrun. The Volsung looked up at that moment and as he encountered Brunhild's reproachful eyes Grimhild's spell was broken and the past came back in a flood of bitter recollection. It was too late, however : both were in honour bound, he to Gudrun and she to Gunnar, whom she passively followed to the high seat, to sit beside him as the scalds entertained the royal couple with the ancient lays of their land.

The days passed, and Brunhild remained apparently indifferent, but her heart was hot with anger, and often did she steal out of her husband's palace to the forest, where she could give vent to her grief in solitude.

Meanwhile, Gunnar perceived the cold indifference of his wife to his protestations of affection, and began to have jealous suspicions, wondering whether Sigurd had honestly told the true story of the wooing, and fearing lest he had taken advantage of his position to win Brunhild's love. Sigurd alone continued the even tenor of his way, striving against none but tyrants and oppressors, and cheering all by his kindly words and smile.

The Quarrel of the Queens

On a day the queens went down together to the Rhine to bathe, and as they were entering the water Gudrun claimed precedence by right of her husband's

286

courage. Brunhild refused to yield what she deemed her right, and a quarrel ensued, in the course of which Gudrun accused her sister-in-law of not having kept her faith, producing the ring Andvaranaut in support of her charge. The sight of the fatal ring in the hand of her rival crushed Brunhild, and she fled homeward, and lay in speechless grief day after day, until all thought she must die. In vain did Gunnar and the members of the royal family seek her in turn and implore her to speak; she would not utter a word until Sigurd came and inquired the cause of her un-utterable grief. Then, like a long-pent-up stream, her love and anger burst forth, and she overwhelmed the hero with reproaches, until his heart so swelled with grief for her sorrow that the tight bands of his strong armour gave way.

> " Out went Sigurd
> From that interview
> Into the hall of kings,
> Writhing with anguish;
> So that began to start
> The ardent warrior's
> Iron-woven sark
> Off from his sides."
> *Sæmund's Edda (Thorpe s tr.).*

Words had no power to mend that woeful situation, and Brunhild refused to heed when Sigurd offered to repudiate Gudrun, saying, as she dismissed him, that she would not be faithless to Gunnar. The thought that two living men had called her wife was unendur-able to her pride, and the next time her husband sought her presence she implored him to put Sigurd to death, thus increasing his jealousy and suspicion. He refused to deal violently with Sigurd, however, because of their oath of good fellowship, and so she turned to Högni for aid. He, too, did not wish to violate his oath, but he induced Guttorm, by means of much persuasion and one of Grimhild's potions, to undertake the dastardly deed.

The Death of Sigurd

Accordingly, in the dead of night, Guttorm stole into Sigurd's chamber, weapon in hand; but as he bent over the bed he saw Sigurd's bright eyes fixed upon him, and fled precipitately. Later on he returned and the scene was repeated; but towards morning, stealing in for the third time, he found the hero asleep, and traitorously drove his spear through his back.

Although wounded unto death, Sigurd raised himself in bed, and seizing his renowned sword which hung beside him, he flung it with all his remaining strength at the flying murderer, cutting him in two as he reached the door. Then, with a last whispered farewell to the terrified Gudrun, Sigurd sank back and breathed his last.

> "'Mourn not, O Gudrun, this stroke is the last of ill;
> Fear leaveth the House of the Niblungs on this breaking of the
> morn;
> Mayst thou live, O woman belovèd, unforsaken, unforlorn!'
>
> .   .   .   .
>
> 'It is Brynhild's deed,' he murmured, 'and the woman that loves
> me well;
> Nought now is left to repent of, and the tale abides to tell.
> I have done many deeds in my life-days; and all these, and my love,
> they lie
> In the hollow hand of Odin till the day of the world go by.
> I have done and I may not undo, I have given and I take not
> again:
> Art thou other than I, Allfather, wilt thou gather my glory in
> vain?'"

Sigurd's infant son was slain at the same time, and poor Gudrun mourned over her dead in silent, tearless

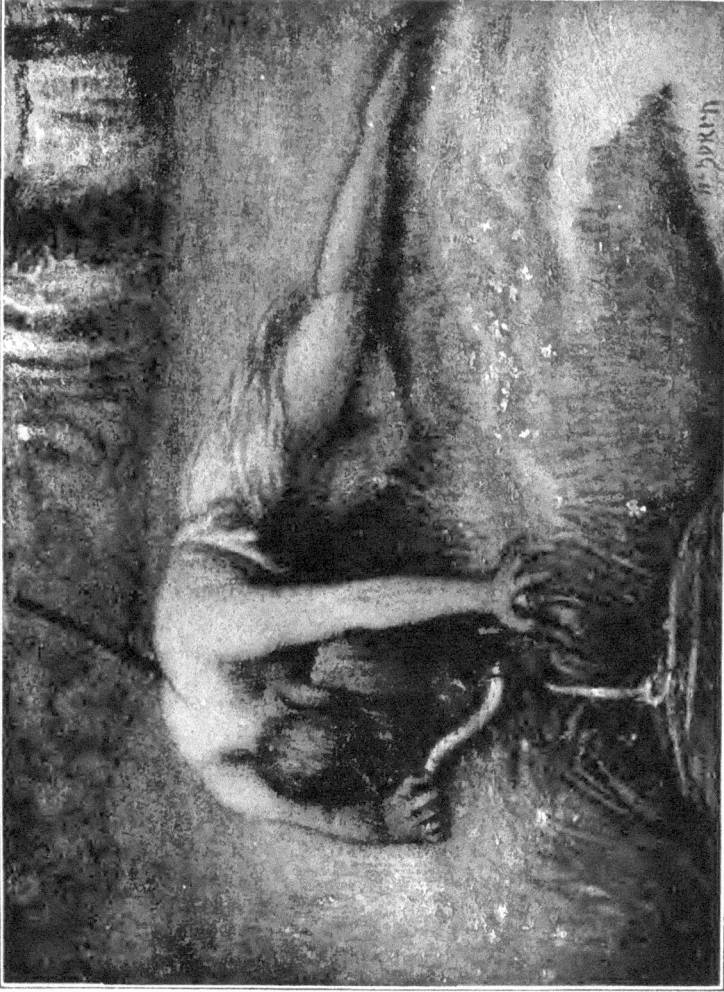

The Death of Siegfried

H. Hendrich

By Permission of the "Illustrirte Zeitung" J. J. Weber Leipzig

grief; while Brunhild laughed aloud, thereby incurring the wrath of Gunnar, who repented, too late, that he had not taken measures to avert the dastardly crime.

The grief of the Niblungs found expression in the public funeral celebration which was shortly held. A mighty pyre was erected, to which were brought precious hangings, fresh flowers, and glittering arms, as was the custom for the burial of a prince; and as these sad preparations took shape, Gudrun was the object of tender solicitude from the women, who, fearing lest her heart would break, tried to open the flood-gate of her tears by recounting the bitterest sorrows they had known, one telling of how she too had lost all she held dear. But these attempts to make her weep were utterly vain, until at length they laid her husband's head in her lap, bidding her kiss him as if he were still alive; then her tears began to flow in torrents.

The reaction soon set in for Brunhild also; her resentment was all forgotten when she saw the body of Sigurd laid on the pyre, arrayed as if for battle in burnished armour, with the Helmet of Dread at his head, and accompanied by his steed, which was to be burned with him, together with several of his faithful servants who would not survive his loss. She withdrew to her apartment, and after distributing her possessions among her handmaidens, she donned her richest array, and stabbed herself as she lay stretched upon her bed.

The tidings soon reached Gunnar, who came with all haste to his wife and just in time to receive her dying injunction to lay her beside the hero she loved, with the glittering, unsheathed sword between them, as it had lain when he had wooed her by proxy. When she had breathed her last, these wishes were faithfully

T   289 executed, and her body was burned with Sigurd's amid the lamentations of all the Niblungs.

In Richard Wagner's story of " The Ring " Brunhild's end is more picturesque. Mounted on her steed, as when she led the battle-maidens at the command of Odin, she rode into the flames which leaped to heaven from the great funeral pyre, and passed for ever from the sight of men.

" They are gone—the lovely, the mighty, the hope of the ancient
  Earth:
  It shall labour and bear the burden as before that day of their
    birth:
  It shall groan in its blind abiding for the day that Sigurd hath
    sped,
  And the hour that Brynhild hath hastened, and the dawn that
    waketh the dead:
  It shall yearn, and be oft-times holpen, and forget their deeds no
    more,
  Till the new sun beams on Baldur and the happy sea-less shore."

The death scene of Sigurd (Siegfried) is far more powerful in the Nibelungenlied. In the Teutonic version his treacherous assailant lures him from a hunting party in the forest to quench his thirst at a brook, where he thrusts him through the back with a spear. His body was thence borne home by the hunters and laid at his wife's feet.

The Flight of Gudrun

Gudrun, still inconsolable, and loathing the kindred who had treacherously robbed her of all joy in life, fled from her father's house and took refuge with Elf, Sigurd's foster father, who, after the death of Hiordis, had married Thora, the daughter of King Hakon. The two women became great friends, and here Gudrun tarried several years, employing herself in embroidering upon tapestry the great deeds of Sigurd, and watching

The End of Brunhild

J. Wagrez

over her little daughter Swanhild, whose bright eyes reminded her vividly of the husband whom she had lost.

Atli, King of the Huns

In the meantime, Atli, Brunhild's brother, who was now King of the Huns, had sent to Gunnar to demand atonement for his sister's death; and to satisfy his claims Gunnar had promised that when her years of widowhood had been accomplished he would give him Gudrun's hand in marriage. Time passed, and Atli clamoured for the fulfilment of his promise, wherefore the Niblung brothers, with their mother Grimhild, went to seek the long-absent princess, and by the aid of the magic potion administered by Grimhild they succeeded in persuading Gudrun to leave little Swanhild in Denmark and to become Atli's wife in the land of the Huns.

Nevertheless, Gudrun secretly detested her husband, whose avaricious tendencies were extremely repugnant to her; and even the birth of two sons, Erp and Eitel, did not console her for the death of her loved ones and the absence of Swanhild. Her thoughts were continually of the past, and she often spoke of it, little suspecting that her descriptions of the wealth of the Niblungs had excited Atli's greed, and that he was secretly planning some pretext for seizing it.

Atli at last decided to send Knefrud or Wingi, one of his servants, to invite the Niblung princes to visit his court, intending to slay them when he should have them in his power; but Gudrun, fathoming this design, sent a rune message to her brothers, together with the ring Andvaranaut, around which she had twined a wolf's hair. On the way, however, the messenger partly effaced the runes, thus changing their meaning; and when he appeared before the Niblungs, Gunnar

accepted the invitation, in spite of Högni's and Grimhild's warnings, and an ominous dream of Glaumvor, his second wife.

Burial of the Niblung Treasure

Before departing, however, Gunnar was prevailed upon to bury secretly the great Niblung hoard in the Rhine, and he sank it in a deep hole in the bed of the river, the position of which was known to the royal brothers only, who took a solemn oath never to reveal it.

" Down then and whirling outward the ruddy Gold fell forth,
  As a flame in the dim grey morning, flashed out a kingdom's worth;
  Then the waters roared above it, the wan water and the foam
  Flew up o'er the face of the rock-wall as the tinkling Gold fell home,
  Unheard, unseen for ever, a wonder and a tale,
  Till the last of earthly singers from the sons of men shall fail."

The Treachery of Atli

In martial array the royal band then rode out of the city of the Niblungs, which they were never again to see, and after many adventures they entered the land of the Huns, and arrived at Atli's hall, where, finding that they had been foully entrapped, they slew the traitor Knefrud, and prepared to sell their lives as dearly as possible.

Gudrun hastened to meet them with tender embraces, and, seeing that they must fight, she grasped a weapon and loyally aided them in the terrible massacre which ensued. After the first onslaught, Gunnar kept up the spirits of his followers by playing on his harp, which he laid aside only when the assaults were renewed. Thrice the brave Niblungs resisted the assault of the Huns, until all save Gunnar and Högni had perished, and the king and his brother, wounded, faint, and weary, fell into the hands of their foes, who cast them, securely bound, into a dungeon to await death.

Atli had prudently abstained from taking any active part in the fight, and he now had his brothers-in-law brought in turn before him, promising them freedom if they would reveal the hiding-place of the golden hoard; but they proudly kept silence, and it was only after much torture that Gunnar spake, saying that he had sworn a solemn oath never to reveal the secret as long as Högni lived. At the same time he declared that he would believe his brother dead only when his heart was brought to him on a platter.

"With a dreadful voice cried Gunnar : ' O fool, hast thou heard it told
    Who won the Treasure aforetime and the ruddy rings of the Gold ?
It was Sigurd, child of the Volsungs, the best sprung forth from the best :
He rode from the North and the mountains, and became my summer guest,
My friend and my brother sworn: he rode the Wavering Fire,
And won me the Queen of Glory and accomplished my desire;
The praise of the world he was, the hope of the biders in wrong,
The help of the lowly people, the hammer of the strong:
Ah, oft in the world, henceforward, shall the tale be told of the deed,
And I, e'en I, will tell it in the day of the Niblungs' Need:
For I sat night-long in my armour, and when light was wide o'er the land
I slaughtered Sigurd my brother, and looked on the work of mine hand.
And now, O mighty Atli, I have seen the Niblung's wreck,
And the feet of the faint-heart dastard have trodden Gunnar's neck;
And if all be little enough, and the Gods begrudge me rest,
Let me see the heart of Högni cut quick from his living breast,
And laid on the dish before me : and then shall I tell of the Gold,
And become thy servant, Atli, and my life at thy pleasure hold.'"

Urged by greed, Atli gave immediate orders that Högni's heart should be brought; but his servants, fearing to lay hands on such a grim warrior, slew the cowardly scullion Hialli. The trembling heart of this poor wretch called forth contemptuous words from Gunnar, who declared that such a timorous organ could never have belonged to his fearless brother. Atli again issued angry commands, and this time the unquivering heart of Högni was produced, whereupon Gunnar, turning to the monarch, solemnly swore that since the secret now rested with him alone it would never be revealed.

The Last of the Niblungs

Livid with anger, the king bade his servants throw Gunnar, with hands bound, into a den of venomous snakes; but this did not daunt the reckless Niblung, and, his harp having been flung after him in derision, he calmly sat in the pit, harping with his toes, and lulling to sleep all the reptiles save one only. It was said that Atli's mother had taken the form of this snake, and that she it was who now bit him in the side, and silenced his triumphant song for ever.

To celebrate his triumph, Atli now ordered a great feast, commanding Gudrun to be present to wait upon him. At this banquet he ate and drank heartily, little suspecting that his wife had slain both his sons, and had served up their roasted hearts and their blood mixed with wine in cups made of their skulls. After a time the king and his guests became intoxicated, when Gudrun, according to one version of the story, set fire to the palace, and as the drunken men were aroused, too late to escape, she revealed what she had done, and first stabbing her husband, she calmly perished in the flames with the Huns. Another version relates, however, that she murdered Atli with Sigurd's sword, and having placed his body on a ship, which she sent adrift, she cast herself into the sea and was drowned.

> "She spread out her arms as she spake it, and away from the earth she leapt
> And cut off her tide of returning: for the sea-waves over her swept,
> And their will is her will henceforward, and who knoweth the deeps of the sea,
> And the wealth of the bed of Gudrun, and the days that yet shall be?"

According to a third and very different version, Gudrun was not drowned, but was borne by the waves to the land where Jonakur was king. There she became his wife, and the mother of three sons, Sörli, Hamdir, and Erp. She recovered possession, moreover, of her beloved daughter Swanhild, who, in the meantime, had grown into a beautiful maiden of marriageable age.

Swanhild

Swanhild became affianced to Ermenrich, King of Gothland, who sent his son, Randwer, and one of his servants, Sibich, to escort the bride to his kingdom. Sibich was a traitor, and as part of a plan to compass the death of the royal family that he might claim the kingdom, he accused Randwer of having tried to win his young stepmother's affections. This accusation so roused the anger of Ermenrich that he ordered his son to be hanged, and Swanhild to be trampled to death under the feet of wild horses. The beauty of this daughter of Sigurd and Gudrun was such, however, that even the wild steeds could not be induced to harm her until she had been hidden from their sight under a great blanket, when they trod her to death under their cruel hoofs.

Upon learning the fate of her beloved daughter, Gudrun called her three sons to her side, and girding them with armour and weapons against which nothing but stone could prevail, she bade them depart and avenge their murdered sister, after which she died of grief, and was burned on a great pyre.

The three youths, Sörli, Hamdir, and Erp, proceeded to Ermenrich's kingdom, but ere they met their foes, the two eldest, deeming Erp too young to assist them, taunted him with his small size, and finally slew him. Sörli and Hamdir then attacked Ermenrich, cut off his hands and feet, and would have slain him but for a one-eyed stranger who suddenly appeared and bade the bystanders throw stones at the young men. His orders were immediately carried out, and Sörli and Hamdir soon fell slain under the shower of stones, which, as we have seen, alone had power to injure them.

"Ye have heard of Sigurd aforetime, how the foes of God he slew;
How forth from the darksome desert the Gold of Waters he drew;
How he wakened Love on the Mountain, and wakened Brynhild the Bright,
And dwelt upon Earth for a season, and shone in all men's sight.
Ye have heard of the Cloudy People, and the dimming of the day,
And the latter world's confusion, and Sigurd gone away;
Now ye know of the Need of the Niblungs and the end of broken troth,
All the death of kings and of kindreds and the Sorrow of Odin the Goth."

Interpretation of the Saga

This story of the Volsungs is supposed by some authorities to be a series of sun myths, in which Sigi, Rerir, Volsung, Sigmund, and Sigurd in turn personify the glowing orb of day. They are all armed with invincible swords, the sunbeams, and all travel through the world fighting against their foes, the demons of cold and darkness. Sigurd, like Balder, is beloved of all ; he marries Brunhild, the dawn maiden, whom he finds in the midst of flames, the flush of morn, and parts from her only to find her again when his career is ended. His body is burned on the funeral pyre, which, like Balder's, represents either the setting sun or the last gleam of summer, of which he too is a type. The slaying of Fafnir symbolises the destruction of the demon of cold or darkness, who has stolen the golden hoard of summer or the yellow rays of the sun.

According to other authorities, this Saga is based upon history. Atli is the cruel Attila, the "Scourge of God," while Gunnar is Gundicarius, a Burgundian monarch, whose kingdom was destroyed by the Huns, and who was slain with his brothers in 451. Gudrun is the Burgundian princess Ildico, who slew her husband on her wedding-night, as has already been related, using the glittering blade which had once belonged to the sun-god to avenge her murdered kinsmen.

CHAPTER XXVII : THE STORY OF FRITHIOF

Bishop Tegnér

PROBABLY no writer of the nineteenth century did so much to awaken interest in the literary treasures of Scandinavia as Bishop Esaias Tegnér, whom a Swedish author characterised as, " that mighty Genie who organises even disorder."

Tegnér's " Frithiof Saga " has been translated once at least into every European tongue, and some twenty times into English and German. Goethe spoke of the work with the greatest enthusiasm, and the tale, which gives a matchless picture of the life of our heathen ancestors in the North, drew similar praise from Longfellow, who considered it to be one of the most remarkable productions of his century.

Although Tegnér has chosen for his theme the Frithiof saga only, we find that that tale is the sequel to the older but less interesting Thorsten saga, of which we give here a very brief outline, merely to enable the reader to understand clearly every allusion in the more modern poem.

As is so frequently the case with these ancient tales, the story begins with Haloge (Loki), who came north with Odin, and began to reign over northern Norway, which from him was called Halogaland. According to Northern mythology, this god had two lovely daughters. They were carried off by bold suitors, who, banished from the mainland by Haloge's curses and magic spells, took refuge with their newly won wives upon neighbouring islands.

Birth of Viking

Thus it happened that Haloge's grandson, Viking,

298

was born upon the island of Bornholm, in the Baltic Sea, where he dwelt until he was fifteen, and where he became the biggest and strongest man of his time. Rumours of his valour finally reached Hunvor, a Swedish princess, who was oppressed by the attentions of a gigantic suitor whom none dared drive away, and she sent for Viking to deliver her.

Thus summoned, the youth departed, after having received from his father a magic sword named Angurvadel, whose blows would prove fatal even to a giant like the suitor of Hunvor. A " holmgang," as a duel was termed in the North, ensued as soon as the hero arrived upon the scene, and Viking, having slain his antagonist, could have married the princess had it not been considered disgraceful for a Northman to marry before he was twenty.

To beguile the time of waiting for his promised bride, Viking set out in a well-manned dragon ship ; and cruising about the Northern and Southern seas, he met with countless adventures. During this time he was particularly persecuted by the kindred of the giant he had slain, who were adepts in magic, and they brought upon him innumerable perils by land and sea.

Aided and abetted by his bosom friend, Halfdan, Viking escaped every danger, slew many of his foes, and, after rescuing Hunvor, whom, in the meantime, the enemy had carried off to India, he settled down in Sweden. His friend, faithful in peace as well as in war, settled near him, and married also, choosing for wife Ingeborg, Hunvor's attendant.

The saga now describes the long, peaceful winters, when the warriors feasted and listened to the tales of scalds, rousing themselves to energetic efforts only when returning spring again permitted them to launch their dragon ships and set out once more upon their piratical expeditions.

> "Then the Scald took his harp and sang,
>   And loud through the music rang
>   The sound of that shining word ;
>   And the harp-strings a clangour made,
>   As if they were struck with the blade
>   Of a sword.
>
> "And the Berserks round about
>   Broke forth into a shout
>   That made the rafters ring :
>   They smote with their fists on the board,
>   And shouted, ' Long live the Sword,
>   And the King ! ' "
>
> *Longfellow's Saga of King Olaf.*

In the old story the scalds relate with great gusto every phase of attack and defence during cruise and raid, and describe every blow given and received, dwelling with satisfaction upon the carnage and lurid flames which envelop both enemies and ships in common ruin. A fierce fight is often an earnest of future friendship, however, and we are told that Halfdan and Viking, having failed to conquer Njorfe, a foeman of mettle, sheathed their swords after a most obstinate struggle, and accepted their enemy as a third link in their close bond of friendship.

On returning home from one of these customary raids, Viking lost his beloved wife ; and, entrusting her child, Ring, to the care of a foster father, after undergoing a short period of mourning, the brave warrior married again. This time his marital bliss was more lasting, for the saga tells that his second wife bore him nine stalwart sons.

Njorfe, King of Uplands, in Norway, also rejoiced in a family of nine brave sons. Now, although their fathers were united in bonds of the closest friendship, having sworn blood brotherhood according to the true Northern rites, the young men were jealous of one another, and greatly inclined to quarrel.

The Game of Ball

Notwithstanding this smouldering animosity, the youths often met ; and the saga relates that they used to play ball together, and gives a description of the earliest ball game on record in the Northern annals. Viking's sons, as tall and strong as he, were inclined to be rather reckless of their opponents' welfare, and, judging from the following account, translated from the old saga, the players were often left in as sorry a condition as after a modern game.

" The next morning the brothers went to the games, and generally had the ball during the day ; they pushed men and let them fall roughly, and beat others. At night three men had their arms broken, and many were bruised or maimed."

The game between Njorfe's and Viking's sons cul-minated in a disagreement, and one of Njorfe's sons struck one of his opponents a dangerous and treacher-ous blow. Prevented from taking his revenge then and there by the interference of the spectators, the injured man made a trivial excuse to return to the ground alone ; and, meeting his assailant there, he slew him.

The Blood Feud

When Viking heard that one of his sons had slain one of his friend's children, he was very indignant, and mindful of his oath to avenge all Njorfe's wrongs, he banished the young murderer. The other brothers, on hearing this sentence, vowed that they would accompany the exile, and so Viking sorrowfully bade them farewell, giving his sword Angurvadel to Thorsten, the eldest, and cautioning him to remain quietly on an island in Lake Wener until all danger of retaliation on the part of Njorfe's remaining sons should be over.

The young men obeyed ; but Njorfe's sons were determined to avenge their brother, and although they had no boats to convey them over the lake, they made use of a conjurer's art to bring about a great frost. Accompanied by many armed men, they then stole noiselessly over the ice to attack Thorsten and his brothers, and a terrible carnage ensued. Only two of the attacking party managed to escape, but they left, as they fancied, all their foes among the dead.

Then came Viking to bury his sons, and he found that two of them, Thorsten and Thorer, were still alive ; whereupon he secretly conveyed them to a cellar beneath his dwelling, and in due time they recovered from their wounds.

Njorfe's two surviving sons soon discovered by magic arts that their opponents were not dead, and they made a second desperate but vain attempt to kill them. Viking saw that the quarrel would be incessantly renewed if his sons remained at home ; so he now sent them to Halfdan, whose court they reached after a series of adventures which in many points resemble those of Theseus on his way to Athens.

When spring came round Thorsten embarked on a piratical excursion, in the course of which he encountered Jokul, Njorfe's eldest son, who, meanwhile, had taken forcible possession of the kingdom of Sogn, having killed the king, banished his heir, Belé, and changed his beautiful daughter, Ingeborg, into the similitude of an old witch.

Throughout the story Jokul is represented as somewhat of a coward, for he resorted by preference to magic when he wished to injure Viking's sons. Thus he stirred up great tempests, and Thorsten, after twice suffering shipwreck, was only saved from the waves by the seeming witch, whom he promised to marry in gratitude for her good offices. Thorsten, advised by Ingeborg, now went in search of Belé, whom he found and replaced upon his hereditary throne, having sworn eternal friendship with him. After this, the baleful spell was removed, and Ingeborg, now revealed in her native beauty, was united to Thorsten, and dwelt with him at Framnäs.

Thorsten and Belé

Every spring Thorsten and Belé set out together in their ships ; and, upon one of these expeditions, they joined forces with Angantyr, a foe whose mettle they had duly tested, and proceeded to recover possession of a priceless treasure, a magic dragon ship named Ellida, which Ægir, god of the sea, had once given to Viking in reward for hospitable treatment, and which had been stolen from him.

> "A royal gift to behold, for the swelling planks of its framework
> Were not fastened with nails, as is wont, but *grown* in together.
> Its shape was that of a dragon when swimming, but forward
> Its head rose proudly on high, the throat with yellow gold
>   flaming;
> Its belly was spotted with red and yellow, but back by the rudder
> Coiled out its mighty tail in circles, all scaly with silver;
> Black wings with edges of red; when all were expanded
> Ellida raced with the whistling storm, but outstript the eagle.
> When filled to the edge with warriors, it sailed o'er the waters,
> You'd deem it a floating fortress, or warlike abode of a monarch.
> The ship was famed far and wide, and of ships was first in the
>   North."
>
> *Tegnér, Frithiof Saga (Spalding's tr.).*

The next season, Thorsten, Belé, and Angantyr conquered the Orkney Islands, which were given as a kingdom to the latter, he voluntarily pledging himself to pay a yearly tribute to Belé. Next Thorsten and Belé went in quest of a magic ring, or armlet, once forged by Völund, the smith, and stolen by Soté, a famous pirate.

This bold robber was so afraid lest some one should gain possession of the magic ring, that he had buried himself alive with it in a mound in Bretland. Here his ghost was said to keep constant watch over it, and when Thorsten entered his tomb, Belé, who waited outside, heard the sound of frightful blows given and returned, and saw lurid gleams of supernatural fire.

When Thorsten finally staggered out of the mound, pale and bloody, but triumphant, he refused to speak of the horrors he had encountered to win the coveted treasure, but often would he say, as he showed it, " I trembled but once in my life, and 'twas when I seized it ! "

Birth of Frithiof and Ingeborg

Thus owner of the three greatest treasures of the North, Thorsten returned home to Framnäs, where Ingeborg bore him a fine boy, Frithiof, while two sons, Halfdan and Helgé, were born to Belé. The lads played together, and were already well grown when Ingeborg, Belé's little daughter, was born, and some time later the child was entrusted to the care of Hilding, who was already Frithiof's foster father, as Thorsten's frequent absences made it difficult for him to undertake the training of his boy.

> " Jocund they grew, in guileless glee;
> Young Frithiof was the sapling tree;
> In budding beauty by his side,
> Sweet Ingeborg, the garden's pride."
> *Tegnér, Frithiof Saga (Longfellow's tr.).*

Frithiof soon became hardy and fearless under his

Ingeborg

M. E. Winge

foster father's training, and Ingeborg rapidly developed the sweetest traits of character and loveliness. Both were happiest when together ; and as they grew older their childish affection daily became deeper and more intense, until Hilding, perceiving this state of affairs, bade the youth remember that he was a subject of the king, and therefore no mate for his only daughter.

> "To Odin, in his star-lit sky,
> Ascends her titled ancestry;
> But Thorsten's son art thou; give way!
> For 'like thrives best with like,' they say."
>
> *Tegnér, Frithiof Saga* (*G. Stephens's tr.*).

Frithiof's Love for Ingeborg

These wise admonitions came too late, however, and Frithiof vehemently declared that he would win the fair Ingeborg for his bride in spite of all obstacles and his more humble origin.

Shortly after this Belé and Thorsten met for the last time, near the magnificent shrine of Balder, where the king, feeling that his end was near, had convened a solemn assembly, or Thing, of all his principal subjects, in order to present his sons Helgé and Halfdan to the people as his chosen successors. The young heirs were very coldly received on this occasion, for Helgé was of a sombre and taciturn disposition, and inclined to the life of a priest, and Halfdan was of a weak, effeminate nature, and noted for his love of pleasure rather than of war and the chase. Frithiof, who was present, and stood beside them, was the object of many admiring glances from the throng.

> "But close behind them Frithiof goes,
> Wrapp'd in his mantle blue;
> His height a whole head taller rose
> Than that of both the two.

u

He stands between the brothers there—
As though the ripe day stood
Atween young morning rosy-fair,
And night within the wood."

Tegnér, Frithiof Saga (G. *Stephens's tr.*).

After giving his last instructions and counsel to his sons, and speaking kindly to Frithiof, for whom he entertained a warm regard, the old king turned to his lifelong companion, Thorsten, to take leave of him, but the old warrior declared that they would not long be parted. Belé then spoke again to his sons, and bade them erect his howe, or funeral mound, within sight of that of Thorsten, that their spirits might commune over the waters of the narrow firth which would flow between them, that so they might not be sundered even in death.

Helgé and Halfdan

These instructions were piously carried out when, shortly after, the aged companions breathed their last ; and the great barrows having been erected, the brothers, Helgé and Halfdan, began to rule their kingdom, while Frithiof, their former playmate, withdrew to his own place at Framnäs, a fertile homestead, lying in a snug valley enclosed by the towering mountains and the waters of the ever-changing firth.

"Three miles extended around the fields of the homestead; on three sides
Valleys and mountains and hills, but on the fourth side was the ocean.
Birch-woods crowned the summits, but over the down-sloping hill-sides
Flourished the golden corn, and man-high was waving the rye-field."

Tegnér, Frithiof Saga (*Longfellow's tr.*).

FRITHIOF'S SUIT

But although surrounded by faithful retainers, and blessed with much wealth and the possession of the famous treasures of his hero sire, the sword Angurvadel, the Völund ring, and the matchless dragon ship Ellida, Frithiof was unhappy, because he could no longer see the fair Ingeborg daily. All his former spirits revived, however, when in the spring, at his invitation, both kings came to visit him, together with their fair sister, and once again they spent long hours in cheerful companionship. As they were thus constantly thrown together, Frithiof found opportunity to make known to Ingeborg his deep affection, and he received in return an avowal of her love.

> " He sat by her side, and he pressed her soft hand,
> And he felt a soft pressure responsive and bland;
> Whilst his love-beaming gaze
> Was returned as the sun's in the moon's placid rays."
> *Tegnér, Frithiof Saga (Longfellow's tr.).*

Frithiof's Suit

When the visit was ended and the guests had departed, Frithiof informed his confidant and chief companion, Björn, of his determination to follow them and openly ask for Ingeborg's hand. His ship was set free from its moorings and it swooped like an eagle over to the shore near Balder's shrine, where the royal brothers were seated in state on Belé's tomb to listen to the petitions of their subjects. Straightway Frithiof presented himself before them, and manfully made his request, adding that the old king had always loved him and would surely have granted his prayer.

> " No king was my sire, not a jarl, ev'n—'tis true;
> Yet Scald-songs his mem'ry and exploits renew;
> The Rune-stones will tell
> On high-vaulted cairn what my race hath done well.

" With ease could I win me both empire and land ;—
But rather I stay on my forefathers' strand ;
While arms I can wield—
Both poverty's hut and king's palace I'll shield.

" On Belé's round barrow we stand ; each word
In the dark deeps beneath us he hears and has heard ;
With Frithiof pleadeth
The old Chief in his cairn : think ! your answer thought
needeth."

Tegnér, Frithiof Saga (G. Stephens's tr.).

Then he went on to promise lifelong fealty and the service of his strong right arm in exchange for the boon he craved.

As Frithiof ceased King Helgé rose, and regarding the young man scornfully, he said : " Our sister is not for a peasant's son ; proud chiefs of the Northland may dispute for her hand, but not thou. As for thy arrogant proffer, know that I can protect my kingdom. Yet if thou wouldst be my man, place in my household mayst thou have."

Enraged at the insult thus publicly offered, Frithiof drew his invincible sword ; but, remembering that he stood on a consecrated spot, he struck only at the royal shield, which fell in two pieces clashing to the ground. Then striding back to his ship in sullen silence, he embarked and sailed away.

" And lo ! cloven in twain at a stroke
Fell King Helge's gold shield from its pillar of oak :
At the clang of the blow,
The live started above, the dead started below."

Tegnér, Frithiof Saga (Longfellow's tr.).

Sigurd Ring a Suitor

After his departure came messengers from Sigurd Ring, the aged King of Ringric, in Norway, who, having lost his wife, sent to Helgé and Halfdan to ask

Frithiof cleaves the Shield of Helgé

Knut Ekwall

Ingeborg's hand in marriage. Before returning answer to this royal suitor, Helgé consulted the Vala, or prophetess, and the priests, who all declared that the omens were not in favour of the marriage. Upon this Helgé assembled his people to hear the word which the messengers were to carry to their master, but unfortunately King Halfdan gave way to his waggish humour, and made scoffing reference to the advanced age of the royal suitor. These impolitic words were reported to King Ring, and so offended him that he immediately collected an army and prepared to march against the Kings of Sogn to avenge the insult with his sword. When the rumour of his approach reached the cowardly brothers they were terrified, and fearing to encounter the foe unaided, they sent Hilding to Frithiof to implore his help.

Hilding found Frithiof playing chess with Björn, and immediately made known his errand.

> " ' From Bele's high heirs
> I come with courteous words and prayers
> Disastrous tidings rouse the brave ;
> On thee a nation's hope relies.
>
> . . . . . .
>
> In Balder's fane, grief's loveliest prey,
> Sweet Ing'borg weeps the livelong day :
> Say, can her tears unheeded fall,
> Nor call her champion to her side ? ' "
> *Tegnér, Frithiof Saga (Longfellow's tr.).*

While the old man was speaking Frithiof continued to play, ever and anon interjecting an enigmatical reference to the game, until at this point he said :

> " Björn ; thou in vain my queen pursuest,
> She from childhood dearest, truest !
> She's my game's most darling piece, and
> Come what will—I'll save my queen ! "
> *Tegnér, Frithiof Saga (G. Stephens's tr.).*

Hilding did not understand such mode of answering, and at length rebuked Frithiof for his indifference. Then Frithiof rose, and pressing kindly the old man's hand, he bade him tell the kings that he was too deeply offended to listen to their appeal.

Helgé and Halfdan, thus forced to fight without their bravest leader, preferred to make a treaty with Sigurd Ring, and they agreed to give him not only their sister Ingeborg, but also a yearly tribute.

At Balder's Shrine

While they were thus engaged at Sogn Sound, Frithiof hastened to Balder's temple, to which Ingeborg had been sent for security, and where, as Hilding had declared, he found her a prey to grief. Now although it was considered a sacrilege for man and woman to exchange a word in the sacred building, Frithiof could not forbear to console her; and, forgetting all else, he spoke to her and comforted her, quieting all her apprehensions of the gods' anger by assuring her that Balder, the good, must view their innocent passion with approving eyes, for love so pure as theirs could defile no sanctuary; and they ended by plighting their troth before the shrine of Balder.

> " ' Thou whisp'rest " Balder,"—His wrath fearest ;—
> That gentle god all anger flies.
> We worship here a Lover, dearest !
> Our hearts' love is his sacrifice;
> That god whose brow beams sunshine-splendour,
> Whose faith lasts through eternity,—
> Was not his love to beauteous Nanna
> As pure, as warm, as mine to thee ?
>
> " ' His image see !—himself broods o'er it—
> How mild, how kind, his bright eyes move !
> An off'ring bear I here before it,
> A warm heart full of purest love.

FRITHIOF BANISHED

Come, kneel with me ! no altar incense
To Balder's soul more grateful is
Than two hearts, vowing in his presence
A mutual faith as true as his!'"
Tegnér, Frithiof Saga (G. Stephens's tr.).

Reassured by this reasoning, which received added
strength from the voice which spoke loudly from her
own heart, Ingeborg could not refuse to see and con-
verse with Frithiof.   During the kings' absence the
young lovers met every day, and they exchanged love-
tokens, Frithiof giving to Ingeborg Völund's arm-ring,
which she solemnly promised to send back to her
lover should she be compelled to break her promise to
live for him alone.   Frithiof lingered at Framnäs until
the kings' return, when, yielding to the fond entreaties
of Ingeborg the Fair, he again appeared before them,
and pledged himself to free them from their thraldom
to Sigurd Ring if they would only reconsider their
decision and promise him their sister's hand.

"' War stands and strikes
His glitt'ring shield within thy boundaries ;
Thy realm, King Helge, is in jeopardy :
But give thy sister, and I'll lend mine arm
Thy guard in battle.   It may stead thee well :
Come ! let this grudge between us be forgotten,
Unwilling bear I such 'gainst Ing'borg's brother.
Be counsell'd, King ! be just ! and save at once
Thy golden crown and thy fair sister's heart !
Here is my hand : by Asa-Thor I swear
Never again 'tis stretch'd in reconcilement !'"
Tegnér, Frithiof Saga (G. Stephens's tr.).

Frithiof Banished

But although this offer was received with acclamation
by the assembled warriors, Helgé scornfully demanded
of Frithiof whether he had spoken with Ingeborg and
so defiled the temple of Balder.

A shout of "Say nay, Frithiof ! say nay !" broke

from the ring of warriors, but he proudly answered :
" I would not lie to gain Valhalla. I have spoken to
thy sister, Helgé, yet have I not broken Balder's peace."

A murmur of horror passed through the ranks at
this avowal, and when the harsh voice of Helgé was
raised in judgment, none was there to gainsay the
justice of the sentence.

This apparently was not a harsh one, but Helgé well
knew that it meant death, and he so intended it.

Far westward lay the Orkney Islands, ruled by Jarl
Angantyr, whose yearly tribute to Belé was withheld
now that the old king lay in his cairn. Hard-fisted he
was said to be, and heavy of hand, and to Frithiof was
given the task of demanding the tribute face to face.

Before he sailed upon the judgment-quest, however,
he once more sought Ingeborg, and implored her to
elope with him to a home in the sunny South, where
her happiness should be his law, and where she should
rule over his subjects as his honoured wife. But Ingeborg sorrowfully refused to accompany him, saying
that, since her father was no more, she was in duty
bound to obey her brothers implicitly, and could not
marry without their consent.

The fiery spirit of Frithiof was at first impatient
under this disappointment of his hopes, but in the end
his noble nature conquered, and after a heartrending
parting scene, he embarked upon Ellida, and sorrowfully sailed out of the harbour, while Ingeborg, through
a mist of tears, watched the sail as it faded and disappeared in the distance.

The vessel was barely out of sight when Helgé sent
for two witches named Heid and Ham, bidding them
by incantations to stir up a tempest at sea in which it
would be impossible for even the god-given vessel
Ellida to live, that so all on board should perish. The

Ingeborg watches her lover depart
Knut Ekwall   312

By Permission of F. Bruckmann, Munich

witches immediately complied ; and with Helgé's aid they soon stirred up a storm the fury of which is unparalleled in history.

> " Helgé on the strand
> Chants his wizard-spell,
> Potent to command
> Fiends of earth or hell.
> Gathering darkness shrouds the sky ;
> Hark, the thunder's distant roll !
> Lurid lightnings, as they fly,
> Streak with blood the sable pole.
> Ocean, boiling to its base,
> Scatters wide its wave of foam ;
> Screaming, as in fleetest chase,
> Sea-birds seek their island home."
>
> *Tegnér, Frithiof Saga (Longfellow's tr.).*

> " Then the storm unfetter'd wingeth
> Wild his course ; in Ocean's foam
> Now he dips him, now up-swingeth,
> Whirling toward the God's own home :
> Rides each Horror-spirit, warning,
> High upon the topmost wave—
> Up from out the white, vast, yawning,
> Bottomless, unfathom'd grave."
>
> *Tegnér, Frithiof Saga (G. Stephens's tr.).*

The Tempest

Unfrighted by tossing waves and whistling blasts, Frithiof sang a cheery song to reassure his terrified crew ; but when the peril grew so great that his exhausted followers gave themselves up for lost, he bethought him of tribute to the goddess Ran, who ever requires gold of them who would rest in peace under the ocean wave. Taking his armlet, he hewed it with his sword and made fair division among his men.

> " Who goes empty-handed
> Down to sea-blue Ran ?
> Cold her kisses strike, and
> Fleeting her embrace is."
>
> *Tegnér, Frithiof Saga (G. Stephens's tr.).*

He then bade Björn hold the rudder, and himself climbed to the mast-top to view the horizon. While perched there he descried a whale, upon which the two witches were riding the storm. Speaking to his good ship, which was gifted with power of understanding and could obey his commands, he now ran down both whale and witches, and the sea was reddened with their blood. At the same instant the wind fell, the waves ceased to threaten, and fair weather soon smiled again upon the seas.

Exhausted by their previous superhuman efforts and by the labour of baling their water-logged vessel, the men were too weak to land when they at last reached the Orkney Islands, and had to be carried ashore by Björn and Frithiof, who gently laid them down on the sand, bidding them rest and refresh themselves after all the hardships they had endured.

> " Yet more wearied than their Dragon
> Totter Frithiof's gallant men ;
> Though each leans upon his weapon,
> Scarcely upright stand they then.
> Björn, on pow'rful shoulder, dareth
> Four to carry to the land ;
> Frithiof, all alone, eight beareth,—
> Sets them so round the upblaz'd brand.
>
> ' Nay ! ye white-fac'd, shame not !
> Waves are mighty Vikings ;
> Hard's the unequal struggle—
> Ocean's maids our foes.
> See ! there comes the mead-horn,
> Wand'ring on bright gold-foot ;
> Shipmates ! cold limbs warm,—and
> Here's to Ingeborg ! ' "
> *Tegnér, Frithiof Saga (G. Stephens's tr.).*

The arrival of Frithiof and his men, and their mode of landing, had been noted by the watchman of Angantyr, who immediately informed his master of all he had seen. The jarl exclaimed that the ship which had weathered such a gale could be none but Ellida, and that its captain was doubtless Frithiof, Thorsten's gallant son. At these words one of his Berserkers, Atlé, caught up his weapons and strode from the hall, vowing that he would challenge Frithiof, and thus satisfy himself concerning the veracity of the tales he had heard of the young hero's courage.

Atlé's Challenge

Although still greatly exhausted, Frithiof immediately accepted Atlé's challenge, and, after a sharp encounter with swords, in which Angurvadel was triumphant, the two champions grappled in deadly embrace. Widely is that wrestling-match renowned in the North, and well matched were the heroes, but in the end Frithiof threw his antagonist, whom he would have slain then and there had his sword been within reach. Atlé saw his intention, and bade him go in search of the weapon, promising to remain motionless during his absence. Frithiof, knowing that such a warrior's promise was inviolable, immediately obeyed ; but when he returned with his sword, and found his antagonist calmly awaiting death, he relented, and bade Atlé rise and live.

> "Then storm they, nothing yielded,
>   Two autumn-billows like !
> And oft, with steel round shielded,
>   Their jarring breasts fierce strike.

> " All like two bears they wrestle,
>   On hills of snow; and draw
> And strain, each like an eagle
>   On the angry sea at war.
> The root-fast rock resisted
>   Full hardly them between
> And green iron oaks down-twisted
>   With lesser pulls have been.

315

"From each broad brow sweat rushes ;
    Their bosoms coldly heave ;
And stones and mounds and bushes
    Dints hundred-fold receive."
        Tegnér, Frithiof Saga (*G. Stephens's tr.*).

Together the appeased warriors now wended their way to Angantyr's hall, which Frithiof found to be far different from the rude dwellings of his native land. The walls were covered with leather richly decorated with gilt designs. The chimney-piece was of marble, and glass panes were in the window-frames. A soft light was diffused from many candles burning in silver branches, and the tables groaned under the most luxurious fare.

High in a silver chair sat the jarl, clad in a coat of golden mail, over which was flung a rich mantle bordered with ermine, but when Frithiof entered he strode from his seat with cordial hand outstretched. "Full many a horn have I emptied with my old friend Thorsten," said he, "and his brave son is equally welcome at my board."

Nothing loth, Frithiof seated himself beside his host, and after he had eaten and drunk he recounted his adventures upon land and sea.

At last, however, Frithiof made known his errand, whereupon Angantyr said that he owed no tribute to Helgé, and would pay him none ; but that he would give the required sum as a free gift to his old friend's son, leaving him at liberty to dispose of it as he pleased. Meantime, since the season was unpropitious for the return journey, and storms continually swept the sea, the king invited Frithiof to tarry with him over the winter ; and it was only when the gentle spring breezes were blowing once more that he at last allowed him to depart.

Frithiof's Return to Framnäs

Knut Ekwall

Frithiof's Home-coming

Taking leave of his kind host, Frithiof set sail, and wafted by favourable winds, the hero, after six days, came in sight of Framnäs, and found that his home had been reduced to a shapeless heap of ashes by Helgé's orders. Sadly Frithiof strode over the ravaged site of his childhood's home, and as he viewed the desolate scene his heart burned within him. The ruins were not entirely deserted, however, and suddenly Frithiof felt the cold nozzle of his hound thrust into his hand. A few moments later his favourite steed bounded to his master's side, and the faithful creatures were well-nigh frantic with delight. Then came Hilding to greet him with the information that Ingeborg was now the wife of Sigurd Ring. When Frithiof heard this he flew into a Berserker rage, and bade his men scuttle the vessels in the harbour, while he strode to the temple in search of Helgé.

The king stood crowned amid a circle of priests, some of whom brandished flaming pine-knots, while all grasped a sacrificial flint knife. Suddenly there was a clatter of arms and in burst Frithiof, his brow dark as autumn storms. Helgé's face went pale as he confronted the angry hero, for he knew what his coming presaged. "Take thy tribute, King," said Frithiof, and with the words, he took the purse from his girdle and flung it in Helgé's face with such force that blood gushed from his mouth and he fell swooning at Balder's feet.

The silver-bearded priests advanced to the scene of violence, but Frithiof motioned them back, and his looks were so threatening that they durst not disobey.

Then his eye fell upon the arm-ring which he had given to Ingeborg and which Helgé had placed upon the arm of Balder, and striding up to the wooden image he said : "Pardon, great Balder, not for thee was the ring wrested from Völund's tomb!" Then he seized the ring, but strongly as he tugged it would not come apart. At last he put forth all his strength, and with a sudden jerk he recovered the ring, and at the same time the image of the god fell prone across the altar fire. The next moment it was enveloped in flames, and before aught could be done the whole temple was wreathed in fire and smoke.

> "All, all's lost ! From half-burned hall
> Th' fire-red cock up-swingeth !—
> Sits on the roof, and, with shrilly call
> Flutt'ring, his free course wingeth."
> *Tegnér's Frithiof Saga* (*G. Stephens's tr.*).

Frithiof, horror-stricken at the sacrilege which he had involuntarily occasioned, vainly tried to extinguish the flames and save the costly sanctuary, but finding his efforts unavailing he escaped to his ship and resolved upon the weary life of an outcast and exile.

> "Thou may'st not rest thee,
> Thou still must haste thee,
> Ellida !—out
> Th' wide world about.
> Yes ! rock on ! roaming
> Mid froth salt-foaming
> My Dragon good !
>
> "Thou billow bold
> Befriend me !—Never
> I'll from thee sever !—
> My father's Mound
> Dull stands, fast-bound,
> And self-same surges
> Chaunt changeless dirges ;
> But blue shall mine
> Through foam-flow'rs shine,

Frithiof at the Shrine of Balder

Knut Ekwall

318

FRITHIOF AN EXILE

'Mid tempests swimming,
And storms thick dimming,
And draw yet mo
Down, down, below.—
My Life-Home given,
Thou shalt, far-driven !
My Barrow be—
Thou free broad Sea ! "

Tegnér, Frithiof Saga (G. Stephens's tr.).

Frithiof an Exile

Helgé started in pursuit with ten great dragon-ships, but these had barely got under way when they began to sink, and Björn said with a laugh, " What Ran enfolds I trust she will keep." Even King Helgé was with difficulty got ashore, and the survivors were forced to stand in helpless inactivity while Ellida's great sails slowly sank beneath the horizon. It was thus that Frithiof sadly saw his native land vanish from sight ; and as it disappeared he breathed a tender farewell to the beloved country which he never expected to see again.

After thus parting from his native land, Frithiof roved the sea as a pirate, or viking. His code was never to settle anywhere, to sleep on his shield, to fight and neither give nor take quarter, to protect the ships which paid him tribute and to plunder the others, and to distribute all the booty to his men, reserving for himself nothing but the glory of the enterprise. Sailing and fighting thus, Frithiof visited many lands, and came at last to the sunny isles of Greece, whither he would fain have carried Ingeborg as his bride ; and the sights called up such a flood of sad memories that he was well-nigh overwhelmed with longing for his beloved and for his native land.

319

At the Court of Sigurd Ring

Three years had passed away and Frithiof determined to return northward and visit Sigurd Ring's court. When he announced his purpose to Björn, his faithful companion reproached him for his rashness in thinking to journey alone, but Frithiof would not be turned from his purpose, saying : " I am never alone while Angurvadel hangs at my side." Steering Ellida up the Vik (the main part of the Christiania Fiord), he entrusted her to Björn's care, and, enveloped in a bear-hide, which he wore as a disguise, he set out on foot alone for the court of Sigurd Ring, arriving there as the Yuletide festivities were in progress. As if nothing more than an aged beggar, Frithiof sat down upon the bench near the door, where he quickly became the butt of the courtiers' rough jokes. When one of his tormentors, however, approached too closely, the seeming beggar caught him in a powerful grasp and swung him high above his head.

Terrified by this exhibition of superhuman strength, the courtiers quickly withdrew from the dangerous vicinity, while Sigurd Ring, whose attention was attracted by the commotion, sternly bade the stranger-guest approach and tell who thus dared to break the peace in his royal hall.

Frithiof answered evasively that he was fostered in penitence, that he inherited want, and that he came from the wolf ; as to his name, this did not matter. The king, as was the courteous custom, did not press him further, but invited him to take a seat beside him and the queen, and to share his good cheer. " But first," said he, " let fall the clumsy covering which veils, if I mistake not, a proper form."

Frithiof gladly accepted the invitation thus cordially

Frithiof at the Court of Ring
Knut Ekwall

By Permission of F. Bruckmann, Munich

given, and when the hairy hide fell from off his head and shoulders, he stood disclosed in the pride of youth, much to the surprise of the assembled warriors.

But although his appearance marked him as of no common race, none of the courtiers recognised him. It was different, however, with Ingeborg. Had any curious eye been upon her at that moment her changing colour and the quick heaving of her breast would have revealed her deep emotion.

> "The astonish'd queen's pale cheeks, how fast-changing rose-tints
>   dye!—
> So purple Northlights, quiv'ring, on snow-hid meadows lie ;
> Like two white water-lilies on storm-wave wild that rest,
> Each moment rising, falling,—so heaves her trembling breast !
> _Tegnér, Frithiof Saga_ (G. _Stephens's tr._).

Frithiof had barely taken his seat at the board when with flourish of trumpets a great boar was brought in and placed before the king. In accordance with the Yule-tide custom of those days the old monarch rose, and touching the head of the animal, he uttered a vow that with the help of Frey, Odin, and Thor, he would conquer the bold champion Frithiof. The next moment Frithiof, too, was upon his feet, and dashing his sword upon the great wooden bench he declared that Frithiof was his kinsman and he also would vow that though all the world withstood, no harm should reach the hero while he had power to wield his sword.

At this unexpected interruption the warriors had risen quickly from the oaken benches, but Sigurd Ring smiled indulgently at the young man's vehemence and said : "Friend, thy words are overbold, but never yet was guest restrained from uttering his thoughts in this kingly hall." Then he turned to Ingeborg and bade her fill to the brim with her choicest mead a huge horn, richly decorated, which stood in front of her, and present it to the guest. The queen obeyed with downcast eyes, and the trembling of her hand caused the liquid to overflow. Two ordinary men could hardly have drained the mighty draught, but Frithiof raised it to his lips, and when he removed the horn not one drop of the mead remained.

Ere the banquet was ended Sigurd Ring invited the youthful stranger to remain at his court until the return of spring, and accepting the proffered hospitality, Frithiof became the constant companion of the royal couple, whom he accompanied upon all occasions.

One day Sigurd Ring set out to a banquet with Ingeborg. They travelled in a sleigh, while Frithiof, with steel-shod feet, sped gracefully by their side, cutting many mystic characters in the ice. Their way lay over a dangerous portion of the frozen surface, and Frithiof warned the king that it would be prudent to avoid this. He would not listen to the counsel, however, and suddenly the sleigh sank in a deep fissure, which threatened to engulph it with the king and queen. But like falcon descending upon its quarry, Frithiof was at their side in a moment, and without apparent effort he dragged the steed and its burden on to the firm ice. "In good sooth," said Ring, "Frithiof himself could not have done better."

The long winter came to an end, and in the early spring the king and queen arranged a hunting-party in which all the court were to take part. During the progress of the chase the advancing years of Sigurd Ring made it impossible for him to keep up with the eager hunt, and thus it happened that he dropped behind, until at length he was left with Frithiof as his sole companion. They rode slowly together until they reached a pleasant dell which invited the weary king to repose, and he declared that he would lie down for a season to rest.

> "Then threw Frithiof down his mantle, and upon the greensward spread,
> And the ancient king so trustful laid on Frithiof's knee his head;
> Slept, as calmly as the hero sleepeth after war's alarms
> On his shield, calm as an infant sleepeth in its mother's arms."
>
> *Tegnér, Frithiof Saga (Longfellow's tr.).*

Frithiof's Loyalty

While the aged king was thus reposing, a bird sang to Frithiof from a tree near by, bidding him take advantage of his host's powerlessness to slay him, and recover the bride of whom he had been unfairly deprived. But although Frithiof's hot young heart clamoured for his beloved, he utterly refused to entertain the dastardly suggestion, but, fearing lest he should be overcome by temptation, despite his horror at the thought, he impulsively flung his sword far from him into a neighbouring thicket.

A few moments later Sigurd Ring opened his eyes, and informed Frithiof that he had only feigned sleep; he told him also that having recognised him from the first, he had tested him in many ways, and had found his honour equal to his courage. Old age had now overtaken him and he felt that death was drawing nigh. In but a short time, therefore, Frithiof might hope to realise his dearest hope, and Sigurd Ring told him that he would die happy if he would stay by him until the end.

A revulsion of feeling had, however, overtaken Frithiof, and he told the aged king that he felt that Ingeborg could never be his, because of the wrath of Balder. Too long had he stayed; he would now go once more upon the sea and would seek death in the fray, that so he might appease the offended gods.

Full of his resolve, he quickly made preparations to

323

depart, but when he returned to the court to bid farewell to his royal hosts he found that Sigurd Ring was
at the point of death. The old warrior bethought him
that "a straw death" would not win the favour of
Odin, and in the presence of Frithiof and his court he
slashed bravely the death runes on his arm and breast.
Then clasping Ingeborg with one hand, he raised the
other in blessing over Frithiof and his youthful son,
and so passed in peace to the halls of the blessed.

> " Gods all, I hail ye !
> Sons of Valhalla !
> Earth disappears ; to the Asa's high feast
> Gjallar-horn bids me ;
> Blessedness, like a
> Gold-helmet, circles their up-coming guest ! "
> *Tegnér, Frithiof Saga* (G. *Stephens's tr.*).

Betrothal of Frithiof and Ingeborg

The warriors of the nation now assembled in solemn
Thing to choose a successor to the throne. Frithiof had
won the people's enthusiastic admiration, and they
would fain have elected him king ; but he raised Sigurd
Ring's little son high on his shield when he heard the
shout which acclaimed his name, and presented the boy
to the assembly as their future king, publicly swearing
to uphold him until he was of age to defend the realm.
The lad, weary of his cramped position, boldly sprang
to the ground as soon as Frithiof's speech was ended,
and alighted upon his feet. This act of agile daring in
one so young appealed to the rude Northmen, and a
loud shout arose, " We choose thee, shield-borne
child ! "

> " But thron'd king-like, the lad sat proud
> On shield-floor high ;
> So the eaglet glad, from rock-hung cloud,
> The Sun will eye !

Frithiof watches the sleeping King

Knut Ekwall

BETROTHAL OF FRITHIOF AND INGEBORG

At length this place his young blood found
　Too dull to keep ;
And, with one spring, he gains the ground—
　A royal leap ! "
　　　　Tegnér, Frithiof Saga (G. Stephens's tr.).

According to some accounts, Frithiof now made war against Ingeborg's brothers, and after conquering them, allowed them to retain their kingdom on condition that they paid him a yearly tribute. Then he and Ingeborg remained in Ringric until the young king was able to assume the government, when they repaired to Hordaland, a kingdom Frithiof had obtained by conquest, and which he left to his sons Gungthiof and Hunthiof.

Bishop Tegnér's conclusion, however, differs very considerably, and if it appears less true to the rude temper of the rugged days of the sea-rovers, its superior spiritual qualities make it more attractive. According to Tegnér's poem, Frithiof was urged by the people of Sigurd Ring to espouse Ingeborg and remain amongst them as guardian of the realm. But he answered that this might not be, since the wrath of Balder still burned against him, and none else could bestow his cherished bride. He told the people that he would fare over the seas and seek forgiveness of the god, and soon after, his farewells were spoken, and once more his vessel was speeding before the wind.

Frithiof's first visit was paid to his father's burial mound, where, plunged in melancholy at the desolation around, he poured out his soul to the outraged god. He reminded him that it was the custom of the Northmen to exact blood-fines for kinsmen slain, and surely the blessed gods would not be less forgiving than the earth-born. Passionately he adjured Balder to show him how he could make reparation for his

325

unpremeditated fault, and suddenly, an answer was vouchsafed, and Frithiof beheld in the clouds a vision of a new temple.

> " Then sudden, o'er the western waters pendent,
> An Image comes, with gold and flames resplendent,
> O'er Balder's grove it hovers, night's clouds under,
> Like gold crown resting on a bed of green.
> At last to a temple settling, firm 'tis grounded—
> Where Balder stood, another temple's founded."
> Tegnér, Frithiof Saga (G. Stephens's tr.).

The hero immediately understood that the gods had thus indicated a means of atonement, and he grudged neither wealth nor pains until a glorious temple and grove, which far exceeded the splendour of the old shrine, rose out of the ruins.

> " Finish'd great Balder's Temple stood !
> Round it no palisade of wood
> Ran now as erst ;
> A railing stronger, fairer than the first,
> And all of hammer'd iron—each bar
> Gold-tipp'd and regular—
> Walls Balder's sacred House.   Like some long line
> Of steel-clad champions, whose bright war-spears shine
> And golden helms afar—so stood
> This glitt'ring guard within the holy wood !

> " Of granite blocks enormous, join'd with curious care
> And daring art, the massy pile was built ; and there
> (A giant-work intended
> To last till time was ended,)
> It rose like Upsal's temple, where the north
> Saw Valhall's halls fair imag'd here on earth.

> " Proud stood it there on mountain-steep, its lofty brow
> Reflected calmly on the sea's bright-flowing wave.
> But round about, some girdle like of beauteous flow'rs,
> Went Balder's Dale, with all its groves' soft-murmur'd sighs,
> And all its birds' sweet-twitter'd songs,—the Home of Peace."
> Tegnér, Frithiof Saga (G. Stephens's tr.).

BETROTHAL OF FRITHIOF AND INGEBORG

Meantime, while the timbers were being hewed, King Helgé was absent upon a foray amongst the Finnish mountains. One day it chanced that his band passed by a crag where stood the lonely shrine of some forgotten god, and King Helgé scaled the rocky summit with intent to raze the ruined walls. The lock held fast, and, as Helgé tugged fiercely at the mouldered gate, suddenly a sculptured image of the deity, rudely summoned from his ancient sleep, started from his niche above.

Heavily he fell upon the head of the intruder, and Helgé stretched his length upon the rocky floor, nor stirred again.

When the temple was duly consecrated to Balder's service, Frithiof stood by the altar to await the coming of his expected bride. But Halfdan first crossed the threshold, his faltering gait showing plainly that he feared an unfriendly reception. Seeing this, Frithiof unbuckled his sword and strode frankly to Halfdan with hand outstretched, whereupon the king, blushing deeply, grasped heartily the proffered hand, and from that moment all their differences were forgotten. The next moment Ingeborg approached and the renewed amity of the long-sundered friends was ratified with the hand of the bride, which Halfdan placed in that of his new brother.

> "Over the copper threshold Halfdan now,
> With pallid brow
> And fearful fitful glance, advanceth slow
> Tow'rds yonder tow'ring ever-dreaded foe—
> And, silent, at a distance stands,—
> Then Frithiof, with quick hands,
> The corslet-hater, Angurvadel, from his **thigh**
> Unbuckleth, and his bright shield's golden round
> Leaning 'gainst the altar, thus draws nigh ;—

327

While his cow'd enemy
He thus accosts, with pleasant dignity.—
' Most noble in this strife will he be found
Who first his right hand good
Offers in pledge of peaceful brotherhood ! '—
Then Halfdan, deeply blushing, doffs with haste
His iron-gauntlet and,—with hearty grasp embrac'd,—
Each long, long, sever'd hand
Its friend-foe hails, steadfast as mountain-bases stand !

" And as th' last deep accents
Of reconcilement and of blessing sounded ;
Lo ! Ing'borg sudden enters, rich adorn'd
With bridal ornaments, and all enrob'd
In gorgeous ermine, and by bright-ey'd maidens
Slow-follow'd, as on heav'n's broad canopy,
Attending star-trains guard the regent-moon !—
But the young bride's fair eyes,
Those two blue skies,
Fill quick with tears,
And to her brother's heart she trembling sinketh ;—
He, with his sister's fears
Deep-mov'd, her hand all tenderly in Frithiof's linketh,
His burden soft transferring to that hero's breast,
Its long-tried faith fit place for Ing'borg's rest."

Tegnér, Frithiof Saga (**G. *Stephens's tr.*).

CHAPTER XXVIII : THE TWILIGHT OF THE GODS

The Decline of the Gods

ONE of the distinctive features of Northern mythology is that the people always believed that their gods belonged to a finite race. The Æsir had had a beginning ; therefore, it was reasoned, they must have an end ; and as they were born from a mixture of the divine and giant elements, being thus imperfect, they bore within them the germ of death, and were, like men, doomed to suffer physical death in order to attain spiritual immortality.

The whole scheme of Northern mythology was therefore a drama, every step leading gradually to the climax or tragic end, when, with true poetic justice, punishment and reward were impartially meted out. In the foregoing chapters, the gradual rise and decline of the gods have been carefully traced. We have recounted how the Æsir tolerated the presence of evil, personated by Loki, in their midst ; how they weakly followed his advice, allowed him to involve them in all manner of difficulties. from which they could be extricated only at the price of part of their virtue or peace, and finally permitted him to gain such ascendency over them that he did not scruple to rob them of their dearest possession, purity, or innocence, as personified by Balder the good.

Too late the gods realised how evil was this spirit that had found a home among them, and too late they banished Loki to earth, where men, following the gods' example, listened to his teachings, and were corrupted by his sinister influence.

> " Brothers slay brothers ;
> Sisters' children

Shed each other's blood.
Hard is the world;
Sensual sin grows huge.
There are sword-ages, axe-ages;
Shields are cleft in twain;
Storm-ages, murder-ages;
Till the world falls dead,
And men no longer spare
Or pity one another."

Norse Mythology (*R. B. Anderson*).

The Fimbul-winter

Seeing that crime was rampant, and all good banished from the earth, the gods realised that the prophecies uttered of old were about to be fulfilled, and that the shadow of Ragnarok, the twilight or dusk of the gods, was already upon them. Sol and Mani grew pale with affright, and drove their chariots tremblingly along their appointed paths, looking back with fear at the pursuing wolves which would shortly overtake and devour them; and as their smiles disappeared the earth grew sad and cold, and the terrible Fimbul-winter began. Then snow fell from the four points of the compass at once, the biting winds swept down from the north, and all the earth was covered with a thick layer of ice.

"Grim Fimbul raged, and o'er the world
Tempestuous winds and snowstorms hurled;
The roaring ocean icebergs ground,
And flung its frozen foam around,
E'en to the top of mountain height;
    No warming air
    Nor radiance fair
Of gentle Summer's soft'ning light,
Tempered this dreadful glacial night."

Valhalla (*J. C. Jones*).

This severe winter lasted during three whole seasons without a break, and was followed by three others, equally severe, during which all cheer departed from the earth, and the crimes of men increased with fearful rapidity, whilst, in the general struggle for life, the last feelings of humanity and compassion disappeared.

The Wolves Let Loose

In the dim recesses of the Ironwood the giantess Iarnsaxa or Angur-boda diligently fed the wolves Hati, Sköll, and Managarm, the progeny of Fenris, with the marrow of murderers' and adulterers' bones ; and such was the prevalence of these vile crimes, that the well-nigh insatiable monsters were never stinted for food. They daily gained strength to pursue Sol and Mani, and finally overtook and devoured them, deluging the earth with blood from their dripping jaws.

> "In the east she was seated, that aged woman, in Jarnrid,
> And there she nourished the posterity of Fenrir ;
> He will be the most formidable of all, he
> Who, under the form of a monster, will swallow up the moon."
> *Voluspa (Pfeiffer's tr.)*.

At this terrible calamity the whole earth trembled and shook, the stars, affrighted, fell from their places, and Loki, Fenris, and Garm, renewing their efforts, rent their chains asunder and rushed forth to take their revenge. At the same moment the dragon Nidhug gnawed through the root of the ash Yggdrasil, which quivered to its topmost bough ; the red cock Fialar, perched above Valhalla, loudly crowed an alarm, which was immediately echoed by Gullin-kambi, the rooster in Midgard, and by Hel's dark-red bird in Nifl-heim.

> "The gold-combed cock
> The gods in Valhal loudly crowed to arms ;
> The blood-red cock as shrilly summons all
> On earth and down beneath it."
> *Viking Tales of the North (R. B. Anderson)*.

Heimdall Gives the Alarm

Heimdall, noting these ominous portents and hearing the cock's shrill cry, immediately put the Giallar-horn to his lips and blew the long-expected blast, which was heard throughout the world. At the first sound of this rally Æsir and Einheriar sprang from their golden couches and sallied bravely out of the great hall, armed for the coming fray, and, mounting their impatient steeds, they galloped over the quivering rainbow bridge to the spacious field of Vigrid, where, as Vafthrudnir had predicted long before, the last battle was to take place.

The Terrors of the Sea

The terrible Midgard snake Iörmungandr had been aroused by the general disturbance, and with immense writhings and commotion, whereby the seas were lashed into huge waves such as had never before disturbed the deeps of ocean, he crawled out upon the land, and hastened to join the dread fray, in which he was to play a prominent part.

> "In giant wrath the Serpent tossed
> In ocean depths, till, free from chain,
> He rose upon the foaming main ;
> Beneath the lashings of his tail,
> Seas, mountain high, swelled on the land ;
> Then, darting mad the waves acrost,
> Pouring forth bloody froth like hail,
> Spurting with poisoned, venomed breath
> Foul, deadly mists o'er all the Earth,
> Thro' thundering surge, he sought the strand."
> *Valhalla* (*J. C. Jones*).

One of the great waves, stirred up by Iörmungandr's struggles, set afloat Nagilfar, the fatal ship, which was constructed entirely out of the nails of those dead folks whose relatives had failed, through the ages, in their

332

duty, having neglected to pare the nails of the deceased, ere they were laid to rest. No sooner was this vessel afloat, than Loki boarded it with the fiery host from Muspells-heim, and steered it boldly over the stormy waters to the place of conflict.

This was not the only vessel bound for Vigrid, however, for out of a thick fog bank towards the north came another ship, steered by Hrym, in which were all the frost giants, armed to the teeth and eager for a conflict with the Æsir, whom they had always hated.

The Terrors of the Underworld

At the same time, Hel, the goddess of death, crept through a crevice in the earth out of her underground home, closely followed by the Hel-hound Garm, the malefactors of her cheerless realm, and the dragon Nidhug, which flew over the battlefield bearing corpses upon his wings.

As soon as he landed, Loki welcomed these reinforcements with joy, and placing himself at their head he marched with them to the fight.

Suddenly the skies were rent asunder, and through the fiery breach rode Surtr with his flaming sword, followed by his sons; and as they rode over the bridge Bifröst, with intent to storm Asgard, the glorious arch sank with a crash beneath their horses' tread.

> "Down thro' the fields of air,
> With glittering armour fair,
> In battle order bright,
> They sped while seething flame
> From rapid hoofstrokes came.
> Leading his gleaming band, rode Surtur,
> 'Mid the red ranks of raging fire."
> *Valhalla (J. C. Jones).*

The gods knew full well that their end was now near,

333

and that their weakness and lack of foresight placed them under great disadvantages ; for Odin had but one eye, Tyr but one hand, and Frey nothing but a stag's horn wherewith to defend himself, instead of his invincible sword. Nevertheless, the Æsir did not show any signs of despair, but, like true battle-gods of the North, they donned their richest attire, and gaily rode to the battle-field, determined to sell their lives as dearly as possible.

While they were mustering their forces, Odin once more rode down to the Urdar fountain, where, under the toppling Yggdrasil, the Norns sat with veiled faces and obstinately silent, their web lying torn at their feet. Once more the father of the gods whispered a mysterious communication to Mimir, after which he remounted Sleipnir and rejoined the waiting host.

The Great Battle

The combatants were now assembled on Vigrid's broad plain. On one side were ranged the stern, calm faces of the Æsir, Vanas, and Einheriar ; while on the other were gathered the motley host of Surtr, the grim frost giants, the pale army of Hel, and Loki and his dread followers, Garm, Fenris, and Iörmungandr, the two latter belching forth fire and smoke, and exhaling clouds of noxious, deathly vapours, which filled all heaven and earth with their poisonous breath.

> " The years roll on,
> The generations pass, the ages grow,
> And bring us nearer to the final day
> When from the south shall march the fiery band
> And cross the bridge of heaven, with Lok for guide,
> And Fenris at his heel with broken chain ;
> While from the east the giant Rymer steers
> His ship, and the great serpent makes to land ;
> And all are marshall'd in one flaming square
> Against the Gods, upon the plains of Heaven."
>
> *Balder Dead* (*Matthew Arnold*).

Odin and Fenris
Dorothy Hardy

334

THE GREAT BATTLE

All the pent-up antagonism of ages was now let loose in a torrent of hate, each member of the opposing hosts fighting with grim determination, as did our ancestors of old, hand to hand and face to face. With a mighty shock, heard above the roar of battle which filled the universe, Odin and the Fenris wolf came into impetuous contact, while Thor attacked the Midgard snake, and Tyr came to grips with the dog Garm. Frey closed with Surtr, Heimdall with Loki, whom he had defeated once before, and the remainder of the gods and all the Einheriar engaged foes equally worthy of their courage. But, in spite of their daily preparation in the heavenly city, Valhalla's host was doomed to succumb, and Odin was amongst the first of the shining ones to be slain. Not even the high courage and mighty attributes of Allfather could withstand the tide of evil as personified in the Fenris wolf. At each succeeding moment of the struggle its colossal size assumed greater proportions, until finally its wide-open jaws embraced all the space between heaven and earth, and the foul monster rushed furiously upon the father of gods and engulphed him bodily within its horrid maw.

> " Fenrir shall with impious tooth
> Slay the sire of rolling years :
> Vithar shall avenge his fall,
> And, struggling with the shaggy wolf,
> Shall cleave his cold and gory jaws."
> *Vafthrudni's-mal* (*W. Taylor's tr.*).

None of the gods could lend Allfather a helping hand at that critical moment, for it was a time of sore trial to all. Frey put forth heroic efforts, but Surtr's flashing sword now dealt him a death-stroke. In his struggle with the arch-enemy, Loki, Heimdall fared better, but his final conquest was dearly bought, for he, too, fell dead. The struggle between Tyr and Garm

335

had the same tragic end, and Thor, after a most terrible encounter with the Midgard snake, and after slaying him with a stroke from Miölnir, staggered back nine paces, and was drowned in the flood of venom which poured from the dying monster's jaws.

> " Odin's son goes
> With the monster to fight ;
> Midgard's Veor in his rage
> Will slay the worm ;
> Nine feet will go
> Fiörgyn's son,
> Bowed by the serpent
> Who feared no foe."
>
> *Sæmund's Edda (Thorpe's tr.).*

Vidar now came rushing from a distant part of the plain to avenge the death of his mighty sire, and the doom foretold fell upon Fenris, whose lower jaw now felt the impress of that shoe which had been reserved for this day. At the same moment Vidar seized the monster's upper jaw with his hands, and with one terrible wrench tore him asunder.

The Devouring Fire

The other gods who took part in the fray, and all the Einheriar having now perished, Surtr suddenly flung his fiery brands over heaven, earth, and the nine kingdoms of Hel. The raging flames enveloped the massive stem of the world ash Yggdrasil, and reached the golden palaces of the gods, which were utterly consumed. The vegetation upon earth was likewise destroyed, and the fervent heat made all the waters seethe and boil.

> " Fire's breath assails
> The all-nourishing tree,
> Towering fire plays
> Against heaven itself."
>
> *Sæmund's Edda (Thorpe's tr.).*

REGENERATION

The great conflagration raged fiercely until everything was consumed, when the earth, blackened and scarred, slowly sank beneath the boiling waves of the sea. Ragnarok had indeed come ; the world tragedy was over, the divine actors were slain, and chaos seemed to have resumed its former sway. But as in a play, after the principals are slain and the curtain has fallen, the audience still looks for the favourites to appear and make their bow, so the ancient Northern races fancied that, all evil having perished in Surtr's flames, from the general ruin goodness would rise, to resume its sway over the earth, and that some of the gods would return to dwell in heaven for ever.

> " All evil
> Dies there an endless death, while goodness riseth
> From that great world-fire, purified at last,
> To a life far higher, better, nobler than the past.
> *Viking Tales of the North* (*R. B. Anderson*).

Regeneration

Our ancestors believed fully in regeneration, and held that after a certain space of time the earth, purged by fire and purified by its immersion in the sea, rose again in all its pristine beauty and was illumined by the sun, whose chariot was driven by a daughter of Sol, born before the wolf had devoured her mother. The new orb of day was not imperfect, as the first sun had been, and its rays were no longer so ardent that a shield had to be placed between it and the earth. These more beneficent rays soon caused the earth to renew its green mantle, and to bring forth flowers and fruit in abundance. Two human beings, a woman, Lif, and a man, Lifthrasir, now emerged from the depths of Hodmimir's (Mimir's) forest, whence they had fled for refuge when Surtr set fire to the world. They had sunk into peaceful slumber there, unconscious of the destruction around them, and had remained, nurtured by the morning dew, until it was safe for them to wander out once more, when they took possession of the regenerated earth, which their descendants were to people and over which they were to have full sway.

> " We shall see emerge
> From the bright Ocean at our feet an earth
> More fresh, more verdant than the last, with fruits
> Self-springing, and a seed of man preserved,
> Who then shall live in peace, as then in war."
> *Balder Dead* (*Matthew Arnold*).

A New Heaven

All the gods who represented the developing forces of Nature were slain on the fatal field of Vigrid, but Vali and Vidar, the types of the imperishable forces of Nature, returned to the field of Ida, where they were met by Modi and Magni, Thor's sons, the personifications of strength and energy, who rescued their father's sacred hammer from the general destruction, and carried it thither with them.

> " Vithar's then and Vali's force
> Heirs the empty realm of gods ;
> Mothi's thew and Magni's might
> Sways the massy mallet's weight,
> Won from Thor, when Thor must fall."
> *Vafthrudni's-mal* (*W. Taylor's tr.*).

Here they were joined by Hoenir, no longer an exile among the Vanas, who, as developing forces, had also vanished for ever ; and out of the dark underworld where he had languished so long rose the radiant Balder, together with his brother Hodur, with whom he was reconciled, and with whom he was to live in perfect amity and peace. The past had gone for ever, and the surviving deities could recall it without bitterness. The memory of their former companions was, however, dear to them, and full often did they return to their old haunts to linger over the happy associations. It was thus that walking one day in the long grass on Idavold, they found again the golden disks with which the Æsir had been wont to sport.

> "We shall tread once more that well-known plain
> Of Ida, and among the grass shall find .
> The golden dice with which we play'd of yore ;
> And that will bring to mind the former life
> And pastime of the Gods, the wise discourse
> Of Odin, the delights of other days."
>
> *Balder Dead* (*Matthew Arnold*).

When the small band of gods turned mournfully towards the place where their lordly dwellings once stood, they became aware, to their joyful surprise, that Gimli, the highest heavenly abode, had not been consumed, for it rose glittering before them, its golden roof outshining the sun. Hastening thither they discovered, to the great increase of their joy, that it had become the place of refuge for all the virtuous.

> "In Gimli the lofty
> There shall the hosts
> Of the virtuous dwell,
> And through all ages
> Taste of deep gladness."
>
> *Literature and Romance of Northern*
> *Europe* (*Howitt*).

One too Mighty to Name

As the Norsemen who settled in Iceland, and through whom the most complete exposition of the Odinic faith has come down to us in the Eddas and Sagas, were not definitely converted until the eleventh century,— although they had come in contact with Christians during their viking raids nearly six centuries before,— it is very probable that the Northern scalds gleaned

339

some idea of the Christian doctrines, and that this knowledge influenced them to a certain extent, and coloured their descriptions of the end of the world and the regeneration of the earth. It was perhaps this vague knowledge, also, which induced them to add to the Edda a verse, which is generally supposed to have been an interpolation, proclaiming that another God, too mighty to name, would arise to bear rule over Gimli. From his heavenly seat he would judge mankind, and separate the bad from the good. The former would be banished to the horrors of Nastrond, while the good would be transported to the blissful halls of Gimli the fair.

> " Then comes another,
> Yet more mighty.
> But Him I dare not
> Venture to name.
> Few farther may look
> Than to where Odin
> To meet the wolf goes."
>
> *Literature and Romance of Northern*
> *Europe (Howitt).*

There were two other heavenly mansions, however, one reserved for the dwarfs and the other for the giants ; for as these creatures had no free will, and but blindly executed the decrees of fate, they were not thought to be responsible for any harm done by them, and were therefore held to be undeserving of punishment.

The dwarfs, ruled by Sindri, were said to occupy a hall in the Nida mountains, where they drank the sparkling mead, while the giants took their pleasure in the hall Brimer, situated in the region Okolnur (not cool), for the power of cold was entirely annihilated, and there was no more ice.

Various mythologists have, of course, attempted to

explain these myths, and some, as we have already stated, see in the story of Ragnarok the influence of Christian teachings, and esteem it only a barbaric version of the end of the world and the coming judgment day, when a new heaven and earth shall arise, and all the good shall enjoy eternal bliss.

CHAPTER XXIX : GREEK AND NORTHERN MYTHOLOGIES

Comparative Mythology

DURING the past fifty years learned men of many nations have investigated philology and comparative mythology so thoroughly that they have ascertained beyond the possibility of doubt "that English, together with all the Teutonic dialects of the Continent, belongs to that large family of speech which comprises, besides the Teutonic, Latin, Greek, Slavonic, and Celtic, the Oriental languages of India and Persia." " It has also been proved that the various tribes who started from the central home to discover Europe in the north, and India in the south, carried away with them, not only a common language, but a common faith and a common mythology. These are facts which may be ignored but cannot be disputed, and the two sciences of comparative grammar and comparative mythology, though but of recent origin, rest on a foundation as sound and safe as that of any of the inductive sciences." " For more than a thousand years the Scandinavian inhabitants of Norway have been separated in language from their Teutonic brethren on the Continent, and yet both have not only preserved the same stock of popular stories, but they tell them, in several instances, in almost the same words."

This resemblance, so strong in the early literature of nations inhabiting countries which present much the same physical aspect and have nearly the same climate, is not so marked when we compare the Northern myths with those of the genial South. Still, notwithstanding the contrast between Northern and Southern Europe, where these myths gradually ripened and attained their full growth, there is an analogy between the

342

two mythologies which shows that the seeds from whence both sprang were originally the same.

In the foregoing chapters the Northern system of mythology has been outlined as clearly as possible, and the physical significance of the myths has been explained. Now we shall endeavour to set forth the resemblance of Northern mythology to that of the other Aryan nations, by comparing it with the Greek, which, however, it does not resemble as closely as it does the Oriental.

It is, of course, impossible in a work of this character to do more than mention the main points of resemblance in the stories forming the basis of these religions; but that will be sufficient to demonstrate, even to the most sceptical, that they must have been identical at a period too remote to indicate now with any certainty.

The Beginning of Things

The Northern nations, like the Greeks, imagined that the world rose out of chaos; and while the latter described it as a vapoury, formless mass, the former, influenced by their immediate surroundings, depicted it as a chaos of fire and ice—a combination which is only too comprehensible to any one who has visited Iceland and seen the wild, peculiar contrast between its volcanic soil, spouting geysers, and the great icebergs which hedge it round during the long, dark winter season.

From these opposing elements, fire and ice, were born the first divinities, who, like the first gods of the Greeks, were gigantic in stature and uncouth in appearance. Ymir, the huge ice giant, and his descendants, are comparable to the Titans, who were also elemental forces of Nature, personifications of subterranean fire; and both, having held full sway for a time, were obliged to yield to greater perfection. After a

343

fierce struggle for supremacy, they all found themselves defeated and banished to the respective remote regions of Tartarus and Jötun-heim.

The triad, Odin, Vili, and Ve, of the Northern myth is the exact counterpart of Jupiter, Neptune, and Pluto, who, superior to the Titan forces, rule supreme over the world in their turn. In the Greek mythology, the gods, who are also all related to one another, betake themselves to Olympus, where they build golden palaces for their use ; and in the Northern mythology the divine conquerors repair to Asgard, and there construct similar dwellings.

Cosmogony

Northern cosmogony was not unlike the Greek, for the people imagined that the earth, Mana-heim, was entirely surrounded by the sea, at the bottom of which lay coiled the huge Midgard snake, biting its own tail ; and it was perfectly natural that, viewing the storm-lashed waves which beat against their shores, they should imagine these to be caused by his convulsive writhing. The Greeks, who also fancied the earth was round and compassed by a mighty river called Oceanus, described it as flowing with " a steady, equable current," for they generally gazed out upon calm and sunlit seas. Nifl-heim, the Northern region of perpetual cold and mist, had its exact counterpart in the land north of the Hyper-boreans, where feathers (snow) continually hovered in the air, and where Hercules drove the Ceryneian stag into a snowdrift ere he could seize and bind it fast.

The Phenomena of the Sky

Like the Greeks, the Northern races believed that the earth was created first, and that the vaulted heavens were made afterwards to overshadow it entirely. They

344

The Ride of the Valkyrs

H. Hendrich

By Permission of the " Illustrirte Zeitung " J. J. Weber, Leipzig

also imagined that the sun and moon were daily driven across the sky in chariots drawn by fiery steeds. Sol, the sun maiden, therefore corresponded to Helios, Hyperion, Phœbus, or Apollo, while Mani, the Moon (owing to a peculiarity of Northern grammar, which makes the sun feminine and the moon masculine), was the exact counterpart of Phœbe, Diana, or Cynthia.

The Northern scalds, who thought that they descried the prancing forms of white-maned steeds in the flying clouds, and the glitter of spears in the flashing light of the aurora borealis, said that the Valkyrs, or battle maidens, galloped across the sky, while the Greeks saw in the same natural phenomena the white flocks of Apollo guarded by Phaetusa and Lampetia.

As the dew fell from the clouds, the Northern poets declared that it dropped from the manes of the Valkyrs' steeds, while the Greeks, who observed that it generally sparkled longest in the thickets, identified it with Daphne and Procris, whose names are derived from the Sanskrit word which means "to sprinkle," and who are slain by their lovers, Apollo and Cephalus, personifications of the sun.

The earth was considered in the North as well as in the South as a female divinity, the fostering mother of all things ; and it was owing to climatic difference only that the mythology of the North, where people were daily obliged to conquer the right to live by a hand-to-hand struggle with Nature, should represent her as hard and frozen like Rinda, while the Greeks embodied her in the genial goddess Ceres. The Greeks believed that the cold winter winds swept down from the North, and the Northern races, in addition, added that they were produced by the winnowing of the wings of the great eagle Hræ-svelgr.

The dwarfs, or dark elves, bred in Ymir's flesh, were

345

like Pluto's servants in that they never left their underground realm, where they, too, sought the precious
metals, which they moulded into delicate ornaments
such as Vulcan bestowed upon the gods, and into
weapons which no one could either dint or mar. As
for the light elves, who lived above ground and cared
for plants, trees, and streams, they were evidently the
Northern equivalents to the nymphs, dryads, oreades,
and hamadryads, which peopled the woods, valleys, and
fountains of ancient Greece.

Jupiter and Odin

Jupiter, like Odin, was the father of the gods, the god
of victory, and a personification of the universe. Hlidskialf, Allfather's lofty throne, was no less exalted than
Olympus or Ida, whence the Thunderer could observe
all that was taking place ; and Odin's invincible spear
Gungnir was as terror-inspiring as the thunderbolts
brandished by his Greek prototype. The Northern
deities feasted continually upon mead and boar's flesh,
the drink and meat most suitable to the inhabitants of
a Northern climate, while the gods of Olympus preferred the nectar and ambrosia which formed their only
sustenance.

Twelve Æsir sat in Odin's council hall to deliberate
over the wisest measures for the government of the
world and men, and an equal number of gods assembled
on the cloudy peak of Mount Olympus for a similar
purpose. The Golden Age in Greece was a period of
idyllic happiness, amid ever-flowering groves and under
balmy skies, while the Northern age of bliss was also a
time when peace and innocence flourished on the earth,
and when evil was as yet entirely unknown.

The Creation of Man

Using the materials near at hand, the Greeks modelled their first images out of clay ; hence they naturally imagined that Prometheus had made man out of that substance when called upon to fashion a creature inferior to the gods only. As the Northern statues were hewn out of wood, the Northern races inferred, as a matter of course, that Odin, Vili, and Ve (who here correspond to Prometheus, Epimetheus, and Minerva, the three Greek creators of man) made the first human couple, Ask and Embla, out of blocks of wood.

The goat Heidrun, which supplied the heavenly mead, is like Amalthea, Jupiter's first nurse, and the busy, tell-tale Ratatosk is equivalent to the snow-white crow in the story of Coronis, which was turned black in punishment for its tattling. Jupiter's eagle has its counterpart in the ravens Hugin and Munin, or in the wolves Geri and Freki, which are ever crouching at Odin's feet.

Norns and Fates

The close resemblance between the Northern Orlog and the Greek Destiny, goddesses whose decrees the gods themselves were obliged to respect, and the equally powerful Norns and Mœræ, is too obvious to need pointing out, while the Vanas are counterparts of Neptune and the other ocean divinities. The great quarrel between the Vanas and the Æsir is merely another version of the dispute between Jupiter and Neptune for the supremacy of the world. Just as Jupiter forces his brother to yield to his authority, so the Æsir remain masters of all, but do not refuse to continue to share their power with their conquered foes, who thus become their allies and friends.

Like Jupiter, Odin is always described as majestic and middle-aged, and both gods are regarded as the divine progenitors of royal races, for while the Heraclidæ claimed Jupiter as their father, the Inglings, Skioldings, etc., held that Odin was the founder of their families. The most solemn oaths were sworn by Odin's spear as well as by Jupiter's footstool, and both gods rejoice in a multitude of names, all descriptive of the various phases of their nature and worship.

Odin, like Jupiter, frequently visited the earth in disguise, to judge of the hospitable intentions of mankind, as in the story of Geirrod and Agnar, which resembles that of Philemon and Baucis. The aim was to encourage hospitality ; therefore, in both stories, those who showed themselves humanely inclined are richly rewarded, and in the Northern myth the lesson is enforced by the punishment inflicted upon Geirrod, as the scalds believed in poetic justice and saw that it was carefully meted out.

The contest of wit between Odin and Vafthrudnir has its parallel in the musical rivalry of Apollo and Marsyas, or in the test of skill between Minerva and Arachne. Odin further resembled Apollo in that he, too, was god of eloquence and poetry, and could win all hearts by means of his divine voice ; he was like Mercury in that he taught mortals the use of runes, while the Greek god introduced the alphabet.

Myths of the Seasons

The disappearance of Odin, the sun or summer, and the consequent desolation of Frigga, the earth, is merely a different version of the myths of Proserpine and Adonis. When Proserpine and Adonis have gone, the earth (Ceres or Venus) bitterly mourns their absence, and refuses all consolation. It is only when they return from their exile that she casts off her mourning garments and gloom, and again decks herself in all her jewels. So Frigga and Freya bewail the absence of their husbands Odin and Odur, and remain hard and cold until their return. Odin's wife, Saga, the goddess of history, who lingered by Sokvabek, " the stream of time and events," taking note of all she saw, is like Clio, the muse of history, whom Apollo sought by the inspiring fount of Helicon.

Just as, according to Euhemerus, there was an historical Zeus, buried in Crete, where his grave can still be seen, so there was an historical Odin, whose mound rises near Upsala, where the greatest Northern temple once stood, and where there was a mighty oak which rivalled the famous tree of Dodona.

Frigga and Juno

Frigga, like Juno, was a personification of the atmosphere, the patroness of marriage, of connubial and motherly love, and the goddess of childbirth. She, too, is represented as a beautiful, stately woman, rejoicing in her adornments ; and her special attendant, Gna, rivals Iris in the rapidity with which she executes her mistress's behests. Juno has full control over the clouds, which she can brush away with a motion of her hand, and Frigga is supposed to weave them out of the thread she has spun on her jewelled spinning wheel.

In Greek mythology we find many examples of the way in which Juno seeks to outwit Jupiter. Similar tales are not lacking in the Northern myths. Juno obtains possession of Io, in spite of her husband's reluctance to part with her, and Frigga artfully secures the victory for the Winilers in the Langobarden Saga. Odin's wrath at Frigga's theft of the gold from his

349

statue is equivalent to Jupiter's marital displeasure at
Juno's jealousy and interference during the war of
Troy. In the story of Gefjon, and the clever way in
which she procured land from Gylfi to form her
kingdom of Seeland, we have a reproduction of the
story of Dido, who obtained by stratagem the land
upon which she founded her city of Carthage. In
both accounts oxen come into play, for while in the
Northern myth these sturdy beasts draw the piece of
land far out to sea, in the other an ox hide, cut into
strips, serves to enclose the queen's grant.

Musical Myths

The Pied Piper of Hamelin, who could attract all
living creatures by his music, is like Orpheus or
Amphion, whose lyres had the same power ; and Odin,
as leader of the dead, is the counterpart of Mercury
Psychopompus, both being personifications of the wind,
on whose wings disembodied souls were thought to be
wafted from this mortal sphere.

The trusty Eckhardt, who would fain save Tannhäuser
and prevent his returning to expose himself to the
enchantments of the sorceress, in the Hörselberg, is like
the Greek Mentor, who not only accompanied Telema-
chus, but gave him good advice and wise instructions, and would have rescued Ulysses from the hands
of Calypso.

Thor and the Greek Gods

Thor, the Northern thunder-god, also has many
points of resemblance with Jupiter. He bears the
hammer Miölnir, the Northern emblem of the deadly
thunderbolt, and, like Jupiter, uses it freely when
warring against the giants. In his rapid growth Thor
resembles Mercury, for while the former playfully

tosses about several loads of ox hides a few hours after his birth, the latter steals Apollo's oxen before he is one day old. In physical strength Thor resembles Hercules, who also gave early proofs of uncommon vigour by strangling the serpents sent to slay him in his cradle, and who delighted, later on, in attacking and conquering giants and monsters. Hercules became a woman and took to spinning to please Omphale, the Lydian queen, and Thor assumed a woman's apparel to visit Thrym and recover his hammer, which had been buried nine rasts underground. The hammer, his principal attribute, was used for many sacred purposes. It consecrated the funeral pyre and the marriage rite, and boundary stakes driven in by a hammer were considered as sacred among Northern nations as the Hermæ or statues of Mercury, removal of which was punishable by death.

Thor's wife, Sif, with her luxuriant golden hair, is, as we have already stated, an emblem of the earth, and her hair of its rich vegetation. Loki's theft of these tresses is equivalent to Pluto's rape of Proserpine. To recover the golden locks, Loki must visit the dwarfs (Pluto's servants), crouching in the low passages of the underground world ; so Mercury must seek Proserpine in Hades.

The gadfly which hinders Jupiter from recovering possession of Io, after Mercury has slain Argus, reappears in the Northern myth to sting Brock and to endeavour to prevent the manufacture of the magic ring Draupnir, which is merely a counterpart of Sif's tresses, as it also represents the fruits of the earth. The fly continues to torment the dwarf during the manufacture of Frey's golden-bristled boar, a prototype of Apollo's golden sun chariot, and it prevents the perfect formation of the handle of Thor's hammer.

The magic ship Skidbladnir, also made by the dwarfs, is like the swift-sailing Argo, which was a personification of the clouds sailing overhead ; and just as the former was said to be large enough to accommodate all the gods, so the latter bore all the Greek heroes off to the distant land of Colchis.

The Germans, wishing to name the days of the week after their gods, as the Romans had done, gave the name of Thor to Jove's day, and thus made it the present Thursday.

Thor's struggle against Hrungnir is a parallel to the fight between Hercules and Cacus or Antæus ; while Groa is evidently Ceres, for she, too, mourns for her absent child Orvandil (Proserpine), and breaks out into a song of joy when she hears that it will return.

Magni, Thor's son, who when only three hours old exhibits his marvellous strength by lifting Hrungnir's leg off his recumbent father, also reminds us of the infant Hercules ; and Thor's voracious appetite at Thrym's wedding feast has its parallel in Mercury's first meal, which consisted of two whole oxen.

The crossing of the swollen tide of Veimer by Thor reminds us of Jason's feat when he waded across the torrent on his way to visit the tyrant Pelias and recover possession of his father's throne.

The marvellous necklace worn by Frigga and Freya to enhance their charms is like the cestus or girdle of Venus, which Juno borrowed to subjugate her lord, and is, like Sif's tresses and the ring Draupnir, an emblem of luxuriant vegetation or a type of the stars which shine in the firmament.

The Northern sword-god Tyr is, of course, the Greek war-god Ares, whom he so closely resembles that his name was given to the day of the week held sacred to Ares, which is even now known as Tuesday or Tiu's day. Like Ares, Tyr was noisy and courageous; he delighted in the din of battle, and was fearless at all times. He alone dared to brave the Fenris wolf; and the Southern proverb concerning Scylla and Charybdis has its counterpart in the Northern adage, "to get loose out of Læding and to dash out of Droma." The Fenris wolf, also a personification of subterranean fire, is bound, like his prototypes the Titans, in Tartarus.

The similarity between the gentle, music-loving Bragi, with his harp, and Apollo or Orpheus, is very great; so is the resemblance between the magic draught Od-hroerir and the waters of Helicon, both of which were supposed to serve as inspiration to mortal as well as to immortal poets. Odin dons eagle plumes to bear away this precious mead, and Jupiter assumes a similar guise to secure his cupbearer Ganymede.

Idun, like Adonis and Proserpine, or still more like Eurydice, is also a fair personification of spring. She is borne away by the cruel ice giant Thiassi, who represents the boar which slew Adonis, the kidnapper of Proserpine, or the poisonous serpent which bit Eurydice. Idun is detained for a long time in Jötun-heim (Hades), where she forgets all her merry, playful ways, and becomes mournful and pale. She cannot return alone to Asgard, and it is only when Loki (now an emblem of the south wind) comes to bear her away in the shape of a nut or a swallow that she can effect her escape. She reminds us of Proserpine and Adonis escorted back to earth by Mercury (god of the wind), or of Eurydice lured out of Hades by the sweet sounds of Orpheus's harp, which were also symbolical of the soughing of the winds.

Idun and Eurydice

The myth of Idun's fall from Yggdrasil into the darkest depths of Nifl-heim, while subject to the same

z

explanation and comparison as the above story, is still more closely related to the tale of Orpheus and Eurydice, for the former, like Bragi, cannot exist without the latter, whom he follows even into the dark realm of death ; without her his songs are entirely silenced. The wolf-skin in which Idun is enveloped is typical of the heavy snows in Northern regions, which preserve the tender roots from the blighting influence of the extreme winter cold.

Skadi and Diana

The Van Niörd, who is god of the sunny summer seas, has his counterpart in Neptune and more especially in Nereus, the personification of the calm and pleasant aspect of the mighty deep. Niörd's wife, Skadi, is the Northern huntress ; she therefore resembles Diana. Like her, she bears a quiver full of arrows, and a bow which she handles with consummate skill. Her short gown permits the utmost freedom of motion, also, and she, too, is generally accompanied by a hound.

The story of the transference of Thiassi's eyes to the firmament, where they glow like brilliant stars, reminds us of many Greek star myths, and especially of Argus's eyes ever on the watch, of Orion and his jewelled girdle, and of his dog Sirius, all changed into stars by the gods to appease angry goddesses. Loki's antics to win a smile from the irate Skadi are considered akin to the quivering flashes of sheet-lightning which he personified in the North, while Steropes, the Cyclops, typified it for the Greeks.

Frey and Apollo

The Northern god of sunshine and summer showers, the genial Frey, has many traits in common with Apollo, for, like him, he is beautiful and young, rides the golden-bristled boar which was the Northern concep-

354

tion of the sunbeams, or drives across the sky in a golden car, which reminds us of Apollo's glittering chariot.

Frey has some of the gentle Zephyrus's characteristics besides, for he, too, scatters flowers along his way. His horse Blodug-hofi is not unlike Pegasus, Apollo's favourite steed, for it can pass through fire and water with equal ease and velocity.

Fro, like Odin and Jupiter, is also identified with a human king, and his mound lies beside Odin's near Upsala. His reign was so happy that it was called the Golden Age, and he therefore reminds us of Saturn, who, exiled to earth, ruled over the people of Italy, and granted them similar prosperity.

Freya and Venus

Gerda, the beautiful maiden, is like Venus, and also like Atalanta ; she is hard to woo and hard to win, like the fleet-footed maiden, but, like her, she yields at last and becomes a happy wife. The golden apples with which Skirnir tries to bribe her remind us of the golden fruit which Hippomenes cast in Atalanta's way, and which made her lose the race.

Freya, the goddess of youth, love, and beauty, like Venus, sprang from the sea, for she is a daughter of the sea-god Niörd. Venus bestowed her best affections upon the god of war and upon the martial Anchises, while Freya often assumes the garb of a Valkyr, and rides rapidly to earth to take part in mortal strife and bear away the heroic slain to feast in her halls. Like Venus, she delights in offerings of fruits and flowers, and lends a gracious ear to the petitions of lovers. Freya also resembles Minerva, for, like her, she wears a helmet and breastplate, and, like her, also, she is noted for her beautiful blue eyes.

Odur and Adonis

Odur, Freya's husband, is like Adonis, and when he leaves her, she, too, sheds countless tears, which, in her case, are turned to gold, while Venus's tears are changed into anemones, and those of the Heliades, mourning for Phaeton, harden to amber, which resembles gold in colour and in consistency. Just as Venus rejoices at Adonis's return, and all Nature blooms in sympathy with her joy, so Freya becomes lighthearted once more when she has found her husband beneath the flowering myrtles of the South. Venus's car is drawn by fluttering doves, and Freya's is swiftly carried along by cats, which are emblems of sensual love, as the doves were considered types of tenderest love. Freya is appreciative of beauty and angrily refuses to marry Thrym, while Venus scorns and finally deserts Vulcan, whom she has been forced to marry against her will.

The Greeks represented Justice as a goddess blindfolded, with scales in one hand and a sword in the other, to indicate the impartiality and the fixity of her decrees. The corresponding deity of the North was Forseti, who patiently listened to both sides of a question ere he, too, promulgated his impartial and irrevocable sentence.

Uller, the winter-god, resembles Apollo and Orion only in his love for the chase, which he pursues with ardour under all circumstances. He is the Northern bowman, and his skill is quite as unerring as theirs.

Heimdall, like Argus, was gifted with marvellous keenness of sight, which enabled him to see a hundred miles off as plainly by night as by day. His Giallarhorn, which could be heard throughout all the world, proclaiming the gods' passage to and fro over the quivering bridge Bifröst, was like the trumpet of the goddess Renown. As he was related to the water deities on his mother's side, he could, like Proteus, assume any form at will, and he made good use of this power on the occasion when he frustrated Loki's attempt to steal the necklace Brisinga-men.

Hermod, the quick or nimble, resembles Mercury not only in his marvellous celerity of motion. He, too, was the messenger of the gods, and, like the Greek divinity, flashed hither and thither, aided not by winged cap and sandals, but by Odin's steed Sleipnir, whom he alone was allowed to bestride. Instead of the Caduceus, he bore the wand Gambantein. He questioned the Norns and the magician Rossthiof, through whom he learned that Vali would come to avenge his brother Balder and to supplant his father Odin. Instances of similar consultations are found in Greek mythology, where Jupiter would fain have married Thetis, yet desisted when the Fates foretold that if he did so she would be the mother of a son who would surpass his father in glory and renown.

The Northern god of silence, Vidar, has some resemblance to Hercules, for while the latter has nothing but a club with which to defend himself against the Nemean lion, whom he tears asunder, the former is enabled to rend the Fenris wolf at Ragnarok by the possession of one large shoe.

Rinda and Danae

Odin's courtship of Rinda reminds us of Jupiter's wooing of Danae, who is also a symbol of the earth ; and while the shower of gold in the Greek tale is intended to represent the fertilising sunbeams, the footbath in the Northern story typifies the spring thaw which sets in when the sun has overcome the resistance of the frozen earth. Perseus, the child of this union, has many points of resemblance with Vali, for he, too, is an avenger, and slays his mother's enemies just as surely as Vali destroys Hodur, the murderer of Balder.

The Fates were supposed to preside over birth in Greece, and to foretell a child's future, as did the Norns ; and the story of Meleager has its unmistakable parallel in that of Nornagesta. Althæa preserves the half-consumed brand in a chest, Nornagesta conceals the candle-end in his harp ; and while the Greek mother brings about her son's death by casting the brand into the fire, Nornagesta, compelled to light his candle-end at Olaf's command, dies as it sputters and burns out.

Hebe and the Valkyrs were the cupbearers of Olympus and Asgard. They were all personifications of youth ; and while Hebe married the great hero and demigod Hercules when she ceased to fulfil her office, the Valkyrs were relieved from their duties when united to heroes like Helgi, Hakon, Völund, or Sigurd.

The Cretan labyrinth has its counterpart in the Icelandic Völundarhaus, and Völund and Dædalus both effect their escape from a maze by a cleverly devised pair of wings, which enable them to fly in safety over land and sea and escape from the tyranny of their respective masters, Nidud and Minos. Völund resembles Vulcan, also, in that he is a clever smith and makes use of his talents to work out his revenge. Vulcan, lamed by a fall from Olympus, and neglected by Juno, whom he had tried to befriend, sends her a golden throne, which is provided with cunning springs to seize and hold her fast. Völund, hamstrung by the suggestion of Nidud's queen, secretly murders her sons, and out of their eyes fashions marvellous jewels, which she unsuspectingly wears upon her breast until he reveals their origin.

358

The Storm-Ride

Gilbert Bayes

Myths of the Sea

Just as the Greeks fancied that the tempests were the effect of Neptune's wrath, so the Northern races attributed them either to the writhings of Iörmungandr, the Midgard snake, or to the anger of Ægir, who, crowned with seaweed like Neptune, often sent his children, the wave maidens (the counterpart of the Nereides and Oceanides), to play on the tossing billows. Neptune had his dwelling in the coral caves near the Island of Eubœa, while Ægir lived in a similar palace near the Cattegat. Here he was surrounded by the nixies, undines, and mermaids, the counterpart of the Greek water nymphs, and by the river-gods of the Rhine, Elbe, and Neckar, who remind us of Alpheus and Peneus, the river-gods of the Greeks.

The frequency of shipwrecks on the Northern coasts made the people think of Ran (the equivalent of the Greek sea-goddess Amphitrite) as greedy and avaricious, and they described her as armed with a strong net, with which she drew all things down into the deep. The Greek Sirens had their parallel in the Northern Lorelei, who possessed the same gift of song, and also lured mariners to their death ; while Princess Ilse, who was turned into a fountain, reminds us of the nymph Arethusa, who underwent a similar transformation.

In the Northern conception of Nifl-heim we have an almost exact counterpart of the Greek Hades. Mödgud, the guardian of the Giallar-bridge (the bridge of death), over which all the spirits of the dead must pass, exacts a tribute of blood as rigorously as Charon demands an obolus from every soul he ferries over Acheron, the river of death. The fierce dog Garm, cowering in the Gnipa hole, and keeping guard at Hel's gate, is like

359

the three-headed monster Cerberus; and the nine worlds of Nifl-heim are not unlike the divisions of Hades, Nastrond being an adequate substitute for Tartarus, where the wicked were punished with equal severity.

The custom of burning dead heroes with their arms, and of slaying victims, such as horses and dogs, upon their pyre, was much the same in the North as in the South; and while Mors or Thanatos, the Greek Death, was represented with a sharp scythe, Hel was depicted with a broom or rake, which she used as ruthlessly, and with which she did as much execution.

Balder and Apollo

Balder, the radiant god of sunshine, reminds us not only of Apollo and Orpheus, but of all the other heroes of sun myths. His wife Nanna is like Flora, and still more like Proserpine, for she, too, goes down into the underworld, where she tarries for a while. Balder's golden hall of Breidablik is like Apollo's palace in the east; he, also, delights in flowers; all things smile at his approach, and willingly pledge themselves not to injure him. As Achilles was vulnerable only in the heel, so Balder could be slain only by the harmless mistletoe, and his death is occasioned by Loki's jealousy just as Hercules was slain by that of Deianeira. Balder's funeral pyre on Ringhorn reminds us of Hercules's death on Mount Œta, the flames and reddish glow of both fires serving to typify the setting sun. The Northern god of sun and summer could only be released from Nifl-heim if all animate and inanimate objects shed tears; so Proserpine could issue from Hades only upon condition that she had partaken of no food. The trifling refusal of Thok to shed a single tear is like the pomegranate seeds which Proserpine ate, and the result is equally disastrous in both cases, as it detains Balder and Proserpine underground, and the earth (Frigga or Ceres) must continue to mourn their absence.

Through Loki evil entered into the Northern world; Prometheus's gift of fire brought the same curse upon the Greeks. The punishment inflicted by the gods upon the culprits is not unlike, for while Loki is bound with adamantine chains underground, and tortured by the continuous dropping of venom from the fangs of a snake fastened above his head, Prometheus is similarly fettered to Caucasus, and a ravenous vulture continually preys upon his liver. Loki's punishment has another counterpart in that of Tityus, bound in Hades, and in that of Enceladus, chained beneath Mount Ætna, where his writhing produced earthquakes, and his imprecations caused sudden eruptions of the volcano. Loki, further, resembles Neptune in that he, too, assumed an equine form and was the parent of a wonderful steed, for Sleipnir rivals Arion both in speed and endurance.

The Fimbul-winter has been compared to the long preliminary fight under the walls of Troy, and Ragnarok, the grand closing drama of Northern mythology, to the burning of that famous city. " Thor is Hector ; the Fenris wolf, Pyrrhus, son of Achilles, who slew Priam (Odin) ; and Vidar, who survives in Ragnarok, is Æneas." The destruction of Priam's palace is the type of the ruin of the gods' golden halls ; and the devouring wolves Hati, Sköll, and Managarm, the fiends of darkness, are prototypes of Paris and all the other demons of darkness, who bear away or devour the sun-maiden Helen.

Ragnarok and the Deluge

According to another interpretation, however, Ragnarok and the consequent submersion of the world is but a Northern version of the Deluge. The survivors, Lif and Lifthrasir, like Deucalion and Pyrrha, were destined to repeople the world; and just as the shrine of Delphi alone resisted the destructive power of the great cataclysm, so Gimli stood radiant to receive the surviving gods.

Giants and Titans

We have already seen how closely the Northern giants resembled the Titans. It only remains to mention that while the Greeks imagined that Atlas was changed into a mountain, so the Northmen believed that the Riesengebirge, in Germany, were formed from giants, and that the avalanches which descended from their lofty heights were the burdens of snow which these giants impatiently shook from their crests as they changed their cramped positions. The apparition, in the shape of a bull, of one of the water giants, who came to woo the queen of the Franks, has its parallel in the story of Jupiter's wooing of Europa, and Meroveus is evidently the exact counterpart of Sarpedon. A faint resemblance can be traced between the giant ship Mannigfual and the Argo, for while the one is supposed to have cruised through the Ægean and Euxine Seas, and to have made many places memorable by the dangers it encountered there, so the Northern vessel sailed about the North and Baltic Seas, and is mentioned in connection with the Island of Bornholm and the cliffs of Dover.

While the Greeks imagined that Nightmares were the evil dreams which escaped from the Cave of Somnus, the Northern race fancied they were female dwarfs or trolls, who crept out of the dark recesses of the earth to torment them. All magic weapons in the North were said to be the work of the dwarfs, the underground smiths, while those of the Greeks were manufactured by Vulcan and the Cyclopes, under Mount Ætna, or on the Island of Lemnos.

The Volsunga Saga

In the Sigurd myth we find Odin one-eyed like the Cyclopes, who, like him, are personifications of the sun. Sigurd is instructed by Gripir, the horse-trainer, who is reminiscent of Chiron, the centaur. He is not only able to teach a young hero all he need know, and to give him good advice concerning his future conduct, but is also possessed of the gift of prophecy.

The marvellous sword which becomes the property of Sigmund and of Sigurd as soon as they prove themselves worthy to wield it, and the sword Angurvadel which Frithiof inherits from his sire, remind us of the weapon which Ægeus concealed beneath the rock, and which Theseus secured as soon as he had become a man. Sigurd, like Theseus, Perseus, and Jason, seeks to avenge his father's wrongs ere he sets out in search of the golden hoard, the exact counterpart of the golden fleece, which is also guarded by a dragon, and is very hard to secure. Like all the Greek sun-gods and heroes, Sigurd has golden hair and bright blue eyes. His struggle with Fafnir reminds us of Apollo's fight with Python, while the ring Andvaranaut can be likened to Venus's cestus, and the curse attached to its possessor is like the tragedy of Helen, who brought endless bloodshed upon all connected with her.

Sigurd could not have conquered Fafnir without the magic sword, just as the Greeks failed to take Troy without the arrows of Philoctetes, which are also emblems of the all-conquering rays of the sun. The recovery of the stolen treasure is like Menelaus's recovery of Helen, and it apparently brings as little happiness to Sigurd as his recreant wife did to the Spartan king.

Brunhild

Brunhild resembles Minerva in her martial tastes, physical appearance, and wisdom; but her anger and resentment when Sigurd forgets her for Gudrun is like the wrath of Œnone, whom Paris deserts to woo Helen. Brunhild's anger continues to accompany Sigurd through life, and she even seeks to compass his death, while Œnone, called to cure her wounded lover, refuses to do so and permits him to die. Œnone and Brunhild are both overcome by the same remorseful feelings when their lovers have breathed their last, and both insist upon sharing their funeral pyres, and end their lives by the side of those whom they had loved.

Sun Myths

Containing, as it does, a whole series of sun myths, the Volsunga Saga repeats itself in every phase ; and just as Ariadne, forsaken by the sun-hero Theseus, finally marries Bacchus, so Gudrun, when Sigurd has departed, marries Atli, the King of the Huns. He, too, ends his life amid the flames of his burning palace or ship. Gunnar, like Orpheus or Amphion, plays such marvellous strains upon his harp that even the serpents are lulled to sleep. According to some interpretations, Atli is like Fafnir, and covets the possession of the gold. Both are therefore probably personifications " of the winter cloud which broods over and keeps from mortals the gold of the sun's light and heat, till in the spring the bright orb overcomes the powers of darkness and tempests, and scatters his gold over the face of the earth."

Swanhild, Sigurd's daughter, is another personification of the sun, as is seen in her blue eyes and golden hair ; and her death under the hoofs of black steeds

364

represents the blotting out of the sun by clouds of storm or of darkness.

Just as Castor and Pollux hasten to rescue their sister Helen when she has been borne away by Theseus, so Swanhild's brothers, Erp, Hamdir, and Sörli, hasten off to avenge her death.

Such are the main points of resemblance between the mythologies of the North and South, and the analogy goes far to prove that they were originally formed from the same materials, the principal differences being due to the local colouring imparted unconsciously by the different races.

INDEX TO POETICAL QUOTATIONS

INDEX TO POETICAL QUOTATIONS

GLOSSARY AND INDEX

A

AAGER (ä'ger) and Else. Ballad of, 184

ABEL. Cain in Wild Hunt because of the murder of, 26

ABUNDANTIA (a-bun-dan'shyä). Same as Fulla, 47

ABUNDIA. Same as Fulla, 47

ACHERON (ak'e-ron). Giöll, the Northern, 359

ACHILLES (a-kil'ēz). Balder, the Northern, 360; father of Pyrrhus, 361

ADONIS (a-dō'nis). Odin, the Northern, 348; Idun lost like, 353; Odur, the Northern, 355

ÆGEAN (ē-jē'an). Argo's cruise round the, 362

ÆGEUS (ē-jē'us). Sigmund's sword compared to that of, 363

ÆGIR (ä'jir). Tempests caused by, 185; god of the sea, 185–193, 303; banquet in halls of, 224; Neptune, the Greek, 359

ÆGIS (ē'jis). Fafnir's Helmet of Dread so called, 270

ÆNEAS (ē-nē'as). Vidar, the Northern, 361

ÆSIR (ä'sir). Northern gods called, 5; twelve in number, 11; Asgard, home of, 15; dispute between Vanas and, 15; to be supplanted, 32; inhabitants of Asia Minor, 39; Gylfi visits the, 40; Hrungnir feasts with the, 73; Freya visited by the, 78; recovery of hammer pleases the, 80; Fenris bound by the, 92, 93; Suttung slain by the, 99; Idun welcomed by the, 107; Niörd among the, 111; Ægir not ranked with the, 185; Ægir visits the, 188; reward promised to the, 205; heralds sent out by the, 211; Loki slanders the, 216, 225; battle between the giants and the, 231; beginning and end of the, 329; Giallar-horn summons the, 332; giants come to fight the, 333; courage and death of the, 335; golden disks of the, 339; Greek gods compared to the, 346; Greek equivalent of dispute between the Vanas and the, 347

ÆTNA (et'nà), MOUNT. Northern equivalent for earthquakes in, 361; dwarfs' forge equivalent to Vulcan's in, 362

AFI (ä'fē). Riger visits, 152

AFTERNOON. Division of day, 9

AGNAR. Son of Hrauding, fostered by Frigga, 34, 36; gives Odin a drink, 36; becomes king, 37; Greek equivalent, 348

AI (ä'ē). Riger visits, 151

AKU-THOR (ak'u-thor). The charioteer, 62

ALBERICH (al'bĕr-ik). King of the dwarfs, 242

ALBION (al'bi-on). Conjectured origin of name, 246

ALF-BLOT. Sacrifices offered to elves, 248

ALF-HEIM (alf'hīm). Home of elves in, 11, 246; Frey, ruler of, 117; Frey's return to, 119; Skirnir's return to, 121; Völund goes to dwell in, 178

ALI. Same as Vali, 164

ALLFATHER. The uncreated is, 2; Yggdrasil, created by, 12; Odin called, 16; questions Vafthrudnir, 32; wrath of, 44; Longbeards named by, 46; disposes of Hel, Midgard snake, and Fenris, 90; sends Hermod to Finland, 155; goes with Vidar, to consult Norns, 159; dooms Brunhild to marry, 280; is slain, 335

ALPHEUS (al-fē'us). Greek equivalent of Northern river-god, 359

ALPINE ROSE. Attendants of Holda crowned with the, 52

ALPS. Uller's home on the, 140; supposed meaning of the name, 246

GLOSSARY AND INDEX

370

GLOSSARY AND INDEX

371

GLOSSARY AND INDEX

372

374

GLOSSARY AND INDEX

GLOSSARY AND INDEX

GLOSSARY AND INDEX

378

GLOSSARY AND INDEX

GLOSSARY AND INDEX

381

GLOSSARY AND INDEX

GLOSSARY AND INDEX

383

GLOSSARY AND INDEX

GLOSSARY AND INDEX

2 B

GLOSSARY AND INDEX

GLOSSARY AND INDEX

GLOSSARY AND INDEX

GLOSSARY AND INDEX

392

GLOSSARY AND INDEX

GLOSSARY AND INDEX

Lightning Source UK Ltd.
Milton Keynes UK
UKHW040258181121
394157UK00002B/98